# GROWING UP UNTOUCHABLE IN INDIA

*Vasant Moon on the podium at the presentation of a volume of* Dr. Babasaheb Ambedkar: Writings and Speeches, *which he edited. Behind him is a portrait of Dr. Ambedkar.*

# GROWING UP UNTOUCHABLE IN INDIA

*A Dalit Autobiography*

VASANT MOON

Translated from the Marathi
by
Gail Omvedt

With an Introduction
by
Eleanor Zelliot

ROWMAN & LITTLEFIELD PUBLISHERS, INC.
*Lanham • Boulder • New York • Oxford*

ROWMAN & LITTLEFIELD PUBLISHERS, INC.

Published in the United States of America
by Rowman & Littlefield Publishers, Inc.
4720 Boston Way, Lanham, Maryland 20706
http://www.rowmanlittlefield.com

12 Hid's Copse Road
Cumnor Hill, Oxford OX2 9JJ, England

Copyright © 2000 by Rowman & Littlefield Publishers, Inc.

First published by Granthali in Mumbai as *Vasti* (1995).

British Library Cataloguing in Publication Information Available

**Library of Congress Cataloging-in-Publication Data**
Moon, Vasant.
    [Vasti. English.]
    Growing up untouchable in India : a Dalit autobiography / Vasant Moon ; translated by
Gail Omvedt ; with an introduction by Eleanor Zelliot.
       p.   cm. — (Asian voices)
    ISBN 0-7425-0880-3 (alk. paper) — ISBN 0-7425-0881-1 (pbk. : alk. paper)
    1. Dalits—India.  2. India—Scheduled tribes.  3. Socially handicapped—India.
I. Omvedt, Gail.  II. Title.  III. Series.
HT720.M66  2000
305.5'68—dc21                                         00-032874

Printed in the United States of America

♾™ The paper used in this publication meets the minimum requirements of American
National Standard for Information Sciences—Permanence of Paper for Printed Library
Materials, ANSI/NISO Z39.48–1992.

She was not, after all, very educated. But at a time when education up to fourth grade was understood to be a big thing in the Dalit community, when girls were not at all educated, she had studied up to third grade. From that time she began to write her name as "Purnabai." But the life of our Mother Purna remained unfulfilled.

During our infancy Purnabai's father removed her permanently from the harassment of her drunkard husband. But then she soon lost the shelter of her father and mother. Her lot became one of wandering barefoot and feeding her two small children through performing daily labor. The cracks in her heels vanished only when she died.

At a time when all the children in the neighborhood around her called their mothers "Ma," she taught us to call her "Mother," like children of the elite. She took care of us, raised us, and taught us the new alphabet: the A of "aspiration," the B of "Babasaheb," and the C of "confidence."

# CONTENTS

# INTRODUCTION

Vasant Moon gave the title of *Vasti* (neighborhood) to his autobiography, stressing the importance of his community in Nagpur. For this translation, we have changed the title to *Growing Up Untouchable in India* as more understandable, but the word *vasti* and the concept of a place of belonging are present throughout this English translation of Moon's narrative. There is much in his story of his childhood *vasti* that would probably be true of any poor urban neighborhood: hunger and deprivation, of course, but also much help from neighbors; a sense of "us" and "them"; easy acceptance of petty crime and violence; the saving grace of sports; the even more important factor of an organized group for youngsters led by caring adults; the off-again, on-again aid from relatives; inexplicable cruelty and big-hearted generosity; the women who work at whatever they can find to keep their families alive; and especially the way out and up through education. But in Moon's story there is also much that is peculiarly Indian.

First among these Indian elements is the factor of caste, a hierarchical system unrelated to race but based on ancient principles of hereditary pollution and purity, with Brahmans as the most pure and Untouchables as the most polluted. Second in importance, perhaps even first, is the presence of a hero so important he is described as a "wave," and surely no despised group has ever had such a meaningful leader as Dr. B. R. (Babasaheb) Ambedkar was (and is) for India's awakened and ambitious Dalits. Third, in my judgment, is nature. I have never read such a compelling description of Nagpur's heat, even though I have experienced it; nor has the joy of the monsoon rains been often so vividly presented. And surely every tree, every fruit, every nook and cranny of the world in and around the *vasti* plays an important part in Moon's story.

# WHAT IS UNTOUCHABILITY?

Vasant Moon's story is about a neighborhood, a community of people who are Mahars, "Untouchables," at the bottom of India's caste system. But it is about that group at a time and place when change had taken place and more change was in the air, when the community feeling was stronger than any sense of inferiority, when a child could delight in the wonders of an urban slum. Nevertheless the tale of Moon's growing up must be seen as a statement by a man whose caste was polluting, despised, "untouchable" by higher castes. Moon uses the word "Dalit" for Untouchables, a fairly recent designation adopted by politicized Untouchables and now current throughout the press. (It must be added that the formalized practice of untouchability was made illegal in the Constitution of India, ratified in 1950, just as the practice of discrimination is illegal here in the United States—more about this later.)

The concept of untouchability is one of the most difficult for non-Indians to understand. That there are groups of people who are by birth permanently impure, not to be touched, given the work that is polluting, relegated to the margins of society and yet necessary for the maintenance of that society—this concept bears some relation to racial or ethnic divisions elsewhere, but is far more systematized in the culture of India. The caste system as it exists today in groups of "graded inequality," with Brahmans as most ritually pure and some four hundred specific castes permanently at the bottom, has probably been firmly established for over a thousand years. It continues today, although usually in less blatant form and with much effort on the part of government to make up for past injustice through "reservations," India's version of affirmative action.

In spite of this hierarchical system, India also has a tradition of equality and has seen numerous reform efforts. The best known is Mohandas K. Gandhi's attempt to give Untouchables some respect with the name "Harijan," people of God, a name rejected as patronizing by politically aware Untouchables. Moon's discussion of the refusal to be named "Harijan" even at the cost of being denied a scholarship and his vivid description of the boycotting of Gandhi will shock those who think of Gandhi as the friend of Untouchables. This rejection must be seen in the context of Gandhi's denying Untouchables the right to the political power that Dr. Ambedkar felt was essential for progress. (See Pune Pact in the glossary for the source of the Gandhi–Ambedkar conflict.) Ideologically, "change of heart" on the part of caste Hindus, which was the Gandhian way, versus legal rights and political power for the group on the bottom, which was Ambedkar's plea, is a dichotomy that has relevance in American culture. However, Moon clearly brings out the kindness of several Gandhian teachers. And the strong strain of reform may be seen in all the high-caste teachers who teach without prejudice and all the famous writers who respond to Moon's invitation to come to the *vasti*.

Other terms are also of historic importance. The practice of untouchability was abolished in the Constitution of India and made punishable by law in 1955, so "ex-Untouchable" is a term used by many. Untouchable castes in 1935 were put on a list, or "schedule," to receive benefits, so "Scheduled Castes" is also a term that must be understood. "Compensatory discrimination" has given Scheduled Castes representation in parliamentary bodies and reservations in government-sponsored educational institutions and government administration. The extraordinary progress shown in Moon's narrative of the high places of many of Nagpur's Mahar children—judges and lawyers and doctors and such—indicates the success of India's policy. The dark side of progress is that there is more violence than ever before, but usually in villages when Untouchables claim rights that threaten the caste Hindu status quo. A hint of the violence appears in Moon's story of the ritual killing of a Brahman–Mahar couple, and in the boycott of Mahars who ended the degrading untouchable custom of dragging out dead cattle from the village. And in the "wars" in the streets in 1946 when Ambedkar's followers fought for political rights denied them in the plans for Independent India.

The most recent nomenclature for ex-Untouchables is "Dalit," a term meaning downtrodden or broken down but used with pride as a self-chosen name that reflects no idea of pollution and can include all who identify themselves as oppressed by the caste system. "Dalit" came into currency in the 1970s in movements that took names such as "Dalit Panthers" and "Dalit literature," and now is the preferred name for those such as Vasant Moon who want to free themselves from the concept of pollution and from the patronage of Gandhian ideology.

## WHO ARE THE MAHARS?

Vasant Moon's story of growing up in a *vasti,* an urban neighborhood, adds a new dimension to our understanding of India's Dalits, her Untouchables. In Moon's world, Dalits are not all unhappy victims, not marginalized peoples to be pitied, not a people without hope. Prejudice, violence, crime are not absent from the story of his early life, but they do not dominate, do not destroy his spirit. Poverty is very widespread, but even hunger cannot triumph over the childhood joys of life. *Vasti* is a Marathi word; in Hindi it is *bustee,* usually translated "urban slum," and anyone visiting the Maharpurs of Nagpur, the localities of the Untouchable Mahar caste, with middle-class eyes would call them slums.

But Moon's story reveals a richly complex slum culture, much in the way that some American Black autobiographies do. We have often used the word "community" for the translation of *vasti* because this is its predominant character for Moon—a center of life and activity, of warmth and welcome.

Two things about the Mahars require special comment: the traditional place of the Mahar caste; the special world of the Mahars in eastern Maharashtra. First, it must be understood that there exist hundreds of Untouchable castes, and each one has a world somewhat different from the other. The Mahars of Maharashtra were ubiquitous in the Marathi-speaking area. They were present in every village, and the anthropologist Iravati Karve claimed, "Where there is a Mahar, there is Maharashtra." A Marathi proverb contains the same notion but has a negative meaning, "*jithe gao, tithe Maharwada*": where there is a village, there are Mahars, or, there's something dirty in every village. Their position in the village was as, in British parlance, "inferior village servants," and this meant a number of menial tasks in the service of the village but also a place, albeit low, in the village hierarchy.

The coming of the British offered new occupations in the army and on the docks and railroads and in the mills, while at the same time it destroyed the Mahar work of carrying messages, determining land boundaries, and caring for government officials' horses, leaving the removal of dead animals, the bringing of wood to the burning ground, and agricultural labor to the lot of the Mahar. The mix of new opportunity and lack of any viable traditional work such as that in leather pushed and pulled the Mahar into greater mobility than many other Untouchable castes. And it must be said that the Mahar world of Moon in the region of Vidarbha, eastern Maharashtra, is different even from that of the caste in other parts of the Marathi-speaking region. It makes us realize that each of the hundreds of Untouchable castes in India has a life somewhat or massively different from that of others. Moon's story adds a new dimension to the English sources on Untouchables. Vivid descriptions of the lives of individual Untouchables available to the English-speaking world are rare, and Moon's work adds greatly to the biographies and autobiographies and novels that exist in English. His *vasti* bears little relationship to the world of Viramma's pariah caste in a village in Tamilnadu, or the semirespectable (semicriminal?) world of Freeman's Muli in Orissa, or the despised life of a nomadic caste as depicted in Mane's *Upara*, or the wretched lives of Bhangis (sweepers) in the north as seen by Mulk Raj Anand in *Untouchable,* or recorded in an early work by an Untouchable who escaped, Hazari. So far, these stories, which are noted in "Further Reading" at the end of the book, are the only full-length accounts we have in English of the actual lives of Untouchables (although there are many in Marathi thanks to the Dalit literary movement inspired by Ambedkar). Vasant

Moon's urban life, filled with the explorations of childhood, secure in its neighborliness but subject to the intrusions, good and bad, of the outside world, is a far cry from any Untouchable world as yet presented to us.

The Mahars of Vidarbha were even better off than the Mahars of the other regions of Maharashtra. They accounted for 20 percent of the population in many eastern areas, including the city of Nagpur. They enjoyed better economic circumstances in that a few owned land, some were forest contractors, many were weavers, an occasional Mahar even served as the village headman, a *patil*. The domination of Brahman castes felt in the western part of Maharashtra was lessened by an admixture of high castes from non-Marathi-speaking areas. The orthodox hand of the Brahman *peshwas,* rulers in eighteenth-century Pune, was lighter in Vidarbha, and a century later the liberal hand of the Brahman reformers was grasped eagerly. While in the early twentieth century there occurred an awakening of Mahars in all parts of the Marathi-speaking area, the common man in Vidarbha seems to have had more opportunity to take hold of the new and build a new world.

One more note: Untouchability has some strangely inconsistent aspects. Note that Mahars roll *bidis,* the Indian cigarette. *Bidis* seem not to carry untouchability. And note that Moon's half brother-in-law Madhavrao is a cook for the railway headquartered in Calcutta. Caste is relevant in specific language areas, often not outside. So being a Mahar in a British institution in Bengal opens up the occupation that is not possible among low castes in Nagpur.

## THE MEANING OF BABASAHEB AMBEDKAR

The second profoundly important element of Moon's story is the role of Dr. B. R. Ambedkar (1891–1956), known affectionately as Babasaheb or Baba or even Bhim, an abbreviation of his first name. Bhimrao Ramji Ambedkar's story is found in almost countless volumes published in India and in every recent international encyclopedia on Asia. But here it is chiefly necessary to say that his most unusual education in Bombay, New York, and London made him instantly a hero to Mahars. His degrees—B.A., M.A., Ph.D., D.D.S., Bar-at-Law from America and England, made possible by non-Brahman reform princes—are celebrated even in song today. Also, his organizing work among Untouchable castes, his representations to the British government for "Depressed Class" rights, his satyagraha (nonviolent direct-action campaign) for water rights at the Chaudar pond in Mahad, his temple entry campaigns, and his battles with Gandhi over the rights of Untouchables to political power were known to Untouchables all over Maharashtra.

Toward the end of his life, Dr. Ambedkar's chairing of the Drafting Committee of the Constitution, his service as law minister in Nehru's first cabinet, and his conversion two months before his death to Buddhism were events of such importance to his followers that his role cannot be overestimated. Moon's story gives one an emotional understanding of the importance of this most unusual man to his people. Ambedkar's people now include Dalits in every corner of India, so Moon's evocative remembrances are important to our grasp of the rise of Ambedkar as a symbol in all of India. His statue, his portrait, his legend is now everywhere, from north to south, east to west, in India. Babasaheb Ambedkar is not only a symbol of pride and achievement, he is a symbol of a contribution to the nation, and Moon's autobiography suggests the importance of that need for creative belonging.

## ALL THOSE NAMES

We have left many names in place—names of trees, names of fruits, and the many, many names of the men and women of Moon's childhood. The trees and

*A painting of Dr. Ambedkar handing the constitution to President Rajendra Prasad while India's leaders look on (from the left: Prime Minister Jawaharlal Nehru, Sardar Patel, C.R. Rajagopalachari; on the right: Maulana Azad). The calendar for 1999–2000 that featured this painting gave no artist's name, but the style is that of Lalit S. More, a Dalit artist from Mhow. The calender is produced by Tai Nana Gajbhiye on behalf of the Dr. Babasaheb Ambedkar Urban Bank, Nagpur.*

fruits remind us of the vast differences in the natural worlds of the different continents, and they also let us know how important that world was to Moon. The names of his friends and those who came to the *vasti* are there in the dozens, to be skipped over if one is reading aloud, but otherwise standing as a reminder that these are real people. These names are a litany of remembered friendships, an anthem to the men and women of the Ambedkar movement. They are many, too many to keep straight, and to add to that, affectionate endings and diminutives are used in abundance: Purna becomes Purni; a *ya* ending indicates affection and appears often; and a *ji* is added as a term of respect, as in Gandhiji. Balakrishna becomes Bala, and Vasant Moon himself is fondly called Vasanta. And of course the reader will catch on to the fact that Sitabardi, the name of the *vasti*, is often shorted to Bardi.

And titles—Ustad for the trainers of wrestlers; Master for elementary and secondary school teachers; the suffixes *tai* or *bai* to refer respectfully to women; *ai,* the word for mother, often added to the name of a god or a godlike human or a saint to indicate nurturing qualities. *Rao* is an honorific attached to the end of a name. *Baba* or *babu* can be used to refer to a child; *buwa* or *maharaj* to a holy man, whom we have usually called a "godman," or *bhatji* for a Brahman. A *seth* is a merchant. *Mamaji* is the term for mother's brother. A saheb is a white man or an Indian who has the accouterments of a saheb in clothing or lifestyle; in the case of Ambedkar's title, Babasaheb, it is an indication of respect. We have retained many Marathi names in the text to allow the flavor of Moon's memories to remain strong.

The names involved with religion are especially interesting and important. Note all the godmen who come by: Somabuwa, Premdasbuwa, Bhanudasbuwa, Laldasbuwa, Jayarambuwa—all probably Mahars, although Moon does not tell us this. And then the holy men at a distance: Tajuddin, Tukdoji, Sai Baba, Gajanand Maharaj, and from the past: Kabir, the great radical saint of the north. There is knowledge of some of the gods: Ram, Sita, Lakshman from the *Ramayana* epic, and Radha and Krishna from that romantic Puranic story, but also Matabai, the smallpox goddess. There are Muslim fakirs and the Muslim celebration of Moharram in which all participate. There is Janmashtami to celebrate Krishna's birth, or that of the local avatar of Krishna, Kanoba. There is Holi, that wild celebration vaguely related to religion, and the celebration of the elephant-headed god Ganpati. There is a temple to Maruti, who is supposed to help students pass exams, and the all-important temple of Vitthal or Vithoba and Rukmini, a reflection of the *bhakti* movement that swept all Maharashtra. But what Moon doesn't say is that no Mahar could enter the main temple of Vitthal and Rukmini at Pandharpur until Independence, and no Brahman entered the Maharpura to perform *pujas.* However, all the richness of religious life is described in such a way that one realizes the great change that the conversion to Buddhism brought. And the way in which Moon attempts to bring about a community understanding of Buddhism and to make Buddhism a community affair through theater should be seen as very important.

We have changed the names of the neighborhoods in Nagpur to an English translation when it seemed to us natural and interesting—e.g., Oiltown, Cameltown—but we have left others in place, since Dharmapeth as "Religionville" seemed too cute.

We have also changed the caste names to occupation names, since these give an indication of the standing of the caste. It should be understood that not all members of a caste follow the caste occupation. Of the names we have given, three besides Mahars are for Untouchable castes: Leatherworkers are Chambhars (Chamar in Hindi); Ropemakers are Mangs, who, in Moon's narrative, are seen as selling baskets; Sweepers or Scavengers are Bhangis or Mehtars, both Hindi-speaking castes since no Marathi-speaking caste has a tradition of removing human waste. All three castes now prefer Sanskritic names: Chambhars would like to be called Charmakars; Mangs prefer Matang; and Bhangis use the name Valmiki after the legendary author of the *Ramayana,* who they feel was a member of their caste.

## THE IMPORTANCE OF THE WORLD OUTSIDE NAGPUR, AND OF THE YEARS 1942 AND 1946

But not only is the world of Dalits in eastern Maharashtra illumined, but also the tapestry of pre-Independence Indian events is presented as it touches that world. The importance of English thinkers and institutions is clear, although the English themselves are barely visible in the story. The Independence movement surrounds the *vasti* but does not meet its needs. Reform-minded upper-caste writers stop by, and the modern vehicles of newspapers and railroads are a familiar part of life. Western missionaries hover at the borders of Moon's life. Members of the Rashtriya Swayamsevak Sangh (see the glossary), or the RSS, so dominant today in Indian politics, live in adjacent neighborhoods, as do Muslims and migrants from north and south and east. Because Moon's story is such a rich treasure-house for the history of the period, we have included a rather massive glossary of names and events so that the relationship of Moon's life to Indian and Maharashtrian history and culture is clear.

Two dates are especially important. In 1942, Gandhi declared a "Quit India" campaign, intent on the immediate withdrawal of the British in spite of their war effort. The British arrested the leaders of the Indian National Congress, and consequently they were unable to control the subsequent violence. Several groups did not participate in what was the most massive of all the Gandhian campaigns: the Brahmans tended to avoid Gandhian affairs; the RSS was devoted to spreading the importance of Hindu nationalism, not independence; the Muslims by now were caught up in the idea of a separate homeland; and Ambedkar's followers wanted their human rights guaranteed before Independence brought new governors. Moon describes vividly the atmosphere of that time.

In 1946 the Cripps Mission had dismissed Ambedkar's pleas for Untouchables to be in a separate electorate so that they could be sure to elect their own leaders. Ambedkar's Scheduled Castes Federation had not been able to secure enough political power through votes. It is quite clear that caste Hindus voted for Scheduled Caste candidates who did not embrace Ambedkar's radical beliefs nor were from his party. In consequence, satyagrahas were held in front of legislative buildings in an effort to force awareness of the Ambedkar ideal. Again, Moon's story throws light on this event, which was almost totally ignored by the press and the historians.

## A PERSONAL NOTE

I met Vasant and Meenakshi Moon first in 1964, when I was taken to their home, then in Chanda, by the Manik Panchbhai whom Moon describes as a faithful worker for the 1956 Buddhist conversion. Moon even then was known as the historian of the Ambedkar movement, collecting material wherever he was sent in his government positions as deputy commissioner, or *naib tahsildar* (later, as *tahsildar*), in various *tahsils* or counties. Since that time, I have met the family on every one of the twenty or so trips I have taken to India. I have been in their home in Nagpur and studied in the library Moon built on the roof of his house to keep safe all the documents he so carefully collected. I have been in their home in Bombay, now Mumbai, which was a center for writers and poets and activists of all sorts. And, sadly, I have been in a hospital room because Vasant Moon was stricken by a stroke several years ago, as a result of which he no longer has the keen memory that produced this volume, although he is still active.

I can testify that Moon's early memories still hold relevance for his life. One day on a long train journey we took from Bombay to Nagpur, Moon started folding paper into animal shapes as he had been taught in school, and for hours he amused everyone in our carriage, including the formerly solemn businessmen. I also remember the famous *mandes* that he writes about so vividly, and indeed these almost transparent chapatis do seem to be somewhat miraculously produced from dough flung on a heated, upturned earthen pot. But this

*Vasant Moon (on the left) receiving the congratulations of K.R. Narayan, the president of India and a Dalit, on the occasion of the publication of his Marathi biography of Dr. Babasaheb Ambedkar for the National Book Trust. Photograph courtesy of Vasant Moon.*

was thirty-five years ago, and I have not seen them since. What has persisted is the love of mutton in Moon's community, and it has been a rare dinner that, even in the poorest of homes, I have not as an honored guest been served a spicy mutton dish.

And I have most recently been invited to attend Buddhist writers' conferences organized by Meenakshi Moon, whose magazine *Maitrani* (Womanfriend) and whose literary and feminist activities are testimony to the continuing creativity of the family and of the movement that this narrative celebrates. In fact, if I have a disagreement with Moon about the contemporary Ambedkar movement, it would be that I am more optimistic. The literary movement he notes as such a vital part early on of the awakening of the Ambedkar movement still exists. It has resulted not only in much poetry and many short stories, but also in professional theater and many autobiographies, and has inspired others from nomadic castes, the Pickpocket caste, and most recently a tribal woman to write. There is still life in the *vastis;* the Buddhist movement has recently seen a great interest in the religious life among women; and Dr. Ambedkar himself is more famous than ever, often considered together with Nehru and Gandhi as one of the three shapers of the twentieth century in India.

Eleanor Zelliot
Laird Bell Professor of History, Emerita
Carleton College

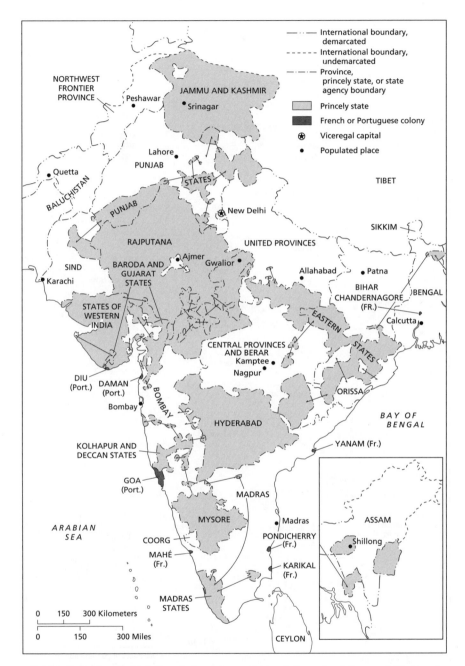

International boundary, demarcated
International boundary, undemarcated
Province, princely state, or state agency boundary
Princely state
French or Portuguese colony
⊛ Viceregal capital
• Populated place

NORTHWEST FRONTIER PROVINCE
Peshawar
JAMMU AND KASHMIR
• Srinagar

Lahore
PUNJAB

Quetta

BALUCHISTAN

PUNJAB
STATES

TIBET

⊛ New Delhi

SIKKIM

RAJPUTANA

UNITED PROVINCES

SIND
Karachi

BARODA AND GUJARAT STATES
Ajmer  Gwalior
Allahabad  • Patna

BIHAR
CHANDERNAGORE (FR.)

BENGAL
Calcutta

STATES OF WESTERN INDIA

EASTERN
STATES

CENTRAL PROVINCES AND BERAR
Kamptee
Nagpur

ORISSA

DIU (Port.)
DAMAN (Port.)

BOMBAY

Bombay

HYDERABAD

BAY OF BENGAL

KOLHAPUR AND DECCAN STATES

YANAM (Fr.)

GOA (Port.)

MADRAS

ARABIAN SEA

MYSORE

Madras

ASSAM
Shillong

COORG

PONDICHERRY (Fr.)

MAHÉ (Fr.)

KARIKAL (Fr.)

0  150  300 Kilometers
0  150  300 Miles

MADRAS STATES

CEYLON

*British India in 1947, before Independence. Adapted from the Library of Congress's* India: A Country Study *(New York, 1992, p. 66), which is based on Joseph E. Schwartzberg, ed.,* A Historical Atlas of South Asia.

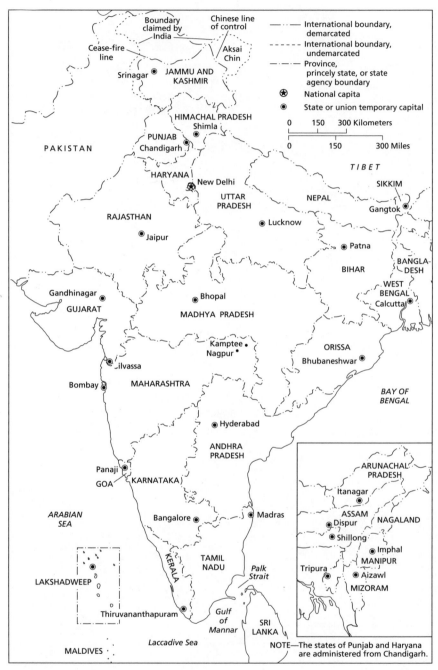

*Administrative Divisions of India, 1995. Adapted from the* Library of Congress's India: A Country Study, *1995.*

# Chapter 1

## THE NEIGHBORHOOD

It was built in a square made by four roads. No one can say when people first settled here. Old people used to tell how the generation before them could hear from their rooftops the sound of the cannon on top of Sitabardi hill when the Bhosle kingdom was defeated in 1857. Now this generation also is ready for its end.

This community in a square of two hundred by two hundred yards made by north-south and east-west roads has been established for generations; people have never built their huts or tried to carry on their daily affairs beyond the roads. If the family grew, if space became insufficient, they would rent a room in a neighbor's house, but never leave the community.

There were two smaller main roads splitting the settlement through the middle. Hardly roads, alleys. Even from before my childhood, that is from sixty years ago, the city government had decided to build a twenty-foot road through the community, but they never did; the houses were there for years. Just like the people of the area, the houses were not easily moved or shoved aside.

Besides the roads that framed the four sides of this quadrangular settlement, there were many alleys and lanes crossing through it; the lanes that entered the main cement road (at that time it was a tar road) were very useful for taunting the police and then running to hide. On the side of the alleys were two three-foot drains carrying away waste water. There was no big drain in the settlement.

It was not possible to build a big veranda or compound in front of houses so crowded and pressing against one another. But the main road in front of the drains used to be empty for chatting in the evening. There was a unique happiness in spreading a mat to sit watching stars in the dark, interminable peace of the night sky.

The clamor of car and truck traffic came mainly from the road to the south. But even today not much noise reaches inside. At midnight the whistle of the trains going on the north-south line east of us would split the darkness. Just before dawn, high-flying airplanes would tell us that it was four A.M. At night, finishing their meals and sitting gossiping, people would prepare to sleep when the factory whistle blew at eleven.

Most of the houses in the settlement were old, earthen, flat-roofed; there were many one-storied brick houses. But every house had a tiled roof. Some Mahar merchants had two-storied houses. The second stories used to be built of wood. Houses were built against houses. From each window women could lean out to chat with the women of the house beside them.

At the east end of the settlement stood a very long apartment building; beyond that lived a mixed colony of Brahmans, Marwaris, Bengalis, and Madrasis. A north-south road ran by Dhanwate's house on the corner parallel to the railway tracks. Towards the northeast was a long-established Mahar temple of Vitthal and Rukmini, and beyond that a public toilet that had existed from the time of the establishment of the municipality. These were toilets that told stories of their unbroken link to the cultural life of a community of four or five thousand people, that stored the remains of the sorrows and joys of their history. With eight rooms there were facilities for men on one side, women on the other. Women found it a convenient place to voice their domestic complaints. Men from the other side could listen to their laments. Occasionally a husband would hear his own wife telling calumnies against him to someone or other.

The road going from the north of the settlement divided the Weaver ward from the Mahar colony. The Weavers had a fondness for wrestling. Each house had a wrestling ground. Whether it was a Hindu-Muslim riot in Nagpur or a Hindu-Mahar quarrel, the Weavers would always come out to defend the Hindu side. But see how time takes its revenge! The same Weavers who rose up to oppose reserved seats for Dalits and were ready in 1946 to massacre Mahars are the ones who are now demanding reservations for themselves. Next to this Weaver colony lay the settlements of Brahmans and other caste Hindus.

From there on the left was a rough road going north-south. This road, which split the main road to go to the Bhide Girls' High School, joins the other main road going north, which comes from the east below an iron bridge and goes directly through Dharampeth towards Amraoti.

The Matamai temple of Maharpura was near the road on the west. If an epidemic of cholera, diarrhea, or smallpox occurred, the uneducated women would take a pot of water to Matamai. Sometimes they would sacrifice chickens. Ragho's wife would always take water to Matamai. At the time of an epidemic she would gather women together and, filling a large pot, bathe

*A Nagpur neighborhood somewhat like Sitabardi, with the addition of a small Buddhist vihar replacing the temples of Moon's childhood. Photo by Eleanor Zelliot, 1964.*

Matamai. The women would sing songs to Matamai at that time, and she would be possessed by the goddess. Letting her hair loose and freeing her sari she would began to moan and women would ask her, "Mai, what do you want?" And whatever she demanded they would give. The goddess's expectations were limited to chickens and goats.

However, after 1930 the wave of Ambedkar Baba came, and Matamai was forced into retirement. Today her temple has crumbled into stones.

From the point of view of the settlement, the field to the south was very useful. This empty field was called the Tar. If anyone asked, "Auntie, where is Pandya," she would generally say, "He's not in the house; he must be playing on the Tar." This Tar had an unbroken link with the settlement. On its eastern edge were two small factories with lathe machines. One of these belonged to Balkrishna Patil-Mahar. It stood where the Anand cinema theater is today. Near the road beyond the field was a very tall *pipal* tree. On the northwest corner of the settlement was a hedge owned by a tall and hefty woman called Longlady. All the people of the settlement would get fuel from Longlady's hedge. No one knew when Longlady's husband had died. But the widow Longlady supervised by herself the storehouse of wood and coal. One day there was a huge storm, of the kind known in Vidarbha as a Matya. This Matya lifted the drying saris of Longlady and threw them against the *pipal* tree. People used to say that a ghost lived in that tree. In the moonlight we used to lie on the Tar near the road and look at the *pipal*. I could see many shapes on that tree: Longlady's trapped saris, torn remnants of kites, pairs of birds flapping in the endless night. I thought that ghosts must indeed be awake on the path.

Who can say what kind of culture gets into the minds of children? In the community, Dhanya's father used to tell stories from the *Mahabharata*, the *Ramayana,* and other epics. I used to go every night at a fixed time to listen to them. After coming back I would eat and go to sleep on the Tar. Sleeping on the dry ground, we friends used to chat until one or two in the morning. In the moonlit night our attention would go to the *pipal* tree. In the clear sky as we looked towards the moon, flocks of herons could be seen circling. Today such flocks do not appear anywhere. At that time, they gave the illusion, against the *pipal*, that Ram, Laxman, and Sita were appearing to us. Ghosts, gods—they were the same to me. Radha and Krishna could also be seen on the tree.

On the western side of the Tar was a *shembdi* tree. Fruits shaped like plums with oozing sap grew on that tree. Once ripe, they were tempting to eat. The children of the settlement on their way to school would shake off the fruits, put them in their pockets, and later eat them.

A fodder market would be held on Mondays and Thursdays on the Tar. This market extended up to where Netaji market is today. Beyond that lay a vegetable market. The municipality would give a contract for operating the market. Ganu Mistri of Maharpura held the contract for many years. On the day of the fodder market carts would come from the villages, and auctions would take place. The carts would be filled and leave. But the dung and the stumps and leaves of the fodder would be spilled. Ganu Mistri and the people of his household would collect these. They would dry them. Ganya would come in the evening to keep watch. Some kids of the settlement always played nasty tricks. They would stay awake at night, and when Ganya slept they would throw pebbles at him. They would silently tie a string to his legs and make a "firecracker." When this firecracker was lit his toes would be burned. He would rise up with a shout. By then Paikya and Modkya would have run away. But Ganya knew all of this. He knew who was harassing him. Especially on the day of Holi, he would have to remain awake. Still, by dawn he would doze off. Once, when the kids went to have their fun, an accident took place. On the lighting of the firecracker the fodder caught fire. Ganu felt the heat and woke up. But how to report such an embarrassing deed?

That Tar field came to be called the Gita ground. An old man who recited the Gita would wander there and give a pungent discourse in Hindi. The whole field would be crowded then. Thousands of people would gather in the evenings for his sermons. At other times the Marwari and Gujarati women would come to get a sight of the godman. His name was Vidyananda Swami. He wore a rosary around his throat. In the center was a jewel. When he moved his neck, the jewel would shift to another place. People would consider that a miracle. In the Maharpura the Gita godman was ridiculed as a pompous figure. The truant boys would go from time to time to tease the little girls. Some boys would fall at the feet of Vidyananda. The godman did not pay very much attention to these kids with ragged clothes. In front of the him was a heap of loose coins. These boys had their attention fixed on those coins. They would distract the godman and grab a handful of coins. Even if he noticed it the godman did not have the courage to beat anyone. Maharpura was notorious for such things throughout Nagpur.

The thieves of this settlement were famous. The name of Nagya the Bandit was known through the whole of Madhya Pradesh for great bravery. The police would throw Nagya in jail with his arms in shackles. But he would disappear during the night. Only the chains would be found. It would be said that Nagya the Bandit had gone to another town by train. He carried a bandana with him. If he threw the bandana over some jewelry, took it and left the train, not even the woman wearing the jewelry would be aware of it. By the time the theft was discovered a number of stations would have been passed. This Nagya would wander, openly showing a wallet he had stolen from the governor. He used to roam with his four-year-old son in the market. He would take him on his shoulders and teach him how to steal. Nagya's whole life was spent in and out of jail. He was a true idealist. "Let me die in jail," he used to say. "My son will continue my name." This was how he raised him and this was what happened. Nagya died in jail. Until just recently there were many pickpockets who continued the heritage of Nagya. Today the community feels regret in falling behind even in thievery.

The community produced thieves but no one there was afraid of being molested by robbers. If anyone harassed the girls of the community his life would no longer be secure. Even widowed women used to leave their little girls at home and fearlessly go out to work. They would say to the older people lounging next door, "Oh Ganba Grandfather, just keep an eye on my kid," and he would do this. "Go child, go; don't worry." There were no secrets in the neighborhood. The walls spoke openly.

I remember when I was small, about four or five years old, the community would be almost deserted in the afternoon. In the path next to our house four or five little children were sitting playing cards. Hearing their voices, Grandfather Sadashiv Lohkare roared as he sat, "Who is that playing cards?" And with his voice the kids ran away. The older people of the settlement were like that. They would give tongue-lashings, and people stood in awe of them.

No one at that time ever imagined that the road running between the community and the Gita ground would become the main road of Sitabardi. On this road all the main processions of Nagpur could be seen. The *pan* shop of Champabai at the edge of the road was famous. Light-skinned Champabai was married to an old man of her father's age. She used to keep peppermints and chocolates in the *pan* shop. The schoolchildren would collect a few pennies and buy sweet balls of parched rice from her. Raghuji Raja's procession would parade with spearmen and mace-bearers in front and at the rear and with the beating of drums. This huge parade would stop at Champabai's door. The Raja's retainers would not go without taking a roll of *pan* from Champabai's hand. Once the Raja's court had gone ahead, then Champabai would turn again to her business. Champabai had no children and no happiness from her husband. Still there was no gossip about her. She would forget herself among the little children of the Maharpura.

It was not that there were no boys to become enamored of Champabai's youth. However, she lived the life of a recluse. There was also no lack of young men to tease her. Shivaram used to drink every Sunday and come and sit on the field in front of Champabai's shop. He would gather the little boys together. He would collect two measures of parched rice, and go to Champabai's and buy some sweets. These he would distribute to the boys, saying, "Look, boys, Champa and Shivaram's marriage is going to happen, beware!" Champa would laugh and say, "What, uncle, such talk gives you grace!" But Champa never had very much to say. She would silently listen to all the talk. Shivaram would tease her a bit, but still would not go beyond limits.

The community nurtured a passion about wrestling from the beginning. There were three wrestling grounds in that small settlement. One was that of the Ladvans, one in the house of Narayan Watchman, and the third of the Bavanes. No one would be turned away from any, but each subcaste wanted its own ground. From plain wrestling to fighting with sticks, to shields and swords, boys could learn all kinds of accomplishments at those wrestling grounds.

Many subcastes existed in the community, eight to ten houses of Ladvans, eight to ten of the Barkes. All these were on the southern side of the neighborhood, while the Zhade-Ghavanes and Somvashis were in the middle, and the entire rest of the neighborhood belonged to the Bavanes. Before I was born, the subcastes didn't eat in each other's houses. At public gatherings they sat in separate rows. The Ladvans, Zhades-Ghavanes, and Barkes would not sit on the mats of the Bavanes. If by mistake anyone sat down in the wrong place, the subcaste *panchayat* would do a purification ceremony. The entire neighborhood would have to be washed with the water from the well near the temple. Later, when taps came, the Barke women would not put their hands on the taps of the Bavane women. Everyone had a fierce pride in his subcaste.

Provocations always sprang up between the Bavanes and Ladvans. The Ladvans and Barkes had an alliance. Maniram Wrestler was a Barke. But he was a match for all the Bavanes. He would go to the Dhobi washing area, pick a fight with the Washermen, and come back. He had no uvula, so his voice came through his nose. Everyone called him Ghenganya wrestler. Four or five wrestlers of the Ladvans and Barkes—Maniram, Sada Ustad, Sadashiv Lohkarya, Chokhoba—were a match for the Bhavanes.

The disagreements that had gone on for years and years to some extent came to an end with the struggle of Babasaheb Ambedkar. Other leaders also organized campaigns against the observance of purity-pollution. The wave of interdining reached the community in 1920. The pollution of untouchability had lessened somewhat. In spite of all of this, the mentality of prejudice had not been wiped out. Whenever the youth got a whim, faults and foibles would be brought up. People from both sides would come to the road. They would be armed with sticks. For an hour or two a rip-roaring fight went on, and then everyone would go home. The next day all would go to work as if nothing had happened the day before.

One event finally settled the quarrel of the Ladvans and Bavanes. There were no youth among the Bavanes to defeat Maniram Dalal Wrestler. One night the Bavanes called a meeting. They called Ustad Dajiba from outside the community. Dajiba was skilled in jousting and fighting with sticks along with wrestling.

The meeting began. Ustad Dajiba looked around. Everything was quiet. One person said, "Maniram Wrestler is throwing his weight around. We want to puncture his balloon. He deliberately picks quarrels with our Bavanes. We need to find a remedy."

"So what are you thinking of?" queried Ustad.

"We need to teach a fellow from the Bavanes. We need your help."

"All right."

"Whatever youth you call will come."

"I want Shivaram."

Shivaram said, "I have children. If anything should happen you'll have to see to them."

"Don't be afraid. I'll take care of everything."

Ustad Dajiba made Shivaram work night and day. Along with wrestling he got training in cudgels and fencing sticks.

Maniram watched Shivaram going every day to the wrestling ground. He grew concerned. If he met Shivaram going and coming, Maniram would give him a strong slap on the back, tease him. Once he tried to trip him up with a blow to his leg. Shivaram was young; he would get angry. But his teacher hadn't given the order to fight. Dajiba used to tell Shivram, "Wait; train yourself well."

Within two months Shivaram learned many skills. But still the time didn't come. Ustad Dajiba had a job as a fitter on the railways, but during early mornings and in the evenings he would teach Shivaram strategy.

After about six months Shivaram became thoroughly skilled. He felt no fear of Maniram. In fact, far from feeling overwhelmed by Maniram, he could not even be moved to react to his jibes. Maniram also got a fairly good idea of Shivaram's skill. Shivaram had to be taught a lesson before he became uncontrollable or it would not be possible to sneer at him.

Maniram Wrestler saw Shivaram going one morning to the toilets. Walking by, he gave him a slap just to show his strength. Shivaram went on guard. "What, brother, you're slapping me? You're playing mischief," Shivaram shouted.

"Oh, you're getting insolent?" Maniram roared.

"What are you saying? What do you want?" said Shivaram.

"Today let us finish it!" Maniram bellowed harshly.

And so the trumpets of war were sounded. Those were the days when fights began with such challenges. A report had to be filed beforehand at the police station. The two wrestlers, who were prepared to die, were ready to fight anywhere at an open challenge. If anything happened in such a match, a statement had to be given to the police that the fighters accepted all responsibility for whatever happened.

Shivaram and Maniram both notified the police. The wrestling match was to be held under an *umbri* tree growing in the corner of the neighborhood. The report spread to all of Nagpur. People came from far away to watch.

At the fixed time, in front of thousands of people, the wrestling match of Shivaram and Maniram began. Both used all their strategies. After wrestling for nearly an hour, Shivaram could not be defeated. Maniram finally said, "Well, Shivaram, take a club." Both took big sticks and began to beat each other. Dust obstructed the eyes of the audience. And then Maniram fell to the ground. A huge blow fell squarely on his head, fracturing it.

Shivaram raised his stick in triumph. Ustad Dajiba and the people of the neighborhood picked up Maniram and took him to Mayo hospital. Many from the neighborhood visited him there. The Bavanes were proud of Shivaram, who became the subject of praise in the neighborhood. Others grew afraid. Once Maniram got out of the hospital, he would definitely seek revenge!

After staying in the hospital for a month, Maniram regained his vigor. People's attention was once more fixed on him. It was a Sunday. Shivaram sat in his house chatting with his children. His wife was sitting in the doorway. From there she saw Maniram. She felt a bit of trembling in her chest. But she was also the wife of a wrestler.

Maniram called out, "Oh Shivaram, are you there, fellow? Hello, sister-in-law, how are you? Feeling fine? There's no quarrel now."

Shivaram said to his wife, "Come inside. This is none of your business." He came outside in his undershirt. Maniram told him to get dressed. Shivaram put on a shirt and came back out. Maniram linked his arm in Shivaram's and started off.

A liquor shop lay at the foot of the Sitabardi hill. Government liquor was sold there: Deer brand and Lion brand, the stronger of the two. Outside the shop you could get a fried spicy gram roll for a few pennies. Around this food stall, the laborers forgot the exhaustion of their toil in the evenings.

Maniram and Shivaram arrived there, drank their fill, and returned arm in arm just as they had gone. When they reached Shivaram's house, Maniram told Shivaram's wife, "Child, don't cook anything. Today Shivaram will eat at my house."

They went to Maniram's two-story brick house. Maniram had told his wife beforehand, "Get mutton ready." They had dinner together; Lion bottles continued appearing throughout the meal. The men's mutual fire was swallowed up along with the food and liquor. Until then, Maniram had fought alone. From that time on, the two together protected the honor of the community. It was as if they had decided that subcaste quarrels should no longer be fought.

After eating, Maniram walked with Shivaram back to his house on the northern side. Shivaram's wife, who had been sitting staring after her husband, stood up. She led the reeling Shivaram to the cot. Lamps were not supposed to be blown out, as a matter of good luck, so with thumb and forefinger she extinguished the wick. Her fingers were used to fire. She applied salve to her thumb, went into the darkness of the house, and fell asleep on the cot.

# Chapter 2

## FEARLESS

I was registered in the first grade at Sitabardi Normal School. Before this I had been living at my grandfather Sadashiv's place for around a year. From the time my mother came to Sitabardi with my little sister and me, the "Maharpura of Bardi" was my home community.

I dimly remember even today my grandfather's form. He must have been nearly six feet tall. He had a light-complexioned, glowing face, and a nature that never picked quarrels. But none of his neighbors would dare provoke him. He was held in such awe that the young boys who gamboled in the lane near the house would run somewhere else if they learned that Sadashiv Lohkare was at home.

Grandfather Sadashiv had grown up in the company of Europeans. From this he got the enjoyment of discipline. I remember how he used to dress me in shorts and a shirt. The shirt would be tucked in. The pants would be buttoned. Taking the straps from my drooping pants he would throw them across my shoulders and button them over my chest, left to right, right to left. Next, he would put handsome socks on my feet and canvas shoes over these. This was the way he used to prepare me for going to school. And he would never forget a small handkerchief in my pocket.

"Vasant should not even get dust on his feet. He will be a saheb." His idea of a saheb was taken from his observation of Europeans. I kept pants, shirts, and boots on throughout the day. Only when climbing over wooden planks would I take my shoes off. No one in the house dared to cross him.

He had me learn the English alphabet in the very first year. The Normal School, a government school, was nearly a furlong from the neighborhood. Students went there to get training as teachers. There were seven classes in our school. The student-teachers who taught these classes were given living facilities in the school. On all four sides were the school classes, the dormitory for

10

the trainees, and in the middle a beautiful garden. Outside was an expansive field for a playground. Today only the building of the Normal School remains. The school itself vanished long ago.

In the second grade, when Dhole Master told me to write the multiplication tables, I wrote in English. Dhole Master said, "This is a Marathi school; don't write English again," and gave me two raps on the hand. There were almost no girls in the school. Did girls just not come, or didn't any live around there? Probably they didn't come. The idea of coeducation had not taken hold. Even so, the daughters of the supervisors of the hostel studied in our classes up to the fourth grade.

For a time, my grandfather was manager of a cinema theater in Kamathi. The Mahar regiment had its main office at Kamathi. However, even before this a military camp existed there. The village got its name, Kamathi, from Camp-ti.

The main communities in Kamathi were Muslim cotton carders and Mahars. The Mahars mainly worked as cooks for European officials in the military or for English missionaries. My grandfather used to drink English liquor with English officials and go to parties. When the party finished he would go back to Nagpur in his own tonga, his horse-drawn cart. He used to keep three or four dogs with him. Sadashiv Lohkare's pomp was like some European officials'. He was known as Dogman Sadashiv or Tongaman Sadashiv.

One day while Grandfather was still alive, ten to fifteen Mahar leaders of Vidarbha came to visit us. Among them were Laxmanrao Ogale of Amravati, Ghadale of Shegaon in Chandrapur, and Dasharath Patil of Bele—all the leading group of Vidarbha. Their feeling of gratitude toward Grandfather was evident. Although I saw all these activists up close at that time, later I didn't keep much connection with them. But their images even now come continuously before my eyes. The love this group gave to me in those one or two years had a big effect on my young mind for many years after.

Laxmanrao Ogale, with his round, light face, his black turban wrapped around his head, a long, closed-throat white coat, and a muslin dhoti wrapped around his loins, seemed when we saw him as some wealthy prince standing before us.

Slight but with a hardy body, wearing an ordinary dark-blue coat, with a white shirt inside, on his head a black hat—such was the avatar of Ghadale.

Dasharath Patil was of course a landlord. He was neither very tall nor short. With a strong body, a habit of eating pure homemade ghee with rice and vegetables, but no meat, and without any vice of *bidis* or cigarettes, he was a unique leader revered everywhere by the Untouchable communities of Vidarbha and Madhya Pradesh. Educated only up to the fourth grade, he had the power of personality and skills to make everyone run around and do what he wanted.

Around 1930 Dasharath Patil gave a call for reform, and Mahars for miles around stopped carrying away dead animals. In every village boycotts were imposed on these rebels by caste Hindus. Mahars who went to the market could not make purchases. Mills in the villages were closed to them; beatings began. Dasharath Patil proclaimed, "Let us have our own markets." A huge, open tract lay in front of his house in Vela. He decided to establish a market there. Dasharath Patil himself, with various well-to-do Mahar farmers, traveled fifteen miles to the small town of Sindi. There he bought enough supplies from his own pocket—household goods, lentils, grain, vegetables, etc.—to fill ten or twelve carts, which he sent with the men to the village. After the carts had gone ahead, Dasharath and others started out. As they approached the village in the middle of the night, Babalya, the village watchman, came with a message.

"Master, all your goods were looted by Hindus on the way. Murderers are hiding to kill you. Don't go to the village."

Patil said, "All right, all of you go on your own. I'll decide what to do."

They entered the nearby forest of *nagfani* trees. People were afraid to go into this forest even during the day. After they had stayed there the whole night, Bablya Watchman came out just before the sun rose. Goons were after him also. But he evaded them and went to the police station to file a report. Dasharath Patil hid for three days in the forest; Bablya brought him food at night.

Finally, the police of Sindi provided protection for Dasharath to come out of the forest. Patil met with the police supervisor and commissioner in Wardha and Nagpur and brought police to provide protection to all the Mahars. He also arranged for work to be provided of breaking rocks and repairing roads as an alternative for the boycotted Mahars.

Dasharath Patil owned hundreds of acres of land and held the Malguzari rights for several villages. He was the Bhim who could rout a meeting of Congress in its stronghold at Hinganghat-Wardha. Babasaheb Ambedkar always began his letters to him with the salutation, "Innumerable salutes to the honorable Dasharath Patil Malguzar." Such was this Dasharath Patil of a rich household. He joined Babasaheb's movement in 1920 and from then on spent his whole life in social service.

This group used to come to Grandfather. They engaged in discussions on a variety of social and political questions. I was not old enough to understand these discussions, but one memory remains permanently stamped on my mind.

It happened after Grandfather died. Ghadale and Ogale had come one day to our house. Grandmother had, as always, kept some turnips to eat. Ghadale said, "Oh, Ogale, this Vasanta is going to be a Brahman. I'll give him a sacred thread from today onwards." And around my neck he put a thread that he himself had made.

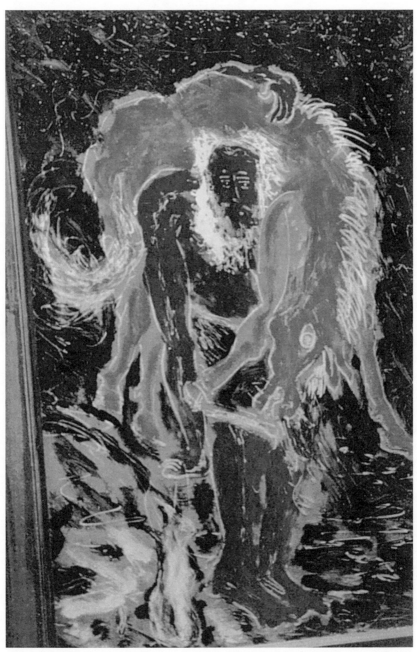

*The traditional Mahar work of carrying dead cattle out of the village, as depicted by a contemporary Dalit artist, Savi Savarkar, of Nagpur and Delhi. Oil on glass, owned by Eleanor Zelliot.*

Then he took me to a barbershop. He instructed the barber to shave my head completely. Only a tuft was left. Grandfather would never have liked this. His thinking was progressive even for his time. No one in our house worshipped the gods. No one brought godmen to our house. If by chance such people came, they ran away after seeing Grandfather.

After keeping the sacred thread for eight or ten days I threw it away. At my next haircut Pralhad Barber cut off the tuft also.

I searched for Ghadale for many years, but never met him again. Ogale died while on tour for public service in Vidarbha. I saw Dasharath Patil into his old age. Even today tears come to my eyes upon remembering all of these men. I feel bad. Why couldn't anyone in the community honor their work while they were alive?

There were no other boys from our community in the Normal School. I was the only Mahar. The boys and girls of Maharpura used to go to the city primary school. In my class, all except me were Brahmans. They all had names like Mohani, Thergavkar, Joshi, Kolhatkar, Ratnaparkhi. There was not even a single boy from the Oilpresser, Gardener, or Farmer castes. There was only one Scavenger boy living in the neighboring handicraft school who was in my class.

The book used for math was that of Mohite Headmaster. Nearly all the teachers were influenced by Gandhi's teachings. They had compassion for Mahar boys. They never treated me scornfully. Today when I hear that teachers or headmasters deliberately fail Untouchable children I become upset.

All the boys used to play during the break and even fight, but no factions existed. The teacher taught us handicrafts: how to prepare clay, how to model it, how to prepare papier-mâché, how to roll it in lumps and make fruit, eggplant, custard apples, frogs, and sparrows out of it. The master himself prepared the clay, so the students learned.

Also work with paper: he taught us how to make different designs with polished, colored thin pieces of paper. How to put cotton thread on the little spinning wheel, how to spin ropes, how to make mats and hangings of bamboo; how to make cloth bags, how to make boats and airplanes, sparrows and rabbits of paper—these were the arts we learned. In doing this we got some practical education along with entertainment. I began to make bags of twine or bits of thread at home and give them to our neighbors. After some time I taught the boys of the neighborhood to prepare figures and models of clay. The boys never went to school. But they began to come to me and I would have them make clay figures. Even at that age it was impressed upon my mind that the knowledge we get grows if we give it to others.

The teachers took care that the poison of casteism never spread among the boys of the class. One day I fell very sick. For three or four days the fever raged.

Nobody, not even my mother, was at home during the day. All the twenty or twenty-five boys in my class came to the Maharpura to visit me. They began to examine me. After that they finished off the cold water in our pot.

"Oh Vasanta, get well fast. We can't get along without you," Bhaskar said. After that the boys left. Bal stayed sitting with me for a long time. Only after all the other boys had gone did he leave. These Brahman boys used to come to school in cars. Even in this there was no feeling that some were great, some small, some rich, and some poor. My bonds of friendship with them remain unbroken.

When an inspector came to the school, he would examine the teacher by seeing how smartly the boys could answer questions. Bal Mohini and I were ahead in the reading. Mohite Master, who taught fourth grade, told us to read the lesson in front of the inspector, and we got good comments. Bal had so many books! I would grab his books and return them after reading them.

Dighade Master used to come to the training classes. During the evening I would play in the courtyard of the Normal School. I happened to meet him. After that he took me to his room. He asked me some questions. From that time on he used to inquire about my well-being. Once he gave me some letters to post. I did so. He asked, "Vasant, who were those letters written to?"

"I don't know," I replied.

"Why?"

"I didn't read the addresses on them."

"Great!" he said. "Students should never read what's written on the letters to others. I was testing you. If you had been tempted to read the addresses, you might have also read what was written on the postcards." Some years later I learned that Dighade was a Mahar. His advice has proved useful up to today.

Beyond Dharampeth, the place behind what is today the law college used to be called the Baramora. Wrestling matches, called "rumblings," were held there. Maniram took part in them. All the young boys in the community would come to watch.

In western Nagpur, from Telankhedi to Ambazari, was a settlement of Cowherds. The Cowherds were famous everywhere for their wrestling skills. No one from any other caste would dare to walk on Cowherd Road. In the morning they would milk the cows and buffaloes, and after an energetic session of an hour or two in the gymnasium they would bring the cans of milk to east and central Nagpur.

Maniram was the only one of our community who dared a wrestling match with the Cowherds. The youth of the Maharpura who were enthusiastic about wrestling put on muslin shirts, turbans, and dhotis and came to the Baramora with ceremony and style. Nearly five to six times their number of Cowherds had gathered there.

Maniram came to the gymnasium, and the ranks of wrestlers started to form. A preplanned quarrel started between the two parties. With insulting language, the Mahars and Cowherds began to taunt each other. "You bastard Scavenger, don't you have any respect?" (In this period all Hindi-speakers, and Muslims too, called Mahars "Scavengers.") All the Cowherds wielded sticks and clubs. The Mahars were caught by surprise. Even so, some Mahars grabbed the sticks of the Cowherds and began to whirl them around. Maniram, of course, was an expert. Warding off eight or ten blows from the Cowherds with his own stick he began to withdraw. By this time the outnumbered Mahar youth had started to run away, and the gang of Cowherds came after Maniram.

Maniram, to save his life, ran into a compound, where his shirt got caught on a wire. A British lawyer for the government, Mr. Dick, lived there. Mr. Dick heard voices shouting, "Kill him! Kill him!" Aware that someone on his grounds was fighting, he fired his gun in the air. All the Cowherd boys who were ready to beat up Maniram ran away.

Barrister Dick was a well-wisher of the Mahar community, but he had very little close connection with the Mahar people, although he had a Mahar cook. Dick enlisted a student of Maniram's named Urkuda, who had arrived looking for his teacher, to bring a tonga. After it came Dick gave Urkuda five rupees and said, "Now take him to Mayo hospital."

Instead, Maniram went directly home, where his mother had some herbs and medicines. She took care of him with these. After three or four days of keeping his body and legs heated, Maniram left the house, with the intention of taking revenge on the Cowherds.

Shouting in his hoarse voice, "I'll see what school the Cowherds have learned in," he left the house with a heavy cudgel—a club rather than a stick. Today's students would not be able even to lift it.

The Cowherds used to bring milk to all the rich people in Bardi from Dharampeth. There was only one road, so they had to enter Bardi in front of what is today the Variety Cinema.

Maniram stood with his club a little ahead of Maharaj Bag. Taunting them with jeers of "Welcome, Cowherds, let's see what you can do to save your milk," he stood on that road from dawn till dusk. The Cowherds who were bringing their milk on their bicycles saw him from a distance. They began to run away in ones and twos. But some daring ones formed groups of four or five and came forward. Maniram whirled the club, and leaving their cycles and milk cans on the road, these Cowherds, too, ran away.

After their milk supply had been stopped for three or four days, the rich folks of Bardi began to raise an outcry, but lacking a compromise with Maniram the Cowherds could not carry on. Dayaram Ustad was the leader of the

Cowherds. He would come with his cart to the Bardi market, held on the Tar in front of the Maharpura. Maniram's merchant business also took place there. One day Dayaram Ustad himself came to Maniram's house. He greeted all respectfully. He gave saris and blouses to Maniram's mother and wife, and a shawl and shoulder cloth to Maniram. Laughing and saying that wrestlers had to respect each other, Maniram accepted these gifts. His honor had been restored.

Maniram was fearless from childhood on. As an adult he got employment as a gangman on the railroad. He would tie a big baton to his cycle and move around, keeping guard in the dead of night along the railway tracks. For a Mahar to own a cycle was a rare thing, but Maniram had a "made in England" bicycle. At the time *nagfani* groves were spread everywhere around the railroad tracks. Even during the day people feared going into those trees. But Maniram didn't know the name of fear. Around 1920 there was a strike in the mills, and Maniram lost his job. The strike ended, but he wasn't taken back. The fodder trade that he began then was continued until the next generation.

# Chapter 3

## CALLOUSNESS AND CLOUDS

Before I was born, Grandfather Sadashiv worked as a tailor at Dhantoli, sewing beautiful slips and blouses. He was living in the neighborhood then. The small Purna used to take rice and vegetables to her father from Bardi. For a few pennies you could get a double roti or bread. Her father would eat half and give half to his daughter.

Once he owed a debt to a Washerman, who planned to bring a lien on the house. In those days court cases were decided quickly, so people held more faith in the police and the legal system. A *sadhu* who was Sadashiv's friend suggested, "Go somewhere for a month." So my grandfather took everyone to Kamathi. He got work as a cinema manager and ended up living there a long time. There also he made friends with Parsis and Europeans.

One day while Sadashiv was eating, his friend came up to him, panting. He said, "Your little girl was wounded by my car." They both ran into the road, picked up Purna from under the car, and took her to Ardeshar Parsi's clinic. She was kept there for nearly a month. Mother used to say, "Since that time it has affected my head." If Mother was alone she went on mumbling for hours on end. This was not a fit of madness. It was an aftereffect of the accident.

Sadashiv lived for seven years at Kamathi in Chintamanbaba's house. Bayjabai lived next door. She took in an orphaned Mahar boy named Husain as a son-in-law. For the marriage of that boy to her daughter, a military band of White people was called. At the time it was considered a great honor to get a military band. The pomp Mahars exhibited when they had the chance was something fantastic. Narayan Kumbhare was the son of that Husain. He became a famous political and social leader, and his daughter is a member of the Legislative Assembly and a staunch Ambedkarite today!

Sadashiv then came again to Bardi to live. His wife, Kamlaja, worked in the mill while he managed the household. By then he had gathered a little property. The couple heard there was a man in Shanivari who was ready for marriage. Sixteen-year-old Purnabai was considered a little old. Waman was a widower. He had four daughters and one son by his first wife. The oldest daughter was older than my mother, but still Sadashiv gave his consent. He must have been concerned whether mother would get married at all after the effects of her accident.

There was one more reason for agreeing to the proposal of Waman. Waman's father, Vithoba Raoji Moon, was a well-known social leader of Nagpur. He had built a bathing place at Ambala tank for the Mahar community; he would collect fees for their ceremonies and so was known as Moonpande (Moonpriest). He would beat the drums known as *pongade* for the processions for Shiva's fair. So he was also called Vithoba Pongade. Along with spreading education among Untouchables, and encouraging them to keep away from carrion, he also organized Mahar conferences. Because Sadashiv was convinced by all of this that his daughter would have a good life in the Moon family, he overlooked Waman's being a widower and had his daughter Purnabai married to him.

Of life with my father, I remember only his drunkenness. I must have been four or five years old; my little sister was two or three years younger. Our father was a driver for the Parsis at a wage of 250 rupees per year, not small for that time. But linked to this fine salary was a strong addiction to drinking. He would go from work to the liquor shop and only from there to the house. At times someone apparently grabbed the rest of the pay from his pocket on his way home. Many times neighbors had to pick him up from the gutter.

One day he came to the house with a bottle. He wouldn't drink at home without giving every kid a little bit to drink. It was a practice in Mahar houses to bring liquor and give some to everyone in the house. That was the "children's cut." He kept giving me drink. Slowly I became tipsy. My mother grabbed me. For some time my eyes remained closed. Everyone came running. Someone gave me some herb medicine and I recovered. My father was indifferent to all of this. When my mother's concern showed on her face, he began to beat her. Every evening he would beat my mother. The first wife's children also occasionally threw oil on this fire by taunting my mother and teasing us.

My mother sent a message to my grandfather Sadashiv: "It's impossible for me to live. The children are in danger." Sadashiv sent for Dasharath Patil, Dr. Adhav, and Bhosle. He told them to go to Shanivar to intervene and bring back his daughter. They brought my mother and us back to Sadashiv and told my grandfather, "Waman can't control himself."

One day my father came and grabbed me and took me with him. But my cousins and my half-brother-in-law Mahadev sneaked me away and brought me back to Grandfather. Sadashiv threatened to take my father to court, but he didn't. And from that time on my little sister and I lived with my mother at my grandfather's.

Then Grandfather died. The pillar of the household had crumbled. The entire family was in a state of disintegration. Soon thereafter a gentleman entered the house. He announced, "I am Laxman Lohkare; this house is mine. I am Sadashiv's son." People were preparing to carry away Sadashiv's body, and there was Laxman Lohkare taking control of the house. He brought his wife and children into the house. He also brought a photographer. He set up the dead Sadashiv and had a photo taken of himself with the dead body; only then did he let the corpse be carried away.

From where did Laxman emerge, I wondered. Mother told us the story one day. Sadashiv had had a relationship with a woman before his marriage to Kamlaja Dhabarde. Though Sadashiv had never married Laxman's mother, his son had used his name.

After Laxman and his family moved in and we were all living in the household together, my days of being callously treated began. Grandmother was at work in the mill but she fell sick from time to time. For a whole year she was bedridden. Laxman's wife, Tulsa, provoked quarrels about this daily.

While Grandmother was sick, the bill for the house tax came. The house was several years behind in a tax of ten rupees. But Grandmother had not even this much money. Laxman realized this and went to the municipality. He paid all the back taxes in his own name and took the receipt. Grandmother was on her deathbed. There was no one to let my mother know what was going on. The neighbors had mostly been won over to Laxman's side.

About that time, when I was studying in third standard, my mother's uncle Narayan Dhabarde came from Vela. He said he would take Grandmother to Vela, her home village, for treatment. Leave aside medicine, there was a huge problem even getting food and drink where we were living. Grandmother, Mother, my sister Malti, and I all went to Vela. It held a central place in the political and social movement as Dasharath Patil's Vela.

Grandmother had four brothers. Narayan Dhabarde was the youngest, the most liberal. The Dhabardes were moneylenders and the richest family for miles around. They owned hundreds of acres of land, with a big house, and a road in front of the house going to the Girda fair. Hundreds of people would come for the fair. They stayed for days and nights on cots at Dhabarde's big house. There was no scarcity of food.

Narayan Dhabarde had two children, a boy and a girl, named Nathu and Nathi. His wife, Radhabai, had them after many years of trying to conceive. Nathi, the older one, was an incomparable beauty. The women of the village would go to the Wainganga river, which flowed beside Vela, to wash their clothes. Nathi would go with them, and there she learned how to swim. The river flooded one day. While the other women sat looking at the fast-flowing Wainganga, Nathi tied up her sari and took a leap. Plowing her way through the water she reached the other side. Then she came back the same way. The news spread through the village in a flash, and Narayan learned about it. He was little educated, but knowledgeable. He called his daughter. His voice used to have force. "Well, Nathi, what if you had been carried away in the flood?"

"Yes, father." Nathi was forthright like her father.

"Great, girl; you're brave. But don't always be so foolhardy."

I saw the marriage of Nathi as a child. There were huge gram sweetballs the size of tennis balls, made with so much ghee and sugar! People were betting over who could eat the most sweetballs. The match began. Ganpat Kamlya and Tanba Moon were in the competition. Usually after two or three sweetballs no one had the strength to eat any more, but these two each ate more than twenty. Slowly, slowly the sweetballs were going down. Narayan Dhabade began to roar at people to serve them more. The attention of everyone in the wedding party was fixed on Ganpat and Tanba. After eating twenty-six sweetballs Tanba accepted defeat. Ganpat ate one more and won the competition. The two sat for a short time. Then they went into the inside room, where they lay down flat. People stood on their backs and pounded them.

Because of her family's great prominence, Nathi's wedding became a subject of wonder throughout the village. Every woman attending the wedding was given a blouse and sari, and every man a dhoti and shoulder cloth. Nathi came bedecked in jewelry from top to toe; she appeared like some princess descending on us. The whole village came as a wave, filling Narayan Dhabarde's house to pay their respects. With songs sung by the Mahar women the atmosphere became mournful, and slowly, whether Mahars or Farmers, Ropemakers or Oilpressers, tears began to flow from everyone's eyes. As one caste, the whole village came with horses, carriages, and carts to join the wedding procession, and Nathi left for her in-laws' place.

Such was my great-uncle Narayan Dharbarde. Grandmother was left for medical treatment with him. At that time very few people went to doctors. Besides this, it was difficult to get a doctor in a village like Vela. A shaman was called. He built a fire and laid Grandmother before it. He became possessed and began to vomit. Some bones appeared to fall out in his vomit. He displayed them to everyone. For two or three months this treatment went on, and one day finally Kamalja breathed her last.

I had left the village before Grandmother died. My third standard Marathi examination was to begin. By the time the exam had finished Mother had completed all the formalities around Grandmother's death and returned. The support that she relied on up to now had thoroughly crumbled. She was without any shelter, like a boat broken away from its moorings.

She had brought one sack of grain and a little money from her uncle's house. She had also taken with her generous promises: "If you need anything send a message. As long as I'm here I won't let you lack anything." But this was not to be so, and she was not about to go back to her drunken husband. Once she came back she had the responsibility of feeding the whole household.

Before the death of her father she had never put a foot outside of the house to work. She was unused to manual labor. The hard toil of splitting rocks would have been too much for her. For some days she sat in thought. Her neighbors gave her advice: "Go to your husband. He will not send you away. Forget what has happened. Start your married life again." However, she didn't listen to anyone. There was no lack of Brahman households around our settlement, but Mother didn't even think about working in one. She knew she would not have gotten any work in housework or cooking. Many Parsi families, who worked in high positions in Tata's Empress Mills or Dadabhai's Model Mill, lived near the Shukrawar tank. They had a separate school. They paid no regard to caste. Mother searched for employment in Parsi households within a mile from our home, but it took a long time to find work.

Mother went out daily to look for work and came back only at seven or eight in the evening. Occasionally she would get one or two rupees' worth of labor. She would feed us a bit, and then go out again the following day.

During this period my little sister and I did some thinking, and we went to the Brahman neighborhood with a bowl. In imitation of the Ropemaker women who came begging to the settlement, we went to the front of a house and yelled, "Oh, madam, give us a piece of bread." An elderly man suddenly sprang at us and said, "Hey, run or I'll whip your ass!" This experience surprised us. We never went out to beg again.

Seeing Mother's helplessness after Grandmother died, Laxman took control of the house. We were now forced to live on the veranda. Laxman's wife was a ferocious shrew. No one could face her curses. A dictionary of swear words would pour out of her mouth. In contrast, Mother didn't even know what a curse was. From her childhood on, Grandfather had raised her like a flower. Now she had to face Tulsa day and night and listen to her. One day Tulsa grabbed her. Mother felt that now she would die. Strength came suddenly into her body. There was an iron poker beside her. She lifted it up and hurled it against Tulsa's throat. The bleeding Tulsa began to yell loudly. All the neighbors gathered to watch. After this incident they began to speak only to Tulsa. After some days had passed a woman acquaintance gave us a small room in the lane behind her house as a place to stay. There was a low door in the decrepit room. We two and Mother somehow lived there with our bodies cramped together. In this manner, days went by, one after another.

# Chapter 4

## HEAT AND RAIN

Starting in March the summer begins to burn in Nagpur. By April it becomes impossible to go outside after nine or ten in the morning. By May the roads are empty in the afternoon.

Naturally no one appeared during afternoons in the open field in front of the settlement. Day after day went by while we played cards or marbles under the pipal tree during the fierce heat of Vaishakh. The turbulent air would give impetus to whirlpools, and then the harshly burning winds would lift up the dust in the field and blow it into the neighborhood. The loud shout "Oh oh, the Matya is coming!" would resound from afar, and the doors in the settlement would slam shut so that dust from outside could not enter. The winds would bring with them the milk cans from the stables of the Cowherds in the market of the Tar and deposit them in the Maharwada, and these cans would be swallowed up in the community.

The flowers of the *shembdi* tree could be seen only in the summer. Crowds of boys and girls would leap up to the trees to eat this ripe red fruit the shape of plums. The winds would blow these fruits to the ground, and then without worrying about hiding, the kids would get a taste of them in the middle of the afternoon.

I passed my days wandering in the lanes of Sitabardi and Dhantoli with Sukhya, sometimes with Gangya, sometimes Bala. If someone's large, spreading mango tree appeared in our path, it was always fun to throw a stone and make a mango fall. If someone yelled from inside we would run away; if not we would leap over the wire of the compound and throw the fallen mango to a friend outside. We only needed to keep a watch that no one came. Beyond this tree grew two or three chinch trees. No matter how many *chinchas* were broken off, still more hung there. With one stone a cluster of *chinchas* would fall. We put the *chinchas* in our pockets and felt pleasure in partaking of their taste on the road or giving them to some smaller friends.

We would go by the Bute School. Rather than taking the long way on the road around it, we would go through the compound behind the school and jump down to the road. Going a little ahead we would cross the gutters of the Sangam *chawls*. Passing the road beyond the Regent Talkies we came to the compound behind the Maharaj Park. (Now a city bus station stands in that spot.) From there we would push our way inside. On the left was a small orchard of mangos and *chikkus*. On the right, the drainage canals. We would go by these canals. If we saw a *chikku* we would evade the watchman and grab it and run. We would watch the deer grazing on the banks of the canal. The net of wires which met to fence the compound would be open at the drains. Placing our feet carefully on their banks we would go between the wires for about twenty feet and then cross over the canal to enter the park. We knew that huge snakes lived in this river for the whole of the year, and that all the polluted water would stagnate in the drains. If anyone fell in, it would be difficult to get him out. Still we got into the habit of going this way.

In Maharaj Park not a trace of the heat of the summer existed. Flower beds and towering trees of varying types spread green everywhere. Glancing at the herds of deer from the fence of their compound we would come to the monkey cages. We would toss the tidbits picked up on the way to the monkeys. Sukya knew the habits of animals very well. He would take some gram bits in his hand and, holding his hand inside the cage and opening his fist, call the monkeys to eat. The monkeys would hold on with one hand and eat with the other. We went there so many times. Because of this the monkeys became familiar to us. We called them by such names as Redcheek, Whiteface, Whitey; we would call to them, tease them, give them some love, and go on.

A high tree stood near the monkey cage. This tree grew huge fruits, twice the size of a large cucumber. The skin was hard like an eggshell, but inside the fruit was white like an apple. The pulp was bittersweet and tasty. These fruits hung from the tree around thirty to forty feet off the ground. But our friends were expert at throwing stones and could throw them exactly in the right way to knock off the fruit. After spending half an hour aiming at the hanging fruits we would leave and eat them on the road and give what was left to the people at home. These fruits were called English *chinchbilai*. I have never seen them anywhere else.

Wandering on from there, we would climb on top of the bear cage. We would tease him for a little while and then throw stones at the *khirni* tree to knock down a *khirni*, grab it, and take it with us. We would fill our pockets with the nuts of the tall *behad* tree and then sit somewhere and crack open the nuts to get at the delicious almond-like pit inside. After some time I would fall into a stupor and lie down under the trees. Gangya, Sukya, Balya also would be lying down. Around eight in the evening someone would get up and say, "Come on, it's gotten very late." Making our way through the darkness of Maharaj Park we would come to the main road and return home.

We would give the fruits of the *behads* left in my pocket to mother, who would say, "The pits of these are very nice, just like almonds."

"Oh yes. That's why I ate so many."

"Oh, Bapu, you get almost drunk from those nuts. Don't eat too many."

When I sat down to supper after washing my hands and feet, I realized I had eaten many more of them than usual.

Balya, or sometimes Gangya, was my friend in wandering. Only one small settlement of huts and some bungalows lay in Ramdas Peth. Beyond Panchshil Talkies the entire area was vacant. We would trample on all the flowers of the *gokaru* forest as we went. In the middle was a palm grove, where tall, tall date trees grew. The yellow-red hanging bundles of dates would call out to us, and we would hurl stones to knock them down. We would fill our pockets and eat them as we walked, giving whatever was left over to our friends. Some boy might eat too many dates and get a nosebleed. His mother would scold him, laughing, "Why ever did you eat so much, huh?" and give him a thump. She would sprinkle cold water over his head, and in five to ten minutes the bleeding would stop and he would go out to play again.

Most of the kids in the neighborhood went to the Tar to sleep in the hot weather. But if any drops of rain started falling on our faces we would spread a mat or blanket in front of the house and sleep there. The afternoon's hot blasts of air would subside after nine at night. At eleven the second shift of workers would leave the mills. Around midnight a cool puff of air would blow over our bodies. Finally, after about two in the morning, a clear, tranquil wind with a cooling touch on our bodies would tell us to sleep.

On such a day a heated wind softens as it rushes in. It brings with it an intoxicating fragrance. It carries an inkling that somewhere rain is sprinkling the earth. It is a sign that now the monsoon will come; the land will become cool; its parched body will grow peaceful. Even then, we don't stop sleeping outside. The summer is stubborn—it does not give in to rain quickly—and people are also stubborn. We wouldn't return to sleeping in the house until the rain actually came.

In those days everyone slept outside without fear. Many left the doors of their houses wide open. Women of all ages and little girls used to sleep fearlessly on small verandas outside or on the roads for relief from the heat. We never heard of any mischief. Big strong men slept on every side, and if there was any twitching, someone could call out.

And then, in the middle of the night, sprinkles of rain would begin. As the moon climbed up in the sky, some clouds would trespass and play mischief by scattering drizzle as they went by. Saying, "Uh oh, water has come," some of the kids would get up and go inside, and as they did so the rain would stop. Then there would be only wind for the whole night. With a small blanket over me I would just remain sleeping.

Huge pitch-black clouds would come into the sky. They completely over-shadow the moon. Just as it feels that now a heavy shower will come, a strong wind blows and all the clouds wildly rush away. Once again the sky glimmers as if washed with clear moonlight. In the last half of Vaishakh month the moon can be seen even when one is lying down on the bedstead. Sometimes the moon seems to be running away; sometimes white and dark clouds seem to be competing with each other. I used to feel curious about what kind of deer were on the moon. I had a hankering to know how the demons could eat up the moon, causing an eclipse. Since the tiled houses were low, I could see the North Star daily. At first the lower part of the Big Dipper would appear, like a small bedstead. The four legs of the bedstead were four stars, or four thieves, with three more thieves to carry them away. Then I would measure out five times the distance of the leg. The solitary North Star would appear different from every other glimmering star. I would remember the story of Dhruv, the North Star, from school. Dhruv won a fixed position, and no one could make him get up or move him from there, and the seven thieves would revolve around him for centuries and centuries.

In between, flocks of herons would caper in the clear moonlight. Like a pure white garland on the blue-black canvas of the sky they could be seen con-tinuously flying, disciplined, in crisscrossed rows. From them we can learn how to walk in ranks. On a tall pipal tree the herons made their nest. Their crying, playing, and leaping went on till the middle of the night. Then they also would become quiet and go to sleep. The heat and hot blasts of air borne on the wind would grow somewhat cool, and slowly my eyes would close. At 2:30 in the morning blew the factory whistle of Model Mill. The mildly blowing winds of dawn would wave their gentle hands over my body, and even with the morn-ing sun I would never feel like getting up. When the sun's rays struck my eyes at 7:00, I would take my mat and go and lie down inside.

There is a different sort of pleasure in the heat of summer, a unique hap-piness. The heat continuously makes sweat flow from the body. But you don't feel clammy in Nagpur as you do in Bombay. The sweat immediately dries up. From time to time thirst comes, and then how peaceful life seems after you ve-hemently gulp down water taken in a metal cup from an earthen pot. That water has a different flavor, linked to the earth; no water from the fridge tastes like it. Two or three hours after the noon meal the flavor of that water is something fantastic. And even in the summer, how wonderful to eat puris fried in oil, along with chicken or a gravy mutton dinner, and then let the water from the earthen jar flow through the stomach for the whole day. In every house such an earthen pot was necessary for water. Even the poor could afford a four-penny pot. And if by accident the pot broke, then you asked for a pitcher full of cool water from the neighbors. Neighborliness means giving a bit of our family's food every day to the neighbors and taking some from them. The love of neighborliness residing in earthen houses would absorb all the summer heat. In those days there was no electricity, no electric lamps, not even fans. Still at the height of afternoon these houses would feel cool. In heavy earthen houses you stay cool during the summer and warm during the winter.

During the heat of the afternoon many women and children would stay in the houses. And sometimes from the north the cries of an assault would be heard. All of Maharpura would start bustling. A pack of monkeys, leaping from one house to another, damaging the tiled roofs, comes capering. There's one pugnacious leader among them. If he runs away then all the monkeys also run. The boys throw stones to drive them away. The monkeys dash through the middle of the community and run to the Nag river through the field on the other side. But in that little time they cause much destruction. To prevent rain leakage during monsoons, the tiles have to be repaired. Men, women, and children in every house climb on the roofs to repair their houses.

And then one day the sky would fill with clouds. Thick clouds would gather and the first rain of the monsoon would begin to fall. The birds would start whirling everywhere. And boys in every house would throw off their clothes and run out to soak themselves in the rain. The mothers would give a push to the lazy ones. The mother who had tried with gentle fingers to scrape away the prickly heat from the back of her child would send the boy to dance in the rain. They believed prickly heat was healed with the first rains. After getting soaked from top to toe we could dance and play in the flowing water. I used to dance for hours and hours under the showers of the cloudy skies.

The first rains spread an intoxicating smell of earth over the settlement. With the first monsoon the settlement becomes quiet. The flow of sweat stops. The drains begin to overflow with three or four days of rainfall. We make our way across the drains with the help of stones.

Now clouds come from time to time, drop some rain, and leave. Other times there is a six- or seven-day downpour. In any case people's business goes on. Gangya and I go out. Water covers the Patwardhan ground. We run back and forth across the whole ground, playing in that water. We proceed on Jail Road up to Khamlya. On coming back we turn at Ajni square. At that time a

tall *kavathe* tree stood there. Gangya loved to climb trees. I have not seen anyone else in our community who could climb up the tall *kavathe* tree and leap
from one branch to another like a monkey as Gangya did. He would break off
the *kavathes* and throw them down and I would pick them up. He and I would
wander along the road eating the nut of the *kavathes*. The rains would stop and
the winds would blow. If we took the shirts off our back and shook them they
wouldn't take long to dry.

Once the rain abated a bit, Gangya and I would go to catch crabs. With a
large pincer in our hands, we would examine the holes in the banks of the Nag
river. We would try to surprise the two eyes inside the hole. If you prick with
the pincer just behind those eyes the crab would come forward. Then we would
grab it and throw it in the bag. We would go far up and down the banks of the
Nag river.

Once when I was about to put my hand inside a hole Gangya yelled,
"Stop! Let me see. Where is the pincer?"

I gave it to him. Two eyes appeared so clearly in the hole. Gangya pricked
with the pincer, but the crab did not come out. When he withdrew the pincer
the two eyes remained there. He exclaimed, "Ahh, Vasanya, run, it's a snake!
Don't stick your hand in there."

Every once in a while ten to twelve boys would go out in a gang to catch
crabs. Catching crabs along with Mangal meant a chance to learn many things.
He knew how, where, and when to grab the crabs and could recognize all the
different kinds. He was known in the community as Crabman Mangal. He
would take small boys with him and wander the banks of the Nag river for the
whole day. He would ask the boys to bring eight or ten bottles from their
houses to put the crabs in, and then would catch selected white and black crabs.
He would light a fire, break off the feet of the crabs, clean them and roast them
on the coals, and then feed all the boys.

The festival of snakes, or Nagpanchmi, was celebrated in every house.
After the sweeping and the sprinkling of water everywhere, a ritual worship
of snakes was performed. In some houses only *muthe* was cooked during Nagpanchmi. Two small *chapatis* would be filled with spices and sealed. They contained sesamum, poppy seeds, coconut, sugar, cashews, and cardamom. Sticks
of the palas tree would be placed over half a pot of boiling water on the
hearth, and the sealed *chapatis* would be put on that and cooked in the steam.
These *muthes* were very tasty and lasted for many days. In some houses *pahile*
or *khis* were prepared. *Khis* is a dish of sweet, thick rice made with cashews,
almonds, and sweets. During Nagpanchmi a rule stipulated that food cooked
in oil should not be eaten at mealtimes. So gram lentils and spiced yogurt
were the only spicy dishes that could be served. Some families were called

"five-spotted," some "seven-spotted," and some "nine-spotted." According to the "spots," so many snakes, so many scorpions, and so many lumps of dough had to be made. These were fried in oil and then soaked in milk to eat. The seven-spotted families were not supposed to eat the snakes and scorpions of the five-spotted families. If some small girl ate one by mistake, then she would be understood to be a daughter of that family, and at weddings and other festivals she would have to be given saris or blouses from them.

While the festival of snakes was going on in every house, we would go outside to see the games. Paikya, Machhinder, Gorakh, and Shamya would gather near the temple, and their contests would begin. Lemons or coconuts would be thrown a certain distance, and whoever could cover the distance with the fewest throws would win fifty, one hundred, or even two hundred rupees. This went on until the afternoon, and then the kids would run to the Morris College grounds to see the magic show. I would go running after all the kids.

A new magician would come to the field beating his tom-tom. He would take a lemon, a knife, and a magic wand out of a small bag. In a loud voice he would hurl his challenge in Hindi: "Come on, beautiful people, who can stand up to me?" He would do a lot of patter. A crowd would gather. He would perform a few sleight-of-hand tricks and then say that there was no one to compete with him and begin to put his things back in the bag. At that moment a youth would come forward from the crowd in the dress of a wizard. He would take up the challenge and come to the field with one or two companions. He would slowly remove his heavy clothes and with a "chhu chhu" would begin hurling chants like a volley of stones. Once these chants began the two would move back and forth. The companions would make a show of being pained in the stomach, or hit in the back. This would go on for a good period of time.

This was a contest between a magician–snake charmer and a sorcerer. The sorcerer had a magic box that held a doll with a charmed egg and a lemon. The sorcerer would throw some magic, and just when the magician would come to pick up the box, he would get a shooting pain in his stomach and fall. Then the magician would run far away to the river. From there he would bring charmed water and cast a spell. He would pick up some dirt, which had an egg in it that had been put there beforehand, and then come and lift up the box. With a knife from his pocket he would cut the lemon. Red blood would gush from it and the sorcerer would gasp and fall unconscious. The magician would leave, and the sorcerer would recover.

One day Waman Rangari of our community, who had become a magician, told me, "There is a red sandalwood tree near Kahate Gokhale Gymnasium. Its sap is put on the knife and the knife is dried; then when it cuts the lemon some acidic process takes place and red juice leaks out. A balloon with red coloring in it is held in your mouth. If you want to spit out a mouthful of blood, you break the balloon. These are all tricks. But people come flocking in crowds to see these magic shows."

The monsoon clouds, after dropping their allotted store of water on the city of Nagpur, would move on. As the water crashed down in torrents during the early rainfall, the clouds and lightning would seem to be having violent intercourse. When the sky with its hundreds of thousands of brandishing hands dashes against the hot earth, isn't it like the sexual play of male and female?

To really see the arrogance of the clouds you should stand on top of Ramtek Hill. When the clouds like combed cotton scatter their spray to lick the body and go, I used to feel that I should dissolve at that instant into the sky. Shouldn't Kalidas, the guru of poets, not feel a trust in the messages brought by the intimate companionship of those clouds that so vehemently drive against the body? These clouds thrust at the hill of Ramtek as if to have an intimate talk with him.

In Maharpura the heat and rain bring both trouble and joy. In infancy, nature is a close friend. It distributes happiness to us with innumerable hands. Everyone has to decide for himself how much to take. The noontime heat of Shravan month pounds on the body and dazes the eyes. As drizzling rain falls the sun comes out from behind the clouds as if to say to the children, "Âbe, the sun is peeing. Come out and play in the water." As they come out the sun is sinking in the west, but everyone begins to look east. There, on the horizon, a rainbow stretches from one end of the earth to the other.

Taking a taste of all this joy, I return to the house. Dark has fallen. Mother has not yet come. My little sister is sitting quietly after bringing water from the tap. The neighbor woman inquires, "Bapu, hasn't your mother come?" We only shake our heads. Once again we'll have to go to sleep hungry today. I slurp cold water into my stomach to still the pangs of hunger and throw myself down on the veranda. My eyes close. Sleep doesn't come. My little sister also lies down. I sense a movement. I think that Mother must have come. I touch her and see that it's our neighbor, Grandmother Bhuri. "Oh, Bapu, get up. Oh girl, get up. Have a bite to eat. Your mother will come now." She puts warm *bhakri* and coconut chutney before us and goes away. We sit waiting. In a little while Mother comes. She is coming back after cooking in the Parsis' bungalows. She gives us the vegetables and chapatis she has brought with her, and then the three of us, mother and children, put enough food into our stomachs to fill them.

Mother says, "I've gotten a job in Mishibaba's house, two rupees plus food."

Eating a little of Grandmother Bhuri's warm *bhakri* and coconut, I gulp down some cold water from the earthen pot. Outside the door, the city's lamp twinkles and burns with a low flame. Electricity has not come to the community. Even in full rain this lamp endures and lives throughout the night. Thinking of the mystery of its life, I lie down. Grandmother Bhuri, Mother, and I, we are all like that lamp, dangling in storm and rain, waiting for the next day.

Outside is the patter of the rain. I hardly know when sleep comes.

# Chapter 5

## DEV MASTER'S CURSE FAILS

Atmaram Patil lived separately from all the neighborhood. His house was next to that of Grandfather Sadashiv. Because Grandfather had supported him in his childhood, Patil honored Grandfather. When Laxman was invading our house, Mother called for Patil. He made a few threats about Laxman, but physical fighting was not in his nature. He always felt that he was different from the rest of the community. He would look at people around him and say, "Everyone drinks yelva. Everyone takes alcohol. They'll never change." Whenever he could, he kept his children from playing with other kids. Two of his three children matriculated before 1930. One was put to work on the lathe machines. Atmaram and Hari did clerical work, and lived like some kind of Brahmans—clean white *dhotis* and white shirts.

The whole house was run according to his son Atmaram's word. Both of his brothers followed blindly whatever he said. Their wives fought continuously, but not a single quarrel broke out among the three brothers. Later the sisters-in-law kept separate hearths, but even then the brothers ate together in the evening. They would talk; they would hear their wives' complaints but not take them very seriously. If there was a white-collar house in the community, this was it. But due to his aloof character, Patil's connection with the other families of the community was nearly broken.

The Patils used to have a fourth brother. His name was Gajanan. Whenever Mother asked him to, Gajanan would take me on his shoulders, give me baths, play with me; he was very warmhearted. He never liked to stay sitting in the house, but always would wander outside. He left on a whim and came back only in the evenings. All of his friends were Brahmans. His other brothers didn't like this. They scolded him for it daily. One day a huge quarrel developed. Atmaram and Bala together beat him ferociously. Balkrishna, who used to run the lathe machine shop, was very sturdy. In the heat of his anger

33

he threw a sledgehammer at Gajanan. Gajanan dodged it and ran away. He never came back. After that, no one uttered a single word about him, but behaved as if nothing had happened. Why should there have been so much cruelty and ferocity? I never got an answer to this. But Hari Patil remained friends with Gajanan. A Brahman named Bhayya Macve, who lived in Hanuman Lane to the west of the neighborhood, also was Gajanan's friend. Hari got some news from him, but never told the rest of the household.

I remained very enthusiastic about Gajanan. Mother always remembered his nature, playful spirit, and courage. I went many times to Bhayya's house and asked about Gajanan. Bhayya would say, "Oh Vasant, Gajanan went to take part in the freedom struggle. He won't come back now."

Bhayya Macwe was tall, with very short hair. His entire dress was pure white, with khadi pajamas and a long Bengali coat. I wasn't old enough to understand what he did in Congress. But eventually I learned that Bhayya had left for Congress work in Uttar Pradesh and Bihar. I would ask his brother frequently about Bhayya and Gajanan. One day he said that they had gone to jail.

After many days Bhayya appeared on the road. I greeted him. "Hello, Bhayya, where are you these days?"

"Oh, Vasanta, one should keep on doing something in life. One should feel meaning in doing something. Where one is is not important. What one does is important."

Bhayya at that time was working among Adivasis in Bihar in the Bhoodan movement to give land to the landless. He said that Gajanan was also there.

I never even learned when Bhayya's dedicated life finished. He died without telling anyone where Gajanan was. After that, one day a letter came to Manohar (Atmaram Patil's son) with information that Gajanan had died in Lucknow and inquiring if he had any heirs. Not one of Gajanan's brothers was alive at the time to hear the news of his death.

Now I began to almost live in Patil's house. When the results of the fourth grade examination came, Mother went to Patil and said, "Brother, Vasanta has passed."

"Good," Patil replied. "Educate him."

"What can I do? I don't even have a penny."

Uncle Hari saw the marks and said, "Come on." He took me directly to the Patwardhan High School. At that time the Patwardhan school was understood to be of the highest standard, not simply in Nagpur but in all of the Central Provinces. Only selected smart students gained admission there. There was no question of reserved seats for Untouchables. Admission was given according to merit alone.

Uncle paid the fee and I got admission. The tuition cost only six annas a month, including the fee for sports equipment. Even so, it was impossible for my mother to manage.

Tucking my shirt into my shorts, I would leave Maharpura. Running between the Modi number three apartments I would enter Patwardhan in the
Somwar market area. Some friends from the normal school also attended there:
Bhaskar Joshi, Prabhakar Thergavkar, Mohani, Shripad Tambe, and some eight
to ten other boys.

For the first class, a very tough teacher named Khedkar Master taught
English. When this gentleman—dressed in coat, pants, tie, and hat, not very tall
but strongly built—entered the classroom the students grew absolutely silent.
He taught us artistic handwriting, and upon examining the notebooks every day
he praised those who had beautiful lettering. At first I wrote a very shapely letter "O" on three-lined paper with a nib. Overall, however, graceful handwriting was not one of my accomplishments.

Uncle provided me with books and notebooks, pencils, slates, and other
equipment. I became friends with Manohar, the oldest son of Uncle Atmaram
Patil, and we always played together in the morning or evening.

Along with my mother, my sister and I were staying on the veranda of
Grandfather's house. Where to keep my books? There was of course Uncle
Hari's house. But I did not have all the things needed for school. For drawing,
I lacked a box of watercolors and a brush. Where to obtain them? The afternoon break began. The boys ran out to play, while thoughts of a brush ran
through my head. My attention could not shift away from the brush that had
fallen from Tambe's bag. Tambe was from a rich family, the youngest son of the
first governor of the Central Provinces. What did he ever lack? He would get
another brush! I snatched his brush and threw it in my bag. I ran outside and
mixed with my friends as if nothing had happened.

At the end of the break the boys came inside. All opened books for the
second subject. That day there was no drawing class. So the deed was done, the
boys got a break, and I went home.

For the whole night thoughts of the brush kept running through my
mind. Why did I steal? Wouldn't Uncle have given me a brush? I felt embar-
rassed to ask Uncle again and again for money. But when I asked he never refused. So why did I do that thing? What would Tambe say tomorrow? If I was
discovered what would the teacher say? Would he allow me to remain in
school? One, two, a thousand thoughts troubled my mind that night. I finally
fell asleep in the middle of the night.

Upon getting up in the morning, I decided to return the brush to Tambe.
After all, Tambe was also a friend. I would say I had taken it by mistake. But by
the time I reached school the class had begun.

Saying, "May I come in, Sir?" I entered—and then what? Khedkar Master
was telling Tambe to search all the children's open bags. I became abashed. I
softly asked a student on the bench, "What is going on?" He said, "Tambe's

brush has been stolen. The teacher has told him to examine everyone's bag." Now there was no meaning in speaking to Tambe. When Tambe came near, I was standing with the brush in my hand and tears streaming down my face.

Khedkar Master was looking at me angrily. Shripad Tambe, a friend, was also looking at me with surprise. The whole class, astonished, was watching. When I came out of my daze, Khedkar Master was giving a sermon on Mahatma Gandhi's experiments with truth.

Khedkar Master instilled us with awe. Since he had come from the military, he imposed harsher discipline than others. He wandered through the classroom and examined everyone's nails. If the nails had grown too long they would have to be clipped by the next day. Not only hands and feet had to be clean; even clothes had to be spotless.

As my clothes grew more worn, I began to avoid washing them. Without soap, clothes naturally had to be washed with hard beating, and beating tore them. My shorts and shirts began to show wear, but I had no other clothes. One day Mr. Khedkar made me stand up. He asked, "Well, you haven't washed your clothes."

"No, sir."

"Why?"

"If they get torn, I have no other ones."

The teacher fell silent. All of these teachers had some kind of social consciousness. He told me to sit down and then told the students purposefully, "Many of you are well-to-do. If someone gives him a shirt and pants outfit it will be a work of merit."

A couple of days later, Bal Mohini took me to his big bungalow in Dharampeth. His mother gave me sweets to eat and a new, unused shirt and pair of shorts as a present. The Mohini family were Gandhians. Some Mahar students were living with them at the time for education. My uncle Vasudevrao had received the benefit of their help. Another classmate, Prabhakar Thergaonkar, whose mother and father were both doctors, took me to his home and gave me some tailored clothes. I also asked for something to eat. I felt happy that I had gotten clothes, and new ones from classmates at that. Mother said, "Son, why be ashamed of begging? At least we don't steal and slander."

I also got some clothes with the help of Pundalik Mul, who would visit the barber shop of Prahlad Mhali at Khalasi Lines. He was a tent contractor who supplied tents and pavilions for huge festivals, especially for the meetings and conferences of Ambedkar. One day, at Prahlad Mhali's urging, he gave me some red and blue tent cloth for pants and shirt. There's no question of worrying about looking good or bad when you don't have cloth to even cover your bottom. I sewed shorts and a shirt from that cloth; they looked like some kind of sports uniform on me. At that time even those clothes felt good to wear. Since the cloth was very strong the outfit lasted a long time, and I found the compassionate help given me by Pundalik Mul very useful.

Though my fee was excused at the school, no government scholarships existed at the time. One day, though, a notice came. Nalsapurkar Master read it, and said to the students, "Let the Harijan boys stand up."

There were six Mahar boys in the class, but no Mangs (Ropemakers) or Chambhars (Leather Workers). Not one student stood up. Then the teacher said, "A scholarship from the Harijan Sevak Sangh has come. We are supposed to send in the names of Harijan students. So which of your names should be written down?"

I never used to easily give answers in class. But I promptly rose and said, "Sir, we are not 'Harijans,' and we don't want the scholarship of the Harijan Sevak Sangh. None of us like to be called Harijans."

Pralhad Rangari also stood up. "We are followers of Babasaheb Ambedkar. None of us want 'Harijan' scholarships. Shende, do you want it?"

Before Shende could speak the teacher said, "Rangari, please sit down. I will ask the questions."

However, no one could defy Rangari. Prahlad used to live in Indora. He could play stick games and do *lathi* fighting. He always carried a dagger. Everyone knew this. No one in the school gave their names for a Harijan scholarship.

Nalsapurkar Master had no married life. He found his joy in teaching English. He would teach lessons like "Walking Tours" or "The Indian Crow" with great intensity. He also taught poems.

> Breathes there the man with soul so dead
> Who never to himself hath said,
> This is my own, my native land?

Such poems enchanted our minds. But we had our own questions. "In a short time Bhim Raj is coming" was the dream dangling before our eyes. Where was our share in our native land? This was something that every Dalit student in those days asked.

Nalsapurkar Master taught English with great dedication. I understood everything he taught, but if he threw out even a simple question I trembled and became tongue-tied. When he asked a question I stood mutely. The teacher would tire himself out asking again and again, but I couldn't get the courage to speak. Once when I made a stumbling effort to give an answer, Nalsapurkar Master said, "Oh speak, little man, speak," and my answer was lost in the uproarious laughter of the class.

*The second volume of* Dr. Babasaheb Ambedkar: Writings and Speeches *was published on Dr. Ambedkar's birthday anniversary, 14 April 1982. Shown at the time of the ceremony are Vasant Moon (center) with his office staff. Photo courtesy of Vasant Moon.*

Dev Master was the teacher for English grammar in the sixth standard. One day Dev Master gave me a curse: "Moon, you cannot pass matric for ten years." There were fluent English-speakers like Kshirsagar, Patwardhan, Tambe, and Buche as students in my class. However in that year, 1949, I easily passed the matric examination, while expert English speakers like Kshirsagar were not even found in the list of results.

See how strange is the course of life! The English language, which gave me so much trouble in high school, was the language of the writings of Babasaheb Ambedkar, which I was given the opportunity to edit, and I successfully did so. I always had doubts lurking in the corner of my mind that I might have made some mistake in English, but I am no longer afraid of that.

# Chapter 6

## RELIGIOUS HYMNS

People of every sect lived in the community. There were those who spread their blankets before the shrine of Tajuddin Baba; there were those who took part in Moharram processions or got possessed; there were hermits wandering apart from their families. Even though they took part in Muslim religious activities, no one became a Muslim. Attababa Spearman used to take a short spear in his hand and live like a Muslim mendicant. But he was in the forefront of all social activities. There were followers of Kabir and of Vithoba in many families. One corner of the community belonged to the Mahanubhav sect. Those who lived as tenants in their houses refrained from eating meat, and when goats were slaughtered openly in the community for Dussera or some other festival, the Mahanubhav group would separate themselves from this violence and live for ten days like Buddhist monks in the mango grove beyond Maharaj Park.

In front of the Hindu temple was a hermitage. A sadhu by the name of Somabuwa lived there. After this godman's wife died, his only daughter, Krishnabai, took care of him. She was crippled. At that time, before 1930, Panchmaji Varade gave them ten rupees a month. Somabuwa caught leprosy as he grew older, and then no one would go near him. He would come and sing *bhajans* with his *ektara* (a one-stringed instrument), and his daughter Krishnabai would go around asking for alms. People would throw grain into his bowl. With this grain he would provide dinner for many other godmen. Because he also received thirty rupees a month from the wealthy Baburao Dhanvate, Somabuwa had amassed much property.

At that time there existed a custom of taking someone as a guru. Premdasbuwa, the disciple of one of the local godmen, Bhanudasbuwa, was blind. With a clean white dhoti, a spotless shirt, a turmeric mark on his forehead and a neatly wrapped turban, he had no fear of speaking to anyone. After Somabuwa's death, the *panch* committee of the community arranged Krishnabai's marriage with the

39

blind Premdasbuwa. (Aside from the people of the Mahanubhav sect, no one had objection to arranging marriages outside their sect; they only followed subcaste rules.) The two of them would take the *ektara* and ask for alms in the colony, and this blind and lame couple would get handfuls of grain. Premdasbuwa had a detailed knowledge of rice varieties. If any rice was put in his hand, he could tell if it was *luchai, basmati, chinnor, shrikamal,* or *ludka.* I used to go to the hermitage and listen to his *bhajans* accompanied by the *ektara.* He had a command of Sanskrit and would chant mantras to the audience while reciting religious stories.

After the call in 1935 for conversion from Hinduism, a great mental upheaval began in Nagpur. Some people in the community—Pralhad Mhali, Pundalik Kavade, and others—read *Janata,* Ambedkar's newspaper. All the newspapers would come to our organization, the Samata Sainik Dal. People gathered in the evenings, and one person would read the news aloud so that everyone could discuss it. People began to think about Ambedkar's call to leave Hinduism. There were many in the community who honored the godmen, who went to the Muslim *durgahs,* who gave vows to Tajuddin Baba. Many people felt that we should become Muslims. There were some who spoke unblemished Urdu and recited poetry. Attababa Spearman, who lived in the neighborhood, was a sannyasi. With a long iron pike in his hand and steel bangles on his arm, this Spearman would wander, saying, "Jay Alakh Hirajan" (eternal victory to the Muslim people). He composed and sang his own hymns. He clashed his bangles together and sang. The Hindi verses of Kabir were on the tip of his tongue. He had made a detailed study of all religions. He had collected many books on Islam, and he also owned other religious books. He would say, "What is in this Hindu religion? If we become Muslims, we'll get the help of the Nizam of Hyderabad!"

In the Vitthal-Rukmini temple ground was the hermitage of Laldasbuwa. This temple had been built by Manke Mahar, a moneylender of Hansapuri. The temple was owned by the committee. But Laldasbuwa took care of it along with his hermitage. This godman belonged to the Kabir sect. He had long hair and a long beard of black and white; he was always cheerful. The temple committee collected money and grain, and every year they held a very big festival. Thousands of people would be fed. People would come from villages around to sing hymns.

Once, the merchant Govinda Bangar had tried to lay claim to the Vitthal-Rukmini temple. "This temple is mine," he began to say. But the whole community united and established a temple committee. People who were considered the wealthiest in the community were made members. Of course Bangar was also included. This committee was later renamed the Vitthal-Rukmini Temple Trust Committee. One of the members, Narayan Watchman, would go

बुद्ध, कबीर, भीमराव, फुले । ज्यांनी नवजीवन फुलविले ।।

*An illustration from a 1999–2000 calander, by artist J. D. Banjari. Above Dr. Ambedkar are (left to right) Kabir, the radical fifteenth-century Hindi poet; the Buddha; and Mahatma Jotirao Phule. The calender is published by Tai Nana Gajbihiye on behalf of the Dr. Babasaheb Ambedkar Urban Bank, Nagpur.*

daily both in the morning and evening to the temple, perform *puja* to Vitthal and Rukmini, and light lamps. Vitthal and Rukmini were in the inside room, and outside was a linga of Shiva and a stone Nandi. The linga required leaves of *bel*, so outside the temple a *bel* tree had been planted. After conversion in 1956, nobody performed *puja*; only Narayan Watchman up to his death maintained the atmosphere of the temple.

I recall a story about Laldasbuwa. He once staged a public competition, wherein an open debate was held with some Brahman pandit. On one side stood a Mahar pandit, on the other side the Brahman. The debate ran heavily into theology. It looked like Laldasbuwa was losing the debate, and then he asked the Brahman, "Bhatji, you have a sacred thread, don't you? Let us see if it's true or false."

"What is this? How can our sacred thread be false?"

"Let us see. You do *puja* to the fire god. So you give your sacred thread to the fire and then I will give mine."

At first the Brahman didn't realize what the Mahar godman was doing. He said, "All right," and both of them threw their threads into the fire. Even though it was a Brahman's sacred thread, still it was made of cotton and burned to ashes. Laldasbuwa's thread did not become ashes but grew red hot and passed the test. The hundreds of people gathered there clapped their hands. The Brahman rose and said, "I have been deceived." Laldasbuwa laughed uproariously. It was no wonder that his thread, which had been made of leather, did not burn so easily!

The kind of atmosphere that was supposed to be in a sannyasi's hermitage did not exist there. We saw the godman smoking the hookah in the evening. Not only was he a sannyasi, but one who had taken vows! At the time of Janmashtami he would organize a feast to celebrate Krishna's birth, and the whole community would join in. Laldasbuwa had the honor of lighting the *holi* fire in front of the temple. He didn't use a match to light it, but would make it burst into flame through his chants. This showed the strength of his chants, all agreed. But a new educated generation had come. The youth of the Ambedkarite movement were not ready to sit quietly, and they exploded the tricks of the godmen. "The godman puts some phosphorous in the tinder; his chants are only a show," they said. And this worked. From then on Laldasbuwa only did *puja*, and the *holi* fire was ignited by the new youth.

There were hymn-singing groups in the community. At the time of the Kartik full moon a ritual of the lamps was conducted. Laxman Kolhatkar, his brother, and many older people in the community joined it. People would come to the Vitthal-Rukmini temple singing hymns. Chants of "Victory to Dhyanba-Tukaram" would be heard. Some of these hymns I found very amusing. The line

"Vithoba, how they beat you; they broke your back"

would be heard, and then someone would sing the response:

"Vithai, she made you well; Chaturai healed your back"

Mother had to get up before dawn to go to work in the mill. Since I slept in the cooking area, I had to get up when Mother woke, and after completing my morning ablutions I would join the procession. Babu Rothe-Mothe Othvala would beat his huge drum while singing; the procession would depart in the morning of the Kartik full moon, and all the bhajan singing groups would join together at Sakkardarya and disperse.

The youth read Ambedkar's call in the *Janata* weekly. There it was written, "The Hindus' gods were not brought for us; don't do their *puja*. Their festivals are not ours; don't observe them." It was not possible for the older generation to forsake the entire Hindu culture one by one. Not only this, the youth were conscious that if such an attempt were made all the wrestlers would be against them.

The Samata Sainik Dal organized a house-to-house publicity campaign. This was in the mid-1930s, before the Scheduled Caste Federation was established. Under the leadership of Waman Godbole, the youth girded their loins. They wondered, Will people really listen to us? The elders could see the activities of the youth in the community. There was a library in the community. There was a youth club for hockey, football, and cricket. The boys were skilled at *hututu* and *khokho*. One boy studying at Patwardhan had built a wrestling ground and trained other boys. Due to all these activities, at least one boy in every house had become a volunteer of the Dal.

Wamanrao Godbole called the young boys to a meeting. He explained Babasaheb's thinking, and told them to spread the word. "From now on, don't celebrate Hindu festivals."

"But what shall we do to begin? People will not give up the practice of *puja*."

"To begin with, stop the festivals in your own homes."

"Then what festivals should we celebrate?"

"Ambedkar Jayanti, Chokhamela Jayanti. Don't celebrate Janmashtrami—Krishna's birthday—or Ram's birthday."

"Janmashtami is coming soon," said Waman Kamble. "They will install idols of Kanoba in every house. How are we going to stop that?"

"We will see what to do about it. If you only do propaganda from this year on, Kanoba will not be worshipped."

The news spread through the whole community. The young boys of the Dal forthrightly told their own mothers and fathers. Most houses did not install Kanoba idols that year.

That same evening there was a meeting of the Dal. The youth on the wrestling ground were called. "Wrestling Master, where are you going?" asked Dasarya Pickpocket of Pralhad Khobragade.

"There is a meeting. We have decided not to install the image of Kanoba. But Gulab Tirpude Ustad says he's going to put up a Kanoba idol in his house. This meeting is called to decide what to do."

"Why can't I come? Oh, brother, let my profession be what it is, but don't I regard Babasaheb as a god? Then why can't I come with you?"

Saying, "Good, come," Prahlad took Dasarya Pickpocket along with him and joined the meeting.

After worship, the Kanobas of the community were put in the water at the confluence of the Nag river. From morning on, women or children would carry the idols on their heads and immerse them like Ganpatis. In the settlement at the head of each lane two to four youth were standing, and at each one the taunt came, "Oh, Ma, your Kanoba has been broken by Ganya." Throughout the community the youth broke the idols of Kanoba. I must have been in the sixth grade then. Our job was to tell the leaders who had Kanobas and where they were going.

Who would dare to lay his hand on the Kanoba of wrestling Ustad Gulab Tirpude? Gulab had put a Kanoba idol on the head of his wife for her to carry to the river. The ustad was walking ahead with a cudgel in his hand and twisting his moustache. He crossed the settlement and reached the main road. Fifty steps ahead, his path would bring him in front of the neighborhood of the caste Hindus. Feeling that his Kanoba was safe, he glanced around him. No one was near. He looked ahead. Many Kanobas were going ahead. Then he heard the cry of his wife, "Oh, oh, come fast! The kids have smashed the idol!" Before Gulab Ustad had even turned his head, Premya Godbole had vanished into the lanes.

This was a subject of discussion for a week in the community. In the study classes of the Dal, Wamanrao said, "In the south, Ramaswami Naiker has broken the idols of Ram and Krishna. He has cut the sacred thread of Brahmans. We should not travel on the paths of others. We only want to reform our community, our neighborhood. Before we adopt another religion, we have to wipe out the culture of this religion."

That year, no one celebrated Krishna's birthday. Not only that, but the very same Gulab Ustad who had so stubbornly held on to Kanoba later became a strong soldier of the Samata Sainik Dal.

After Krishna's birthday came many Hindu festivals. But no one gave them much attention. These festivals were mainly celebrated by making and eating sweets. Nagpanchmi was considered to be our festival because it was a festival of snakes. The Ganesh festival was celebrated enthusiastically in Brahman communities. Other Hindus also made a show of Ganpati. But no one in the community had ever installed a Ganpati.

Holi, though, was celebrated in every house. There were sweets of course, but from small children to older people, everyone played *holi* by throwing colored powder or water and yelling and whooping. It was not a simple thing to start a campaign against this. But the Dal organized against Holi.

In the study classes of the Dal, Keshavrao Patil told us, "In one village a Brahman gave his daughter in marriage to a Mahar schoolteacher. The village Hindus couldn't stand for this. They boycotted him. On the day of Holi the Hindus set the couple on a Ghan monkey, a structure made of a column set into the ground with another piece set crosswise. They put the Brahman girl and the Mahar teacher on either end of the crosspiece and whirled it continuously until they fell unconscious. Then they burned them alive in the *holi* fire. Holi is not our festival."

We listened to such stories. That year the *holi* fires were stopped. The boys even stopped the bringing of color from house to house. No one in the community threw colors. From the age of six until today I have not played *holi*.

It did not take very long for the religious revolt of Maharpura to spread throughout Nagpur. The culture that had been stamped on people's minds for years and years began to be wiped out. And a new generation emerged.

# Chapter 7

## SHOOTING STAR

Kamathi is ten miles from Nagpur. It was previously the headquarters of the
Mahar battalion. Later it was included in the Sagar district of Madhya
Pradesh. At least one man in every Mahar household of Kamathi went to work
for the army. They would get work as cooks, butlers, washermen, drivers, or
other servants of the sahebs. Mahars got a lot of bread, butter, jam, and cheese
there. They would bring these home for their children. They also used the tin
cans brought from the military as pots in their kitchen gardens. Large amounts
of tea were drunk in the military from Chinese porcelain mugs. Anyone who
went to Kamathi would get a huge glass of tea. Kamathi Mahars had two vices,
tea and alcohol.

Grandfather had many friends and relatives in the area surrounding
Kamathi. Bhimrao Nagarale and Gopal Phuljhele were close friends, ready to
give their lives for the family. My mother regarded Bhim as a brother. Uncle
Bhim had much affection for me. He had two wives, Jiri and Gopi. Jiri's son
Shravan used to play with me. Gopi had a son named Anand. Bhim died of
asthma, and after that both sons were afflicted by a life of poverty. Gopi's son
put his mind to his studies and continued his education. Hunger might come
and go, but his education continued. Finally he became a graduate, and after
that an official in Delhi.

Gopal Phuljhele once visited and brought a lot of sweets. I must have been
in fourth grade. We were lying on someone's veranda. Gopal had brought some
woolen clothes made for me. Shining black, round face like a fierce tiger, sturdy
arms and legs, body strong from toil—such was his form. But his voice was
sweet, his nature mild. Once, an old woman who had no heir died in the community. Even her relatives would not lift their hands to help her. Gopal came
forward, gathered all the women together, and saying, "I am her son," washed

her himself and buried her. Seeing our poverty, tears would come into his eyes. He helped mother a little bit and then left for Kamathi.

Gopal died when his sons were small. I used to call his wife "Auntie." I went to Kamathi from time to time. After Gopal's death, the responsibility for the family fell on the older son. Auntie used to make *bidi* cigarettes for work, but her family could not manage on her pay. The older son finally left school and took up the job of painting posters for the cinema.

Gopal's younger son, Chagan, and her daughter, Lila, however, were smart in their studies. They always came first or second in their class. They studied up to eighth standard, but their school fees remained unpaid, so the school expelled them during the ninth standard. One day Lila came to me and said, "Brother, we have been expelled from school. We don't have any money, and the fee is due."

I was in college at the time. In Kamathi, Changdev Vasnik worked as deputy accountant in the general post and telegraph office. All our friends called him Uncle, so I did too. He used to play in the community's *hututu* team. I went to him and said, "Uncle, these two kids' lives will go to waste. Both are smart. They are bright and fiery. Something has to be done." He said, "You come to Kamathi. We'll do something."

So I went to Kamathi. Uncle sent along one activist to help me. We started a campaign and collected money. We presented the money to the headmaster, and both children got readmitted.

The children began again to study. But Chagan got typhoid. His family could not afford medical treatment, so he died at an early age. Lila continued her education. Her voice was as sweet as Lata Mangeshakar's. In school and college she continued to sing. She passed her examinations and became a doctor. She married Suryakant Dongare, who eventually became the deputy speaker of the upper house.

Even a little help can transform life so much.

So many memories remain. An important Mahar leader lived in Kamathi named Babu Hardas L. N. His *samadhi* (memorial) was built on the bank of the Karhan river. Every year on January 14, the day of the Tilsankrant festival, people gathered there in his memory. Thousands of people come even today to pay their respects to him.

Babu Hardas's surname was Nagarale, but he used the English initials "L. N." Babu Hardas L. N. was renowned as the youngest and most determined of the activists of the time. He was of a gallant mentality. With the help of Babu Kalicharan Nandagavali, he founded the organization of *bidi* workers in the Central Provinces and Berar before 1930. He was the secretary of the union, and was the first to organize all the *bidi* workers from Nagpur up to Gondiya and Chandrapur. He was a graduate and the General Secretary of the Independent Labour

Party in the Province. A great enthusiasm and hope was created among the Mahar community about this new young man. Even the Hindus crowded to hear his speeches. He was also a poet and writer. He wrote and published *Songs of the Market* and *Songs of the Hearth*. He organized an Untouchable Literary League in C.P.–Berar in 1936 and put forward the idea of writing a history of the Mahars. Around 1927 he published a small paper called *Maharattha*. His articles can also be read in the 1933 *Janata* weekly.

The drums of the 1937 elections began to sound. The C.P.–Berar Independent Labour Party named Babu Hardas as its candidate for the Kamathi constituency. At that time Congress was so dominant that it was considered the only nationalist party. No other parties except the Independent Labour Party could find candidates. Hardas was given the horse as a symbol. All the work took place without money. Posters were drawn by hand, not printed.

In Kamathi the Congress candidate was a rich Marwari named "Lala." He could not endure the thought that a trifling youth from his own town was standing against him. He sent some activists on behalf of his party to Hardas. "Hardas, Sethji is saying that you should withdraw your candidacy."

"Why? I am standing on behalf of Ambedkar's party."

"This is an insult to the *seth*. The *seth* is ready to give whatever you ask."

"I don't want anything. We left begging a long time ago. From now on whatever we can get by right we will take."

"Nothing good will come of this."

"We'll see about that."

Lala's activists returned and told him the whole story. The *seth*, not one to give up on his prestige, tried everything, from creating splits to bribes to threats.

Hardas, for his part, was not incautious. He prepared himself to face any situation. The youth gathered around him. Some young boys of the Samata Sainik Dal established a "Self-Sacrifice Squad." The boys took turns staying with him night and day.

One day "Babbu" Wrestler came and stood in front of Hardas's door. He had four or five companions with him. Babbu saw the hefty Mahar youth at Hardas's door, but to him they were like mosquitoes. Babbu looked like some *rakshasa*. However, he was a Muslim. He knew Hardas, knew that Hardas worked not only for Mahars but also for Muslim workers.

"Is Hardas at home?"

"Oho, Babbu Ustad, why have you come here?" one activist challenged him.

"I want to meet Hardas."

"Yes, I'm here," came the call of Hardas from his small mud house. Putting on a shirt he came outside. He said to Babbu, "Come, Ustad, sit down, have some tea and then let's talk."

*The* samadhi *of Hardas L. N., one of the most important early Mahar leaders in the Nagpur-Kamathi area, who died in 1939 at age thirty-five. He is the only Dalit leader besides Dr. Ambedkar honored with such a memorial. Photo by Eleanor Zelliot.*

"No, I have other work. But I have come to say one thing. The *seth* is ready to kill you. I have come to warn you to be careful."

"Oho, that can't intimidate me at all. If I die, will the *seth* remain alive?"

"Well, that may be right; that might come afterwards, but before that is the question of living. He even gave me ten thousand rupees. But I won't kill you. You are my friend."

Babbu Ustad left, moving his feet like a lazy elephant. The Self-Sacrifice Squad fighters made a ring around Hardas. For the rest of the day a discussion about what to do went on, and the security was made even stricter.

Babu Hardas L. N. won the election.

On every Thursday the Mandai—a big market without a fair—was held in Kamathi. An abundance of Muslim goons loitered there. They were fascinated by Untouchable girls. If any beautiful young girl came into the market, the Muslim gang tried to kidnap her.

Hardas aroused his companions against this. They urged in every community not to send girls to the Mandai alone. Gangs of Mahar youth began to roam through the market, and if any girl was grabbed, knives flashed. The *goondas* were at first caught by surprise by this counterattack. Later they brought in more boys. Fighting began in the market. Finally the police intervened. Hardas proclaimed, "If the police don't give protection to our women, then we will have to maintain law and order. You should not interfere."

From that time on Mahar girls could wander fearlessly in the Mandai.

Hardas fell sick with tuberculosis. Mahar *bidi* workers in Kamathi were susceptible to many diseases, and TB in particular took many victims. Hardas died in 1938 at a very young age. He was dead by the age of thirty-five. People came from all over Nagpur and Kamathi to his funeral procession as if for a hero returning from the war. Nagpur's textile mills and *bidi* factories in Bhandara, Chandrapur, and Nagpur—all were shut down. During the funeral procession thousands of people sobbed.

Just as a comet appears, bringing light throughout the sky, dazzling our eyes, and then vanishing in an instant, so it happened with Hardas. His body was burned on the banks of the Karhan. A fair began to be held there every year. After that, a new personality came to birth in Kamathi. Vowing to take up the cause of Hardas and carry it forward was the mild and unassuming but gallant Kumbhare, whose name will reappear many times in this memoir. Hardas had departed, but his heritage was carried on by Narayan Hari Kumbhare. And his name is alive in his daughter even today.

# Chapter 8

## CHICKPEAS AND PARCHED RICE

Atmaram Patil had just built his two-story house next to ours. I sat on the steps of our home for hours, becoming distraught and melancholy. There was no sign of food in the house. My sister would fetch the water, wash the clothes, and do the dishes. She had stopped going to school from the third standard. She was lazy. No matter what I said, she was not ready to go to school.

A youth from the Dal, Maroti Bagade, was walking by on the road one day. He saw my melancholy face and said, "Oh, Vasanta, come here."

I walked to him. Nearby was Babulal's snack shop. Maroti bought a whole bag of hot chickpeas and gave me some, saying, "Take this; it's for you and your sister to eat." I brought those chickpeas to the house and both of us spent the day eating them.

The idea of somehow being able to earn a few pennies began to haunt my mind, and I started to roam in the lanes. At that time, a sort of "lotion" was used to fix punctures in bicycle tires. It came in a tube like the toothpaste of today, but since plastic had not been invented, the tube was made of tin. Once the cycle shops had used the tubes they would throw them away. I collected these tubes and earned a few rupees from selling them. Along with trash, when I was in middle school I made an effort to collect all kinds of iron goods for sale.

I roamed the lanes and pathways trying to collect trash to sell. There was a litho press in front of the normal school that printed match labels. The sheets of spoiled labels were thrown outside. I collected them. From this I obtained the habit of collecting matchbooks and cigarette packets. This habit later was transformed into one of collecting pictures. I began the collection with some very good pictures. Mother had an iron box that she had received from her father; it held issues of *The Times of India* with pictures of the Second World War. I used the box to keep my schoolbooks in, but I kept the pictures for many years.

One day Gangya came to tell me that some handcarts were to be taken from Ghat Road to the orange market. Handcarts for carrying trash had one wheel and are used even today. I decided to do the work and went to Ghat Road.

My friends grabbed carts one by one and began to pull them away. But I couldn't pull even one. Even with all my efforts, the cart wouldn't budge. It was beyond my strength. For one thing I was short, and for another I had no strength in my body.

I returned home. When I went to take a bath under Uncle's tap, he said, "Vasanta, the bones in your chest are showing; you ought to eat ghee and such things."

But in those days I never even had the chance to set eyes on ghee. By the time I could afford it, my desire for it had lost its sharpness.

At this time, the militants of the Dal became aware of my economic misery. They had a discussion at the flagpole and then called a meeting of the employed members of the Dal. They told me of their decision, which was for me to go to the houses of the activists with an empty bowl after eight at night. The fresh food made by their wives was given to me. I took this home and shared it with my mother and sister. Many people gave me food to keep me alive. This food always was fresh and hot. No one ever gave me leftover or stale food. Those friends never had the feeling that they were doing me a favor; rather they did it as a duty. They also helped in providing books and notebooks for my education.

Whenever Babasaheb Ambedkar came to Nagpur, all the mill workers would go on strike or take leave. Dadasaheb Gaikwad and P. N. Rajbhoj would come with him. All the men and women of the community would go to the station to welcome them and then take them out in a procession. Women went to these parades with joy as to a wedding, and they would say to the neighbors, "Oh Kamlaji, oh Baiji, why are you still at home? Everyone has gone on ahead." And then everyone would go running to reach the procession. The neighborhood would be empty. And just as Mother went to processions, she also attended meetings. She was, in that way, independent-minded.

Days went on, and we moved from one room to another. Our economic situation was very bad because Mother had no regular work. But she never left the *vasti*. Finally she got a two-room place to rent in Radhabai's house.

Radhabai was a widow. Mother felt a great closeness to her. She would tell us stories about her. "There's a story from the days of your grandfather. Dasharath used to live next door to Radhabai. His wife was light-skinned, with huge eyes, of good height, but he was extremely jealous. He kept her chained up. To keep her from running away with anyone, he kept chains on her feet during the day. One day she came to my father and said, 'Buwaji, my husband is taking a new wife. What should I do? I can't live here.' My father said, 'Okay, you go to your house; I'll set things right.' Then my father went to the police station and made a report. That evening, the police suddenly showed up on horses. They arrested Dasharath and took him away. And from then on her chains were broken."

Mother told us that Radhabai's husband was named Rama. He took a second wife. She was very beautiful. But Rama died soon thereafter. This second wife, Goda, ran away and took another husband. Rama had owned a big estate, and Goda filed a lawsuit laying claim to it. Radhabai appeared at the court session and said, "I am Rama's first wife. Goda should live with me. I am ready to give her everything. But she shouldn't take a second husband. She has no right over this estate." The court accepted Radha's words.

Mother had these kinds of memories of so many people.

There was a servant in the police office by the name of Raghunath Narnavare who lived in the room next to us. Once he saw that Radhabai was a widow he began to give her a lot of trouble. He never paid his rent. When he saw her coming down the steps, he would throw water on her. One day she went to the police and filed a complaint. The police came and threw out Raghunath's goods from the house. The police were like that in those days. Mother would tell this story and say, "Today if you make a report nothing happens. But when Raghunath was thrown out of the house, tears came into Radhabai's eyes."

We began to live as tenants in Radhabai's house. The four-by-four space in the front of our space was used for the kitchen. Beyond that was a six-by-six room for sleeping. At first the rent was twelve annas. Later it was raised to one and three quarter *rupees*. Radha was very sweet. She would never let me leave the house without a couple of bites of food. She was a member of the Mahanubhav sect, and because of her generosity the Mahanubhav priest always stayed in her house.

When Mother got the house she agreed to Radhabai's condition not to cook mutton there. But she honored it only for some days. Gradually she began to bring mutton to cook. I used to wrap the bones in a paper and take them outside to throw them far away. But how to hide the smell of cooking mutton? The rich fragrance spread, and Baina, the wife of our neighbor Bapu, would ask Mother, "What are you doing, Purnabai?" Baina was a Mahanubhav too, but she must have recognized the smell of cooking mutton. Mother would say, "I bought a jackfruit today." She would call fish the "vegetable of leaves and pods" and say eggs were "potatoes."

Except for this one falsehood, I have never seen her lie in her life.

Mother knew so many relatives. Even in her old age she used to tell their stories. Mother's aunt was given in marriage to Godghate Merchant of Colonel

Park. Mother had to go through Colonel Park to get to Model Mill. Once she said, "While coming home from work, I stopped at Colonel Park. They kept me there for four days. 'Oh darling girl, what kind of situation have you come to? What is becoming of you?' they used to say. They bought so much fish for me. When it came time to leave, they gave me a new sari and blouse. Uncle said to me, 'Take whatever house you want; I will give it in writing.' But I was the one who didn't put my mind to it."

Mother remembered another story. "Cousin Sitaram had two wives. The first wife suffered a lot. She used to take a basket of vegetables to sell. But she educated her son. The boy's name was Manik; it's said he studied a lot." Mother never knew that this Manik is Maharashtra's famous poet "Grace."

Mother remembered more. "Sitaram's sister was Uma. She gave her son to a Gudi [Christian orphanage]. But later she brought him back."

At that time two Christian missionary women would come to the community. They went from house to house asking about things. They would give whatever help for education or medicine was needed. These nuns of the French mission were called "Amma." Those families who couldn't care for their children would bring them to the missionary orphanage, or Gudi. A poor man named Kacrya who used to live in our community, begging with his wife to fill their stomach, had two daughters. He took them to that Gudi and became free of their responsibility.

Mother used to say, "People would also tell me, 'Take your children to the Gudi.' But I never did. I said, 'I will endure days of poverty, but I won't give my children to their religion.'" However, even after Kacrya's two daughters grew up they came and met their mother and father. Seeing the change that had taken place in them, people would say, "Because Kacrya gave his daughters to the Gudi they have become gold. The daughters have gotten educated and become great. Otherwise they would have ended up begging on the road." The converted daughters of Kacrya had been saved from hell permanently. Mother had been left bound up in the pride of religion. She freed herself from this bondage on 14 October 1956, the day of the conversion from Hinduism to Buddhism.

From childhood poverty had been my lot. Besides, I had the habit of keeping company with truant boys. I used to return to the house covered with mud and dust. When I came before Mother in such a condition, she would say deliberately, "Wash your legs up above the knees. Wash your arms up above the elbows." Her harping would be continuous. On Sunday she would bring warm water and put it on the rock in front of our house and tell me to sit for my bath. And taking a shard of a broken earthen pitcher, and seating me on the round stone, she would scrub my arms and legs vehemently. Once, I got sick of the scrubbing and resisted, saying "No, no!"

Mother retorted, "Are you sitting there or not?" and came out with a switch in her hand. I stood up in my wet underpants and began to run. She came after me. For some time we played a game of tag. Finally she said menacingly, "Are you coming or not? If not, remember that you'll go hungry." When she glared at me I used to go into a funk. My sister and I were both in awe of her.

Boys and girls used to take baths in the open. The clothes were washed along with the body. The result of wearing half-dry underpants was as might be expected. Ringworm made its home in my groin. At that time there was no effective ointment; what there was made my skin burn. These outbreaks of ringworm and the sores that rose on my arms and legs from hard scrubbing with a shard remained until 1985. Even today they molest me from time to time.

One day on Mother's suggestion I went to see my father in Shanwari. He had an old wooden toy bullock. He took it out of storage and cleaned it. The next day was Tanha Pola, the festival of the bullocks. Boys used to take their toy bullocks and go to all their known relatives in the community, who would give each boy a couple of coins and send them on their way. Father sent me with four or five boys for company. By the time we came back I had collected two rupees and ten annas. Then he brought me to the road in front of the house. Near an electric pole two or three boys were sitting playing cards. Father sat down and gave me a lesson in three-card. He made me put all the money in my hands into that gambling, and I came home empty-handed. Father said, "Well, because that's lost are you lost? Didn't you enjoy yourself?"

My father had three daughters, Savitri, Suru, and Anu, and one son, Dayashankar, from his first wife. My father stayed with Dayashankar's father-in-law in Sadar. One day while I was going to Sadar I met Father alone in the house. On seeing me he brought a quarter kilo of mutton from the bazaar and cooked it himself. Then he opened a bottle of Lion brand liquor. He served me the food and afterwards drank heavily. Then he ate. This was when I understood what great cooking he could prepare. I had not eaten such tasty mutton in a long time. It had a special taste. Then he got the whim that we should go to see his second daughter, Saru, who had been given in marriage to Jayarambuwa of Dharampeth. We left in the afternoon, starting out on the road in front of the high court. By this time Baba was thoroughly drunk. He had been muttering before, but now he began to shout loudly and curse. Waving his hands and yelling, he walked along, and I went mutely along behind him. Baba yelled, "The son of a lion is also a lion!" Since I was getting educated he must have thought this something great. When we got near Dharampeth, he keeled over and fell asleep. I sat near him and mutely watched people passing on the road. After two or three hours he got up and we went to Sarutai's place.

Saru's husband Jayarambuwa was engrossed full-time in *bhajans* and *pujas*. He wore a pure white turban on his head and a rosary of *rudrakshakas* around his neck. He sang religious hymns. He was completely vegetarian. A complete contrast was the older sister Savitri's husband, Hiraman Mhaske, a police constable. But he also sang religious hymns in a sweet voice. He established his own *bhajan* groups. *Bhajan* competitions were held here and there, and he always claimed that he came in first. Jayarambuwa could not stand drunkenness and overeating; on the other hand, Hiramanbuwa could not survive without these.

Anutai's husband, Mahadev, had a nature different from both of these men. I don't recall him offering much *puja* to the gods. He had no habit of drinking. However, he ate mutton and chicken, and even beef and pork were not disagreeable to him! If Hiraman and Mahadev met, it is difficult to say who would be the most fine and lavish. They used to live in Calcutta. Anutai had no children. She used to make all kinds of vows to the gods so that she would get pregnant. Her husband never forbade that. However, he took her to all the main hospitals in Madras, Calcutta, Bombay, etc., for fertility treatment. The couple never had any children. They treated his brother's children very well and helped them a lot, but in the later part of their life they didn't let anyone get close. Mahadev and Anu should have developed an affection for someone and brought him close. But they were afraid he might die after some time and they would have to live alone again. Perhaps because of this, the two had a great love for dogs and cats. All kinds of animals—sometimes parrots, sometimes goats, even cows and buffaloes—could be found in their house. Anutai took so much trouble to teach the parrots and care for them, and if they got away or died she would shed so many tears that they could not be counted. She also refused to let people kill any big snakes that could be found in her house. While I was a college student I used to go to Calcutta, and Mahadev would take me to the Roxy cinema to see English pictures. Along with them I saw the Kali temple, and Dharmatla and other places in Calcutta. I saw the Mahabodhi society at that time.

In Calcutta there was a settlement named Santragacchi. This place had been founded in order to wash, clean, and repair all the trains coming into Howrah station. Huge locomotive sheds were built there, and there was a very big colony of railway employees. Anutai's home was in a one-story *chawl* in that colony. Mahadev would buy Hindi novels and bring them to me. During the afternoons I would sit under a nearby tree and fall under the spell of those novels. I got the chance to read many novelists, like Kaushavkant Kant, Premchand, Sharadchandra, and Ravindranath in those days. Kaushavkant Kant was a very popular writer. His language of Hindi mixed with Urdu and his style were very effective. His thought was very progressive, even revolutionary. But such writers had no place in established literature. Later, when I learned that the orthodox Hindus had gone so far as to murder Kaushavkant, I fell into a great restlessness.

People of various castes and communities from all over India used to live in the railway quarters in Santragacchi. Near our house were many speakers of Tamil, Telugu, Malayali, Bengali, and other languages. There were only one or two houses of Marathi speakers. Because of such multilingual surroundings, Anutai could clearly speak south Indian languages such as Telugu, Tamil, and Malayalam as well as Bengali. I also learned the numbers *vakati, randu, mundu,* and *nalgu* in the Telugu language. I liked Bengali literature, so I thought about learning the language. But I never had the opportunity to study it.

In 1950 the holocaust following Partition was fresh before the eyes of the people of Santragacchi. They showed marks made by knives in their doors and walls. People said, "They would come in the night and mark the doors of Hindus. The assault of the Muslims was just beyond that tree. When the police and military came, they would run away. Then we sent for the Adivasis. They gave us protection with their bows and arrows."

When I was seven or eight, Mother left the house, took me with her, and went to the city hall. There we arrived at an office for registration of land bought and sold. My father and his oldest son, Dayashankar, were present. They had come for the transaction of the big two-story house they owned in Shanichar and the five-room *chawl* behind it. They sold the whole estate to his big brother, Bhanudas. Mother was hopeful of getting some money out of it. But no one even inquired about her or me. Father made some effort to put a few coins in my hand. I threw them away. We returned empty-handed. After that, I never even wanted to look at my father again.

When I was in college my oldest half-brother, Dayashankar, died in Sadar. Mother had had to endure so much, but no malice ever remained in her mind. At the time she was working in the mill. She took leave and went to the inquest at Sadar. I did not feel at all like going. Father was not at Dayashankar's inquest. He must have been at Calcutta. There were few relatives around to perform his rites. There was even a quarrel about who would donate a cloth to cover the body. Mother said, "Not one person came forward to pay the expenses. I was the one who finally gave some money."

For many days there had been no intimacy with our relatives. After this, however, slowly our acquaintance and familiarity began to grow. Once, while I was going to a relative's marriage, a beautiful and bright wheat-complexioned girl was shown to me. This girl was my widowed aunt, the daughter of Bhimabai. She hadn't even passed fourth standard; however, some relatives hoped that I would ask for her hand in marriage. I argued that she should continue her education. Unfortunately, within one year the girl got burned and died while lighting the stove. At that time, love marriages were not very common in college. In the Dalit community, boys and girls were free to get married before receiving their degree. However, I made a mental resolve not to get married until I had obtained employment. I was unaware that such a thing as knowledge of sex existed. Anna Narnavare, who lived next door, showed me an issue of R. D. Karve's *Social Health*. I read it surreptitiously. It included the cross-examination that Dr. Ambedkar had made in defense of Karve in court when legal action had been brought against him. Around that time I also found an old book of Karve's, *Modern Science of Love*, in the market. Reading it greatly changed my view of sexual subjects.

My mother's Aunt Gondan had been given in marriage to a man from Mondha. The peasant and laboring women of Mondha and Hindag used to walk ten to fifteen miles to Bardi market to sell their vegetables. Mother had a lot of affection for Gondan and her sons. If Motiram, Vishram, Doma, or whoever came to Nagpur, she would inquire after them. This family was well off. Silk shirts, silk turbans on their heads, and muslin *dhotis* were the elegant dress of the men. Only the women appeared to work hard.

The people of the community at times called on the activists of the Samata Sainik Dal to overcome obstacles. Weddings in the community meant dinner for hundreds of people. For these, the Dal activists would go happily to help. Three thousand people were fed at Bhanudas Varade's marriage. The Dal youth did the work of serving the people who sat on the ground in dozens of rows.

Once, a gentleman named Puranik living near us fell sick. At midnight his wife began to scream loudly. I ran and asked what happened. The doctor had told Puranik to take pills three times a day for fever. Puranik had thought, Why take these pills again and again? If the three were taken at once then his temperature would quickly drop. He took all three pills at once. A burning heat rose in his body. From midnight onwards we banged on doctors' doors. Every doctor had closed his doors tightly and was deeply asleep. At around four A.M. we reached the house of Dr. Manohar Patwardhan in Tikadi. He said, "I have just come back from seeing a patient. I need a little sleep. But tell me what happened." We told him the whole story. He said, "Give him coffee or lemon sherbet. I will come in the morning and see him." Dr. Patwardhan was thought of as the doctor of the poor and deprived. He was famed for offering effective medicine and for excusing fees. Puranik lived!

Once, while five or six of us boys were crossing the road from Regent Cinema near Variety as usual in our meanderings, a woman appeared, loudly yelling for help. Janya, Pandya, Shankar, and I went running. A young man had fallen in a fainting fit on the ground, and a middle-aged woman was calling out, "Help him!" But the people standing around were only looking on with amusement. We put the man in a rickshaw and took him to a clinic in a nearby textile factory. The woman, wearing white clothes, came with us and said, "You must be volunteers of the Sangh." We replied, "No, we are not a branch of Swayamsevaks. We are activists of the Samata Sainik Dal." The woman looked at us with surprise and said, "It was my understanding that only the Sangh's volunteers do such work."

On another day we had gone to Katol to establish a branch of the student organization in Budhwarpeth. Near the house where I had gone, a bearded sadhu was sitting on a mat by the road. He had gathered students of the community and was talking to them. I was curious about him. In a little while the woman of the house came out and began to massage his legs. This was enough to upset me. I took the students who had come with me and went to the sadhu. After seeing us suddenly appear, the godman fell into confusion and started to go inside. We stopped him and began to ask him questions. He got agitated and, making some excuses, ran away. That day many praised us for challenging that hypocrite sadhu.

There was a watch-repair shop owned by Motiram Nagarkar in Maharpura. He was in Delhi at the time of Partition. He had witnessed the Hindu–Muslim massacres and used to give vivid descriptions of them. One day he said, "Vasanta, do you know our Sulochana, Auntie's daughter?"

"Why, what happened?" Seeing the concern on Motiram's face I wondered whether something bad had happened.

"No, nothing has really happened. But there is a likelihood that it will. She is now only fourteen years old. But her father is arranging her marriage."

"So what? This goes on all the time."

"Do you know how old the fellow is who is asking for her? He's a man of forty-four."

"Well, all right, what can be done?"

"This marriage must be stopped. If you come, it can be done."

The two of us rented bicycles. We cycled the ten or twelve kilometers from Nagpur to Kamathi and reached Sulochana's house. Sulochana's mother and a forty-five-year-old man were sitting there. Sulochana's father had gone to bring things from the market. Sulochana's mother also left in a little while to make tea.

We asked some questions of this gentleman and then told him, "You are the age of her father. It is a crime to make such a marriage." Actually speaking, an ill-matched marriage was no crime, but by throwing various questions at him we convinced him that he was doing something criminal. At that time college students were considered by ordinary people to be very educated. We took an aggressive attitude to bring pressure on him. Who knows what this fellow felt after listening to us, but he took his bundle and, throwing his shawl over his shoulder, left the place.

Sulochana's mother returned. She said, "I was saying no. It was her father who was making haste. My daughter is black. However, is that bad? Her nose and mouth are one in a hundred." This was true. Sulochana was shapely and lustrous. After drinking the tea that Sulochana had made, we returned to Bardi on the cycles.

The next day I went to an advocate named Lobo and told him the story. He had given me some help in an effort to establish a school for orphaned boys. Listening quietly to my story of meddling, he said, "Moon, why did you stop the marriage?"

The question was unexpected. Social issues are not simple; they have so many sides. Not all sides come to our attention. For many days the question of whether Sulochana would ever get married kept passing through my mind.

# Chapter 9

## THE UNCONQUERED

Many activities went on in the community, especially sports. Wrestling grounds and *hututu* sprouted everywhere in Nagpur. The boys of the community were dexterous in both. In the beginning they took part in marches of the Maratha Lancers; later the Ahirrao Club sponsored them at the palace of the Bhosles. The Maratha Mandal and the Bhosle Club also sponsored competitions. However, the Mahar *vastis* were not lagging behind. Tournaments were held at Bhankhed; matches were organized at Babhulkhed by Chitaman Kamble, and at Gita Grounds and Handicraft Grounds in Bardi. And at Kamathi, competitions were held every year on the memorial day of Haridas L. N.

When our Bhagyodaya Club reached the finals of the Maratha Lancers' competition in 1939, then all the Nagpurites gathered to see the match. As the passion for *hututu* grew, youth of all ages had started taking part in the matches. *Hututu* matches were held in the Chokhamela hostel in the new colony beside the railway lines. The hostel had been established around 1925 by Nanasaheb Gavai, Kisan Faguji Bansode, and other Mahar activists with the help of Shahu Maharaj of Kolhapur. The Bardi group decided to send not simply one but two teams. And so the players were split up.

The players in the Bhagyodaya Club seemed each taller than the other. Most were six to six and a half feet tall. When Fattu Gajbhiye of the A team came out, not a single man would escape without being beaten. Fattu Rangari was tall but thin and wiry, agile as a cheetah. Big Nathu Shende was pot-bellied. He was magnificently stout, and if he was caught he would take two to four with him. When Uncle Pralhad or Goma Sontakke guarded the corner, anyone who went inside had no hope of coming out. Along with Bodad Rangari, Yogi Mohil, Pundalik Rangari, and Hari Khobragade to make a military array, this was the A team.

But the B team was not inferior. Actually, once the A team was formed, a B team was not required. But they wanted to give all the players a chance, and so the B team was created. This team had wrestler Mahadev Gajbhiye, whose grasp was fabled; Atmaram Paithankar, who was very black and agile as a snake; Macchindra Mohite, whose stride could catch one at any time; the short brothers Pandurang and Bhanudas Varade, with strong grips; wrestler Tukaram Varade; Premchand Godbole, who shouted abuses and remained enthusiastic to the end; Sadashiv Sontakke; Maroti Bagade; Paiku Shende; the six-footer Govind Meshram; Changdev Meshram; and the dexterous Changdev Vasnik.

The competition began in the courtyard of the Chokhamela hostel, and the Sitabardi folk went to see the prowess of their boys. One game after another took place, but neither team of Bardi appeared ready to retreat. The semifinal rounds came, and both teams won in their class. The next Sunday would see the final match, and this match would be between the A and B teams of the Bhagyodaya Club. With enthusiasm mounting among the spectators, the players returned home.

Naturally, the A team was considered superior to B. However, the B team was determined to make an assault. Both began to practice morning and evening. They started hurling taunts at each other coming and going on the roads. Debates erupted, and wagers were made.

On Sunday there was no place to stand at the Chokhamela hostel grounds. Enthusiasm was at a boiling point. All of Bardi had gathered to see the match. But in those days spectators were disciplined. No match before this had seen such self-restraint. Even with competition there was no quarreling, no fighting. The athletes split off one man after another in a disciplined way up to the end. And the whistle to end the match was blown. People stared in surprise. The A team had been defeated by the B team!

But the real victory was that of Bardi's Bhagyodaya Club, not that of any individual. Both teams took their shields of awards for the final and semifinal rounds and returned in procession to Bardi, tossing the flowers of their victory garlands as they went. The whole community that day was bathed in joy.

The photo of the shield won that day by Bardi's Maharpura is kept even today in many houses.

In 1941 the Chokhamela hostel management, with the collaboration of some Harijan students, decided to call Mahatma Gandhi for the hostel annual gathering. Most of the students, who were strong Ambedkarites and activists of the Samata Sainik Dal, opposed this. However, no one was in the mood to listen. Sadanand Dongare lived in the hostel, but he felt he could not vanquish the idea of bringing Gandhi while staying there. One or two kilometers away from the hostel towards the railway lines, there stood a hostel for Mahars named Gaddi Godam. He took a room there and laid out all his plans. The youth of north and central Nagpur came together.

By the day of Mahatma Gandhi's planned arrival, a huge pavilion had been erected in the central area of the hostel's open ground. A strong line of police was placed outside. Nanasaheb Gavai, Kisan Fagu Bansode, and other Mahar opponents of Ambedkar were members of the managing board. The president was Chaturbhajabhai Jasani of Gondiya. He was a loyal member of Congress and a big leader of Madhya Pradesh. He brought Mahatma Gandhi from Delhi, but he took him off the train two stations early, and because of this the Ambedkarite community, which was spread throughout Nagpur, was led to believe that Gandhi had not come. However, Gandhiji had come to Nagpur in the company of Jasani.

On the east side of the Chokamela hostel lay a parallel railway line running north-south. This line goes via Itwara, Katol, and Kalmeshwar to Delhi and east to Calcutta. Stone rocks had fallen on the railway line. Women and men, young and old gathered on this line, and shouted, "Long Live Ambedkar!" On the north, south, and west of the hostel lay people's houses and narrow roads.

Mahatma Gandhi's car came to the hostel from behind. There the members of the reception committee were waiting to welcome him. While they were trying to shout "Long live Gandhi," a noise like one voice could be heard from the thousands of demonstrators outside: "Mahatma Gandhi go back!" And as this noise reached the neighborhoods around, people began to run towards the hostel.

The hostel was a four-sided block two hundred by two hundred feet in size. The pavilion had been set up in the open ground in the middle. Here, along with the students of the hostel, distinguished guests had been invited to sit. But there were many Ambedkarite Dalits among the students. Until Gandhiji went onto the stage, everything was quiet inside. But once he rose to speak, some of the Ambedkarite students in the audience stood up and began to shout, "Gandhiji, we have many questions for you." Gandhiji was standing quietly. He said, "Yes, ask them." But the turmoil only increased. No one could hear the questions in that confusion. The hundreds of people standing outside on the railway lines began a massive stone-throwing into the hostel. The stones fell inside the pavilion also. There was no sign of halting this attack. Once the stones hit the canvas, it began to collapse. No one would give Gandhi a chance to make his speech. In this confusion, the organizers brought Gandhiji out of the pavilion to protect him. Just as he had come in by the back door, so he left.

With the shouting of "Long live Ambedkar! Bhim Raj is coming soon!" Mahatma Gandhi's car departed. People lifted up Sakharam Meshram, who was trying to quiet them down, and tried to throw him in a well. At that point Narayan Hari Kumbhare intervened to try to calm people down. The incident showed the ferocity of the anti-Gandhi sentiments of the people.

# Chapter 10

## PARADE OF LIONS AND TIGERS

Our branch of the Samata Sainik Dal held its meetings in the field in front of Maharpura, behind where Vasant Talkies is today. This branch was established around 1938 by Asaram Paithankar, Sadanand Dongare, and others. Before that the boys in Maharpura went to the Rashtriya Swayamsevak Sangh, whose branch met in the same field on the western half. Bal Rege was the Sangh organizer.

I started going to the Dal from the third standard on. We gathered every evening on the Dal field. Pandurang Varade had a flag and bamboo stick. We would take these with us and go to the Dal field, where stood an iron pole. The bamboo was raised up on the pole, and we would put a rope through a hook

*Dr. Ambedkar (center, in Western dress) and a group of the Samata Sainik Dal in Mumbai. Date unknown. Photo courtesy of S. D. Gaikwad.*

on its end and raise the flag. All the soldiers of the Dal would stand in ranks before the flag. This we did every day. Only Sunday was a holiday.

Everyone in the community, from schoolchildren to young men, came to the Dal. There was an effort to bring everyone. There was also strict discipline. Every day there was an inquiry: who was present, who was not, why he didn't come. Information about any absent boy was given by a friend the next day to the master. We referred to the teachers in the Dal as "masters"; this continues even today. Our Pandurang Master is still called that.

The flag symbolized our pride. Wamanrao Godbole had come into the Dal around 1941 and had begun to establish Dal branches throughout northern and western Nagpur. After the historic 1942 first Scheduled Castes Federation conference, he brought silk cloth for a blue flag and made a flag with his own hands. In the center of the flag was a sun of white cloth, which symbolized Babasaheb Ambedkar. In the middle of the sun, touching the edges, was a round "SCF," standing for the Scheduled Caste Federation, embroidered in English letters. On the left side of the flag, next to the rope, were eleven stars in the top corner sewn out of white cloth, and the letters "SSD" in the bottom corner. This flag was the united symbol of the Scheduled Caste Federation and the Samata Sainik Dal. The eleven stars symbolized the eleven provinces of India at the time. While raising the flag, care was taken that its edge should not touch the ground or any dirt. Stories of national heroes who had become martyrs for the flag were told in the Dal. In the Ambedkarite movement, the songs written by poets about the blue flag were famous (before 1942, the flag of the Independent Labour Party was red):

> We will give our life for the blue flag
> Millions will bow before the blue flag
> If you still plan to fight us, think about it,
> We will sacrifice all for the blue flag!
> Whatever Bhim wants we will do,
> We will see our blood flow for the blue flag!

These songs seized our minds, inspiring us to dedicate all for the flag. Through rain, cold, or heat, Pandurang Master could be seen going to the Dal grounds with the bamboo staff in his hand. Even if a wedding was held in the community, or someone died, and the whole group attended the ceremony, Pandurang Master would go alone to the Dal grounds with the flag. He would stand raising the flag and saluting it. If anyone came, fine; if not, then he would sing flag songs for an hour, take down the flag, and go home alone. When Pandurang Master left the house you could tell it was 5:00 o'clock; when he came back it was 6:30.

There was a parade of the Dal every day. We learned things that were taught in the military, such as left-right-left, about face, right turn, left turn, slow march, halt, slope arms, with sticks like rifles in our hands.

When the call was given for the 1942 Scheduled Caste Federation conference, all of Nagpur throbbed furiously with inspiration. The Maharpura of Sitabardi was always in the vanguard. Wamanrao Godbole had established branches of the Dal in all of western and southern Nagpur. Every volunteer was told to wear a red shirt and khaki pants. Suddenly, red soldiers began to appear everywhere. People marveled at seeing the bands of red volunteers on every road in Nagpur. Teams of militants began to walk in disciplined ranks through the city with "rap, rap, rap," performing military maneuvers.

The numbers of youth coming to the Dal meetings in the evening began to grow. The Scheduled Caste Federation's conference was set to be held on 17 July 1942. Wamanrao had taken the double responsibility of the arrangements for the conference and the protection of Babasaheb. Wamanrao's organizational skills were marvelous. He assigned tasks to young activists of the Dal, dividing the responsibility for the neighborhoods among them, and he himself traveled everywhere to organize the youth. Branches of the Dal were established in all the neighborhoods, in Dhantoli, Imampada, Zhatakrodi, Yogicity in western Nagpur; in New Fridaydale, Katanbag, Lawyercorner, Cameltown in eastern Nagpur, and in Dharampeth, Ramdaspeth, Oilville, and Mangocreek in western Nagpur.

One day, at six or so in the evening, Wamanrao called together the ten- to fifteen-year-old boys. None of us had had dinner. He selected several boys from the Dal, took us aside, and gave letters to all of us. These letters were for the leaders of every Dal branch. We all left running. The letters were supposed to be delivered in half an hour; hardly anyone had a cycle. We ran to each neighborhood and gave the notes to the designated people.

I reached Wrestler Tukaram in Inamwada just as he was sitting to eat. "Is Mama at home?"

"Why? Vasanta, come, have some food. Subhadra, serve him."

"No, Mama. I have come to deliver this note. Take it."

Tukaram read the letter and immediately got up from his dinner. In the note Wamanrao had written, "Come just as you are."

By ten that night thirty to thirty-five youth from all neighborhoods had gathered in the field. A two-hour meeting ensued. Suggestions were given to everyone and everyone returned home. We got a firsthand experience of what the discipline of the Dal was like.

On Sunday, the branches of all neighborhoods were called to parade in Bardi at nine in the morning. When a thousand youths in red shirts and khaki pants stood in ranks in their companies and Wamanrao gave the order "Attention!" in his high voice, the scene appeared like a red carpet with a khaki fringe below and a black border above.

The flag-raising was completed, and then Bhanudas Varade began to sing the flag song in a world-captivating voice:

> Waving always in the skies
> Our beloved flag of freedom!
> The seventy millions of Dalit people today
> Vow their lives to the flag!
> The sight of you inspires us.
> We'll uproot tradition in an instant!
>
> On the Chaudar lake at Mahad
> King Bhim, our brave leader of Dalits,
> Made the dedication of his life.
> All the community rose up like a storm!
> Seventy million Untouchables roared,
> Became purified with his sight,
> A new spirit filled their bodies,
> A new confidence filled the air!
> "They plundered our freedom,
> Made us slaves for ages and eons,
> With you as witness we will take it back.
> You are our support!
>
> "This is our birthright,
> Let us win equality.
> Take the gift of life,
> Oh brave leader of all!
> The horn has blown anew,
> We salute your name,
> For freedom we will die.
> There is no other thought in the battlefield!"
>
> The net of slavery
> Makes food of the hearts of peasants
> Burns up all the workers
> And the owner gets all the profit!
> All should get the blessing
> Of brotherhood in the motherland,
>
> Let us free everyone now
> The wind of freedom is let loose!
> We have fierce heroic fighting leaders
> Let us all go forward.
> Our aim is to achieve power
> Let us give our lives on the battlefield!

The flag song was usually sung by Bhanudas Varade. When he was absent, the chance to sing it was given to me. We sang five stanzas of that song.

When the flag song was over, each branch went out to the main road in lines of three, in order, one after another. With "left, right, left," the entire red stream began to move ahead. Everyone had a stick in his left hand resting on his left shoulder and the right hand moving up and down to the rhythm of his feet. Each platoon had a leader. The structure was just as in the military, with three platoons making a section, three sections a company, and three companies a brigade. The leaders of the platoons and companies wore long pants. A golden belt of four inches went from left to right on their chests. They wore insignia on their right arms just as military officers had. On the shirts' shoulders was a tab, and on this a blue band with the letters "SSD." The sticks of most of the boys were only as long as their arms. But the cudgels of the young men were extraordinary.

At the time the whole affair was romantic for me. Repressing hunger and thirst, from morning to afternoon, all together on the main roads of Nagpur, we turned the whole city upside down. The boys were hungry. We felt the vehement heat of the harsh March sun. Even then everyone was enthusiastic. By the time we had circled the city and returned, it was two in the afternoon.

After the parade ended and we returned to the community, I asked Ganba about his cudgel. "Is that a metal ring on the front of your stick?"

"Look, kid, you won't understand. There is a ring like this on every militant's stick. A blade is supposed to be fixed on it."

"So where is the blade?"

"Look, friend, is it something to be shown?" And saying this, he lifted his belt and turned it a little aside to show me the blade hidden beneath it. Ganba then said, "Everyone is supposed to keep such an arrangement on his stick; otherwise anyone could strike us down."

It was then that I understood the militancy of the Dal.

On the evening of the second day, Wamanrao held a study session in the Dal branch. "Babasaheb says, sheep and goats are sacrificed, not lions and tigers. Yesterday we had a parade. People saw our strength. Now no one will cross us." Up to then the instructions of the Dal had only been to organize meetings and gatherings. From that time on the Dal took up a broader program of confronting evil, resisting injustice and atrocities.

After many years I read a biography of Hitler. He also had taken out parades in the streets of Berlin. However, I felt the parades of the Dal were closer to those of Russian soldiers. Seeing the military maneuvers of Russian soldiers after 1950 in films, I always used to remember the Samata Sainik Dal. I could understand how meaningful was Babasaheb's intention in choosing red shirts and khaki pants.

# Chapter 11

## FORESHADOWING

Wamanrao Godbole was slightly built, with a slim, sticklike body and a light complexion. He had one year of college education. But because someone in his house had insulted him, this boy ran away. He spent some time in the forests of Itarsi and some time in Mumbai. After that he worked in a company, then got a job as guard in the railways. He kept it to the end.

Wamanrao had a temperamental personality. He could never endure an insult. He picked a quarrel with a neighboring family of wrestlers. Wamanrao paid no attention to his own slight build or the superior strength of the opposing party, and entered the ground suddenly and threw the wrestler. The whole community gathered to watch with surprise. A man whose path everyone feared to cross had been dashed to the ground by Wamanrao.

Wamanrao remained a bachelor his whole life. Not even his enemies could raise a question about his reputation. This reputation was the core of his strength. Wamanrao was respected not only in the Dal but in the whole community. This man had never taken any money from anyone, but had given to whoever had asked him, without any expectation of return.

Due to Wamanrao's fundamental loyalty, Babasaheb in 1956 had given the responsibility for the conversion to him, and later we had heard that he was going to be secretary of the All-India Buddhist People's Committee. But this never came into existence.

It is no wonder that the organization of the Samata Sainik Dal by Wamanrao should be a subject of discussion throughout Nagpur. The activists of the Federation had never seen such management. R. R. Patil was the All-India secretary of the Samata Sainik Dal. He had grown up knowing military discipline. However, even he was stirred after seeing Wamanrao's organizing. Some may also have been moved by doubts that their positions would be threatened. Wamanrao revived the Dal units in such neighborhoods as Indora,

Military Park, and Pacpavali in northern Nagpur. There, also, Dal parades began. Now all of Nagpur began to turn red.

The Federation office near the Buti Municipal Primary School near Maharpura began to hum with meetings of regional working committees. The conference was to take place in July 1942. As preparation, however, Dadasaheb Gaikwad, P. N. Rajbhoj, and others arrived early. All these people would stop at Maharpura on their way to the office. Leaders like Revaram Kavade, Dasharath Patil, Sitaram Hadke, and others made frequent visits, night or day, to Maharpura.

One member of the working committee, Radhabai Kamble, was from our community. When Radhabai rose to give a speech, the whole mass of people became silent. Radhabai, who could barely read and write, could not be defeated in debate by anyone. She had worked in the mill. Previously she had been a member of the Congress INTUC union. But when the Independent Labour Party was established, she began to organize under Revaram Kavade. Mahars made up 40 to 45 percent of Nagpur's mill workers, and 30 percent of these were women. All these came together under Radhabai's leadership. She began to handle all their problems. As the conference drew near, the crowds of women in her house grew.

One day Dasharath Patil, Kavade, and other leaders met our branch. Wamanrao gave them the information about this branch. After the Dal's hour finished, everyone sat down on the field.

"The discipline of the SSD is very good," said Kavade.

"It's a matter of pride that the young people are becoming organized," stated Dasharath Patil.

"This should have happened earlier. It is your work we are doing," Wamanrao proclaimed forthrightly. "We have no interest in your politics. Our effort is only that our boys should learn discipline, get some direction. We don't want to interfere in your politics." The leaders of the working committee gave a sigh of relief.

Wamanrao paused for a while. Then he said, "How has it been decided to organize Babasaheb's reception?"

This question was unexpected by the leaders. They could not answer.

Wamanrao said, "We want to give Babasaheb a 'Guard of Honor.' We have a thousand soldiers today. Babasaheb will definitely like our reception."

"But hasn't the Indora unit also made some preparations?"

"It's not that we have ever had a quarrel with them. But you have seen our arrangements!"

Saying, "Okay, we'll see," the leaders left.

The place in the Civil Lines where the corporation office is today used to be called Nidham Park. Next to it stands Mount Hotel. Babasaheb always stayed in that hotel. In the park a beautiful pavilion was erected, big enough to accommodate two hundred thousand people. On one end stood a huge stage. There were closed curtains on all four sides of the pavilion, with magnificent gates built for people to enter through. On one side was a special place for women to sit. Pundalik Mul (the father of Sushila Mul, now a professor of Pali) had the contract for the pavilion. Shivaji More was the contractor for the loudspeaker, and Sadashiv Mate was the photographer. All were of the Mahar community. Wherever possible, the labor and funds of Untouchables were used.

Babasaheb's reception ceremony was to take place around ten in the morning at the Nagpur railway station. That was the time the mail arrived. So it was necessary for all the volunteers to arrive with discipline before this time. We rose, took our bath, and came to the Dal grounds by seven o'clock. For eight days previously we had kept our khaki shorts and red shirts ironed and ready. Those who could manage it put on a top quality red shirt. I had a cheaper shirt sewn. The cloth for the khaki pants was also according to what each could afford. The platoon leaders were older youth. All these had put on a full pant and full shirt.

Because Babasaheb was to come by railway for the 1942 conference, thousands of people from all over Nagpur began to gather at the Sitabardi station. We boys were all ready in our khaki pants and red shirts. At that time we had no caps. By nine o'clock the volunteers from Inamwada, Dhantoli, and Cameltown—that is, from eastern Nagpur—had come in parades of their units. From the west, units came from faraway places such as Dharampeth, Telangkhedi, Mangocreek, Lendhara, and Jayatala. The whole Gita Ground was covered with the red of the volunteers. Some wore boots on their feet while others had cloth shoes. There were also many bare feet. Many volunteers were poor. They could not buy the red cloth in time. They had dyed their white shirts red.

Wamanrao let loose his call of "Attention!," and all the volunteers who had gathered in ranks became silent and motionless in their places. With "Right dress," the right hand went up. It was placed on the next person's shoulder, the ranks moved, the volunteers moved, and then again, "Position!"

And Wamanrao gave the order for the whole field to move towards the station. "Rup rup" went the feet, and with the noise of a marching band stepping left-right-left, hundreds of volunteers departed to welcome Babasaheb at Sitabardi station. I took a small stick and moved my feet in order along with the "children" among the volunteers.

We reached the station, and there we learned that before we'd arrived, R. R. Patil and his gang had taken Babasaheb away in procession. Wamanrao was not a person to sit quietly. He ordered the volunteers to "double march." All the young volunteers went running from Kasturchand Park field to Mohan Park. Seeing Babasaheb's car on the road, they all sat down in protest.

We small boys arrived after the big ones. Outside the pavilion, hundreds of Dal volunteers were seated. Wamanrao had blocked the main road. The Federation activists were speaking with Wamanrao. Wamanrao was furious. After having agreed to let him have the opportunity of doing the welcoming ceremony, it had been denied. He concluded that he had been betrayed. Finally all the red volunteers gained entrance into the pavilion. Babasaheb called Wamanrao to him, and all became quiet.

The Samata Sainik organized a huge rally one day. Many youth had received education in the university training core. Because of this they had an idea of military training. A military band was developed. Instruments like bugles, drums, and flutes were procured. Rehearsals followed one after another in the morning and evening, then the rally was held.

The parade was to start from the Barsenagar Pacpavali. Five horses were rented. Five Dal members were made captains. Other youth were given huge kettledrums. All were decked out in red full shirts and khaki pants. Pandurang Varade would play the bugle. Pandurang Jivane would play the flute. Keshav Patil, Dongare, and Waman Godbole would give orders—attention, left turn, right turn, etc. The ordinary volunteers carried sticks the height of their shoulders in their hands. They walked, doing left-right, with their sticks on their left shoulders.

At Barsenagar near Pacpavali thousands of people from all over Nagpur had gathered. R. R. Patil was the Dal leader. A salute was given to Kavade Guruji. In ranks of four, about five thousand volunteers parading through Nagpur reached Sitabardi, and the rally was dispersed. I never saw such a captivating sight in my life. The unique features of this procession were the five captains on fine horses wearing yellow-silk sashes sewn by Bardi people, with the letters SSD embroidered on them, hats on their heads, spears in their hands, and a band marching in front.

And once, a ten-day camp of the Dal for all of Nagpur was held at Khaparkheda on the banks of the river for military training. Each neighborhood had its tent. In the morning the military maneuvers began and went on for the whole day. There were study classes and speeches on the movement. Loyalty sank deep and became solidified.

# Chapter 12

## HOLY VICTORY

The Rashtriya Swayamsevak Sangh used to hold its branch meetings on Sitabardi's Gita Ground, near the Bhide girls' school. After the beginning of the Samata Sainik Dal, all the Mahar youth left the RSS chapter. All young and old men of the community began coming to the Dal.

The Rashtriya Swayamsevak Sangh and the Dal units met right next to each other. There was also a cricket pitch on the Patwardhan ground, and with Maharpura teams for cricket, football, and hockey, boys were playing all of them. But the Sangh unit began to feel they were being obstructed by the games of our boys who had left the Sangh for the Dal. If the ball went to their side, they started grabbing it, refusing to give it back and quarreling. And so altercations and fighting began to take place daily.

The youth decided to resolve these quarrels. The only way to permanently settle this fighting was to beat up the Sangh boys. A secret meeting of the Dal was held and it was decided to attack the next day.

Construction had started on a building next to the flag field of the Dal, and sand and gravel were lying around. The Dal volunteers brought sticks one by one, and hid fifty or sixty of them in the sand. Maharpura people were skilled in stick-fighting. Slowly, the youth of the unit gathered. The small boys had no idea; however, on that day all the wrestler trainers of the community were present at the Dal field. A football game began. Dongare, Godbole, and Meshram came to know that some youth from Tekadi Lines and Koshtipura and elsewhere had come to the Sangh meeting. In other words, they also had made preparations to attack us. They had brought their iron swords. We small boys came at a gallop, and all the young kids sitting on the well began to give voice. We said, "The fighting has begun over there"; immediately everyone came running.

When the football went to the Sangh side, they grabbed it and began an argument.

"Hey, you cunt, are you giving it back or what?"

"Yeah, don't swear."

"Why are you starting a fight?"

"Oh, hell, this is too much, it happens every day." So the wrangling began.

Enough! From both sides sticks were pulled out. But as one boy at a time came running with sticks from under the sand and began to whirl them, the Sangh volunteers and their hired bullies were flabbergasted, and all began to run. Some hid in the Bhide girls' school while some went for refuge to Brahman houses in Namjibhai Town. The volunteers ran after them and gave them a thrashing.

After returning, the youth found the sticks, swords, and chains left by the enemy on the battlefield and, considering them to be like gold looted at Dussera, took them home.

The next day the police began a close search in Maharpura. They confiscated many swords. Lawsuits were filed. But the Sangh people could not afford a legal fight. Within two or three days the main activists of the Sangh, like Ghatate, came themselves to our community. They tried to be conciliatory. "There should be no quarrels among us."

"Why should we want quarrels? You play in your boundaries, we will play in ours."

Everyone then went to the ground. The field was divided into two. They played on their western half and we played on our eastern half. The atmosphere again cleared up. Going and coming began. We began to take part in their programs, and they came to ours. Such Sanghists as Dada Joshi, Paturkar, and Ashok Gupte remain acquaintances even today. Even today, with Maharpura renamed Anandnagar (City of Joy) when the Mahars converted to Buddhism in 1956, many swords have been kept in houses as memorials of this victory.

I began to go to school on time. Mother was going daily to look for work. It was impossible for her to manage the road-construction work of rock hauling. She had never carried heavy loads. She was searching for only one kind of work: washing dishes or cooking. Mahar women were not kept as servants in the neighboring Brahman colony. Parsis used to live around Empress Mills. Mother was going there in the hopes that she could get employment with someone. She used to go asking from bungalow to bungalow. Whatever worries and pains she endured she never told. After a whole day she would come back tired in the evening, bringing some prepared food in a tin.

One day she said, "I got some work in Pestonji's bungalow. Only two people live there, the husband and wife. Along with food they'll pay four rupees."

Giving the food she had brought to my sister and me, she went to sleep. The next day before sunrise she left for work. Malti and I got up, took our baths, got ready. There was nothing to eat in the house. Mother had kept some tea for us. We warmed it up and drank it. Our neighbor, Grandmother Rose (her color was very rosy, hence her nickname), saw us and brought over a little food on a plate. We left for school, wondering who would feed us all the other days?

Now our days of hunger began. We started going hungry for two days at a time. At first we were troubled by pangs of starvation. However, once the body gets in the habit of fasting, hunger is not felt. Hunger slowly begins to die. With it, the flowing spirit begins to dry up, free laughter vanishes. We began to put whatever we could get into our stomachs.

While I was coming back from school one day, I started brooding about what to eat. An idea came to me. An old woman was selling bananas. I went over and stood in front of her. I asked the price of the bananas, taking a dozen in my hand. I made a show of taking money out of my pocket. And seeing that the old woman's attention was elsewhere, I started running.

The old woman stumbled to her feet. I could only hear the curses she was hurling. Leaping into Hanuman Lane, I went running. To distract the old women, I threw three or four bananas in the path where she could see them. Collecting these, the woman went back. I watched from a corner wall to make sure she had gone, then I went home. Malti and I ate the remaining bananas. That night Mother brought a tin box. In it was some vegetable curry and rice she had made. If Mother had enough spices, no one could make such tasty food.

While I was eating she said, "I left the job at Pestonji's."

"Then?"

"I got work in a different bungalow."

"But why?"

"The woman was very suspicious. She would say to me, 'Where did the rupee on the tablecloth go?' I said, 'I don't know, Ma'am.' I get very furious if anyone calls me a thief. I will go hungry, but I will not steal. I may die of hunger but not lay my hands on anyone else's goods. So I left the job and took another."

Many thoughts started running through my mind. I felt pride in my mother's honesty. She was telling us how expensive the goods in a Parsi's house were, how she put back the things she found when she was cleaning, how these people keep track of every penny of their expenses, and while listening to all of this we went to sleep in the open veranda in front of the house.

Word about Mother's skill must have spread. Mother's cooking had a special taste. She could cook Parsi, Irani, Muslim, and other types of food. Who knows where she learned it! She must have picked up some knowledge from

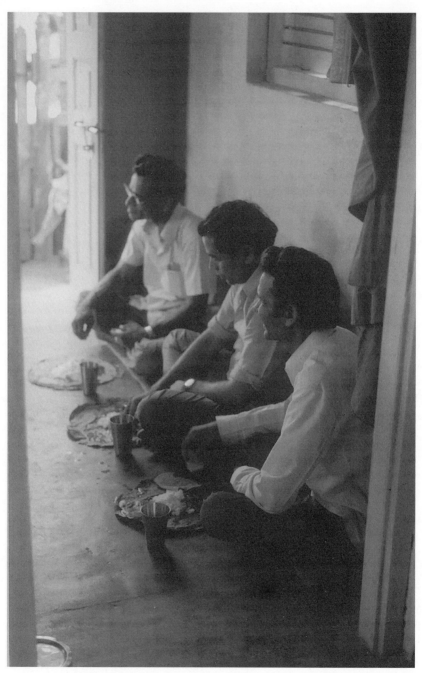

*A meal in a Nagpur Buddhist home. Photo by Eleanor Zelliot, 1964.*

spending so much time in Parsi households. She made simple eggplant, but people could not stop eating it. Those who ate the fish she made will never forget it. In cooking mutton she would stir it from time to time with a spoon, and tell from the smell of the spoon when the mutton was cooked. No one else in the entire Moon family had her skill with vegetables, it was said.

After leaving the Pestonjis, she quickly got a job in a second Parsi home. This family paid three rupees a month. One day Mother was given the son's clothes to wash. The colors faded, so one and a half rupees were cut from her pay. She was given a lot to eat, but there was much trouble. Mother left this job also.

A very famous advocate named Avi J. Cama used to live in Nagpur. She was the first woman advocate of Nagpur. When Mother was working for Ardeshwar Parsi, they would send her to Cama. She had a huge bungalow and a big compound in the Civil Lines. No maids could last long with her either. However, Cama developed an affection for Mother. Hers was a family of two sisters and their mother living together. Avi Cama also was active in the working-class movement with the union leader Raosaheb Phule, and later was the president of the All-India Women's Hockey Federation.

Mother got work from Miss Cama for four rupees a month. From time to time she now also began to get meals. She would save a little from the meals and bring it home for us. Mother would say, "Cama tells me to do all kinds of work. Take out the grass from the yard, do this, do that. Once I got very tired. I was very hungry. There was tea and bread, but Cama said, 'Wait, Purni.' With her own hands she took some fragrant rice and cooked it, poured fresh ghee on it and gave it to me to eat. She was so loving."

Miss Cama had a tempestuous nature. Sometimes Mother also got angry. A couple of explosions might occur, but finally Miss Cama would say, "Purni don't be angry, my nature is like that."

After Mother worked many days, around 1946, Miss Cama got her a job in Model Mill. Mother went to work in the morning and returned at six in the evening. After a month she finally received her first pay. She said, "With a pay of three rupees and dearness allowance of three rupees, we can live happily for the whole month on those six rupees." At that time, even right after the war, the price of rice was six rupees for a huge bag. Mutton was six paise a *sher*, for five rupees you could get a whole goat. For six paise you could get four *shers* of lentils. The day Mother's pay came was the day that ended our life of living like poor Brahmans on alms.

# Chapter 13

## ROBUST AND ROLLICKING

While Mother was wandering about, looking for employment in Parsi bungalows, I was having a problem with my clothes. They began to wear out; when my shorts tore I simply mended them. If they got too torn I would take them to Uncle Kundalik to fix on his sewing machine. Uncle would take a big patch of the right color of fabric from the rags left over from cut cloth, and sew a large oval patch on the seat of the pants and give them back to me.

As my pants grew frayed, Uncle Kundalik realized that I could not buy any new clothes. One day he called me and gave me a pair of newly sewn short pants and a shirt. Uncle said, "Vasanta, if you don't have clothes, tell me. Your grandfather was a saheb. No one here had seen such splendor. He used to maintain horses and a carriage. He had relations with Europeans. But he would help anyone."

I would go at any time of day and sit in Uncle Kundalik's shop. The Kundalik Kavade Tailoring Shop was in the middle section of a fifty-foot-wide apartment building on the main road. He employed two men working on machines. He himself only cut the cloth. Since he had taken a tailoring course in Kolhapur he used to write "Kolhapurkar" before his name on the board. He sewed me pants and shirts whenever I needed them. He used to help many boys like me. His house was spacious and close to Nagpur station. Rekharam Kavade was his maternal uncle. Because of this, meetings with P. N. Rajbhoj, Dadasaheb Gaikwad, Shantabai Dani, and others used to be held at his place.

One day when I was sitting there he said, "This community is one of wrestlers. Behind this house lives Wrestling Ustad Sada, beyond that Ustad Ruda, and beyond that Wrestler Maniram. West of that is Ustad Daji More. Nearby Bhadu Ustad Borkar. And from there Zholba Ustad Meshram, beyond him Sadu Ustad Borkar, behind on the side is Shivaram Ustad Rangari, and behind Bangar's house Wrestler Mahadev Meshram. In the middle of the community is Watchman Narayan Buti Ustad." All of these wrestlers had separate wrestling grounds.

I began to study each wrestler. Narayan Watchman would fill half or more of the road while walking in lanes and alleys. Each Ustad had his specialty. Daji Ustad's was sticks and cudgels; he was skilled in jousting. When wrestling grounds were built in the community, Daji Ustad was in the forefront. Maniram Mohite and Sonba Meshram were all-around wrestlers. Narayan Watchman would become a tiger during Moharram. Uncle Kundalik used to say to my mother, "Auntie, keep a goat ready." And a live goat would be brought and set aside for him. Narayan Buti was the watchman of the community, and was respected even in the police station.

"Uncle, where did our people get educated before?"

"There was a mission school at Shukravari. There our boys used to go to school. Previously there were not many houses in the community. There must have been about fifty. Now there are two hundred. The Sweeper's quarter used to be near the toilets. Bangar Savaji used to loan money to the Ropemakers and Sweepers. A Ropemaker community was near us. Once, there was a big fight over the tap between Maharpura and Oilmaker Town, and the whole community ran into the houses in Oilmaker Town and beat people up." Uncle's eyes glittered. He continued, "No matter how much we fight among ourselves in the community, when the time comes, we all unite.

"Shivaram Ustad was a very talented man. He himself used to make beautiful clay Ganpatis, which people of all castes would buy from him. At the time of plays he would make decorations for the stage. He would also make the curtains."

"Uncle, plays used to be performed here?"

"Oh, just as people here are robust, so they are rollicking. Since the subject of theater has come up, I'll tell you. When I was small—around 1925—the young boys of the community put on a play called *In the Door of the Prison*. This must have been the first play. Haribhau Dongare, Harishchandra Jangam, and Kabhu Khobragade played the women's roles. Fakirchand Meshram also worked in it.

"At that time people would set up Ganpati idols and organize clubs. The kids of the club performed *Raja Harishchandra*. This performance took place in the courtyard of Raghuji Bhosle's palace. The *Raja Harishchandra* play won first prize. Things were very cheap then.

"At that time women used to get three rupees pay in the mills. In Mumbai, Mahars were not supposed to touch the thread, so they didn't get employed in the weaving department. Here, weaving was a major occupation of our people. Because of this there was no ban on weaving work in the mills. The condition of our people improved because of the textile mills; this is important.

Many people in our community even today hold positions as jobbers, masters, and so on in the mills.

"At that time there weren't even any bicycles. After many days, two cycles appeared in Nagpur. Among those one was Masuji's. Dr. Masuji was a god to the Mahar community. If anyone got sick, he would go to Masuji. He had lost one eye in World War I.

"On the side of the orange market was the railway station. The Boy Scouts of our community ran a hostel there on the basis of cooperative principles."

All that Uncle told me was new to me. His stories caused me to realize how much had happened in our community before I was born.

The passion for wrestling slowly lessened. There were now four or five in-dividually managed wrestling grounds. Some youth became members of Kahate Gokhale's gymnasium in Dhantoli.

In the month of Ashada, on full-moon night, the *panchayats* of the sub-castes of the community would cook a goat on the wrestling grounds near the temple. A rule stated that every family in the *panchayat* should symbolically par-ticipate in the killing of the goat. Otherwise they were fined by the caste *pan-chayat*. Even I had to put a knife to the neck of the goat once. Some people were skilled in skinning the goat. The cooked goat meat was distributed equally. Some piece from each part of the goat was put in each plate. The portion made available was called a share, and that day was celebrated with intoxication from liquor and meat.

On that day also the Hindus got wrestling grounds ready, and they would go before the community and show the skills of their crafts. Basayya Ustad, Babulal Ustad, and other Hindu wrestling masters would demonstrate their skill. Dajiba Ustad's stick was so forcefully whirled that it could not even be seen. It was said that no matter how many stones were hurled at it, they couldn't hit him.

Around the time of the Dussera holidays a *mela*, a sort of fair, was held in the community. Poems were sung in the style of Kabir's songs; a spiritual refrain was inserted and drums were beaten. Eight to ten young boys would go singing from house to house in the community. Govind Rangari sang songs in the *mela*. Fakir-chand Chahade danced. In any houses where these songs were sung, singers and householders would challenge each other in song. All of these songs were in Hindi.

> No one respects us in the market,
> We live in mud huts,
> When we live in Sitabardi,
> We get only blows and insults—
> Don't go without showing the wisdom of your guru,
> Roar out your challenge!

As this was sung, a drumlike sound would begin and then a challenger would say,

> Krishna is playing *holi* in Braj,
> He throws red color over the whole world!

Teasing songs were also sung from time to time:

> Let's go to the park, I'll eat some sweets,
> Eat some sweets, spread out my mat,
> If somebody tears up my mat, I'll call a tailor,
> If the tailor's thread breaks I'll call an ironsmith,
> If the smith's hammer breaks I'll call a repairman,
> Come on, let's go to the park, I'll eat some sweets.

And if they saw some beautiful light-skinned boy, they would taunt him with,

> Oh my boy, bring me a little fire,
> Give me a light, bring me tobacco, bring me some cold water
> Oh beautiful boy, come and sit with us.

When the group reached Barber Prahlad's shop, the fun would go on for at least a half to three quarters of an hour, and just as money would be showered on performers in a *tamasha*, a sort of folk theater, Prahlad would make all the young boys happy with a departing gift.

Prahlad Mhali, who had a barber shop on the southeast corner of the community and a house in the northwest, was a person with a passion for the pleasures of life. Prahlad was Grandfather's friend. His shop would be open before six in the morning. Most of the newspapers, not only from Nagpur but also Mumbai, would come to his shop. He would relate the news enthusiastically to people. This haircutter was a very important person in our community.

With his six-foot-tall, strong body and white, round, laughing face, he would come to the shop wearing a shirt and black hat with a *dhoti* held up above one knee. He always went to see English talkies and would not miss a single play that came to Vyankatesh Theater.

One day the Bal Gandharva theater troupe gave a performance of a musical drama. In those days plays went on until morning. Many merry people would come to the play, often after drinking. While Bal Gandharva's song was going on, an excitable man named Narayan Painter threw a shoe at the stage. He felt that Bal Gandharva had made a mistake in the meter while singing! That was all it took; the play stopped, and Bal Gandharva vowed never again to come to Nagpur. Theater vanished from Nagpur.

Prahlad Mhali was distraught without the theater. He satisfied his ardor by going to Amraoti. There, one Sulochana Kulkarni, a Brahman girl who was a student, saw his beautiful form and personality, fell in love with him, and came and lived with him. Prahlad, who already had two wives, maintained her as well up to the end.

Prahlad was a renowned haircutter. The governor used to have his beard trimmed by him. When Babasaheb Ambedkar came to Nagpur, he would call for him. Prahlad gave him loving service. He would tell him all the news. I would go every morning and sit in Prahlad's shop. I was addicted to reading the language of Marathi from primary school onwards, so I would read many newspapers. Prahlad would say, "Vasanta, read out loud." And I would read out the news to everyone sitting there.

When my hair got long, Prahlad would give me a free haircut with his gentle touch. His hand was weighty, but it would go very lightly over my hair, and as he cut my hair, he would talk. He would tell stories from here and there.

One day I said to him, "Grandfather, why don't you arrange a play in our community? You have so much passion for the theater, why don't you organize one?"

"Oh, Vasanta, you don't know; in this community there has been a love for seeing and performing plays for such a long time. According to my memory, from the very beginning—that is around 1927—a play named *Uplift of the Downtrodden* was performed. The Hindi drama *Sorrowful Mohini* also played here."

"Where were these plays rehearsed?"

"In front of our temple in the house of Bhanudas Varade. The club of Bharat Bhagyodaya was in the first floor of that house. Many things went on there, including rehearsals of plays. *Uplift of the Downtrodden,* a musical drama, was performed in 1928. At that time, Sapre Master of Shriram Musical School used to come to perform the music and songs for the plays. Mithu Rangari was a master in the mill. He would help with the plays. Gulab also composed some plays."

And suddenly Prahlad stopped. "Should I show you something amusing?"

"What?"

"Have you ever seen a black rose?"

"Of course not."

"See, then, one is coming before us." I looked towards a very dark gentleman named Gulab (Rose) in front of the shop. Gulab was swearing at Prahlad and laughing. I was getting a taste of his irresistible jokes.

# Chapter 14

## SPORTS AND STUDY

Middle school consisted of fifth through eighth, while ninth through eleventh was high school. A fat teacher named Vaidya in sixth taught Marathi. He would tell Y. G. Joshi's story of the *shenga* tree in a very lively manner. He instructed us to memorize poems. I'd had a craze for memorizing poetry since childhood. At that time, all students were enthusiastic about playing poetry games, and all kept a store of memorized poems. In my class there was a very smart boy named Arvind Buce, who was always first in the class. In the matriculation exam, he won first class first in all of Madhya Pradesh. This boy had a notebook of poems. His specialty was the game in which one stanza had to begin and end with a specific letter, such as "k." He had collected a profusion of such poems. I also collected poems from many old books, but I couldn't achieve such proficiency as Buce. I, Buce, and Bhaskar Joshi were the boys in our class chosen as a team to represent our school in the poetry contest.

Vaidya Master put great stress on clear pronunciation. One day while reading the lesson in class I made a mistake in pronouncing some words. Vaidya Master's insulting remark—"Oh, you would garble the words of the Gayatri mantra itself!"—has remained strongly in my mind. The older people in the community used to say that Brahman teachers, rather than encouraging Mahar students, always destroyed their self-confidence. Atmaram Varade told me, "They would give me the 'horse' punishment [bending the neck and taking both hands behind the legs to grab the ears, and staying in that stooped position]. They would beat me with a cane. One day after another, the 'horse'! How could I learn anything in school? My mother and father would say, 'Go to school.' If not, they would beat me. In the school the teacher beat me. Finally I ran away. This was how my school days ended."

Vaidya Master was very strict and intimidating. But he had a kind nature and, except for this one incident, never gave any trouble on the basis of caste.

And Wagh Master was not a tiger by nature, even though that's what his name means. Around fifty years old, but with more interest in sports than education, he taught English grammar. In the evenings he would call the boys to Patwardhan Ground. There he himself would mix with them and play football.

His favorite game, however, was cricket. He spent all his time after four P.M. on the cricket ground, teaching the students all the details of the sport— how to hold the bat, how to throw the ball, how to catch it, how to hit the ball, how to bowl, etc. I was present many times at his practice, but I could never make the school team. However, a cricket club got organized in our neighborhood, and I played in that.

A new teacher came to teach geography in middle school. He pronounced the word "fruit" as "frood," and made other mistakes, and when he did the boys would laugh. Most of the boys in Patwardhan School were of a high caste background; this was in their view a cause for ridicule. Once, several boys laughed at such impure pronunciation, but the teacher's attention went specifically to me. He came over and gave me a powerful slap on my left cheek. I swallowed the insult and kept quiet.

During the middle break the teacher called me to his room. Probably he felt remorseful that he had hit me. He said, "Moon, I hit you very hard, didn't I? However, if I hadn't done it, the other boys would not have kept quiet. Don't take it badly. This is the way I have talked since childhood; it won't go away."

There were some senior Mahar boys in the school. I told the whole story to one of them, Eknath. He said, "Vasanta, if it were anyone else I would give a blow to the bastard. But he's one of ours who became a Christian. In your class you're the only one who he could see is a Mahar. He wouldn't have had the guts to hit a Brahman. Oh well. He won't do it again."

After Eknath explained this teacher's complex, the fury in my mind was replaced by sympathy.

I kept on going to middle school, but wasted much time in truancy and playing games. I would do exactly the homework the teachers assigned; everything else would be left aside. I had a quick intellect but didn't study. Because of this, I failed the three months' and six months' examinations. When the yearly examination came, the problem arose of how to pass it. What would Uncle say? What would Mother say? Somehow or another I had to pass. So I learned the technique of copying.

My role number was in Vaidya Master's class. The teacher used to sit on his desk and read the paper during exams. Out of awe of him no student had dared to try copying. However, just as it is said that "Stilling hunger is no sin," I was only taking care of my hunger to pass. My only aim was to pass from one class to another, not to come in first, and I began to take the books for that paper hidden in my pocket. I only used this dangerous method for the final examination. Other students gradually became my companions in this. Since the surnames Moon and Mohani were close, Bal Mohani and I used to pass the yearly examinations with each other's help. In eighth, I couldn't help Bal with one paper, and he failed it. I felt that he had failed only because of me. This remained in my mind so strongly that afterward I gave up copying.

Up to eighth, though, this was the secret of my success in examinations.

Whereas Bokil Master had written the algebra and geometry books for middle school, the arithmetic book was Ozha's. These three books served me from fifth to eighth. In ninth, the only optional subjects were arithmetic and chemistry. So I sold my bound algebra and geometry books. I had bought these books for only two and a half rupees, but since they still looked new when I sold them, I got double their value. The new books I obtained for only one and a half times what I got for the old books. I couldn't spend much on books, and would also buy as few notebooks as possible. My handwriting was only so-so. But in the notebooks I wrote two to three lines in each space. I used a narrow nib on my pen to write small letters: the O nib, the U nib, the spear nib, and for Marathi the common yellow nib. I kept them in my desk, and the north Indian janitor of the school would fill them with ink every day. There was living space on the Patwardhan ground for the janitors.

My Marathi was good even in childhood. The Mahar boys who came from the Bhandara-Chandrapur region would pronounce "c" and "j" as "ch" and "jh." In comparison, my white-collar speech was considered pure. From the ninth, I faced the question of what to take as an elective. After passing eighth, most of the Brahman boys would be put in the A class, which was English-medium. In the B class were Marathi-medium students. Students of medium grade like me were in the B class. The lower-marked students and those riotous boys who mainly played sports were in the C class. I felt like taking the science class. My thought was that if Brahman students took it, why shouldn't I? However, when I asked the science teachers, they said, "This subject is very difficult, you will not be able to manage it."

I took algebra and chemistry together. In 1949, nearly 90 percent of the students who took the chemistry test failed it. My chemistry test also received low marks. From that night I started studying for the algebra paper by solving all the problems in Ozha's book and in two days was fully prepared. With a distinction in mathematics, I passed both subjects.

For the optional subject I took manual training, that is, woodworking. I was short in height and weak in my body. The carpenter's plane for finishing the wood was heavy and difficult for me to lift. Even so I took the subject. At first, I had gone and sat in the Sanskrit class. When not a single student from the Mahar community appeared there, I decided I might as well learn wood-working with the other students, and so I changed classes.

My Marathi, which had been thought so fine, got only twenty-nine marks at matric, and I failed. I got higher marks in manual training than in any other subjects. With grace marks in Marathi, I made it to the pass division for matric.

One can never say where the events in our lives will lead us. What took place was what I had never imagined would happen; a different future came to my share. Who would have said, especially in the face of Dev Master's curse, that the work of editing and publishing Babasaheb Ambedkar's English writings would have been given to me? In the moving, shifting world, change is inevitable, and astrologers' predictions are proved fraudulent!

When movements erupt, they burst out on all sides. After the Scheduled Caste Federation was founded in 1942, in the same year a student organization was established by high school and college students. For a full year registration of members took place, and then elections for the student organization were declared.

In our community, every student who had studied as far as middle school and beyond was made a member. The election took place in the Bhide girls' school grounds. Between the two slates of candidates there existed much competitiveness. However, no fighting broke out. After the election, everyone behaved as if nothing had happened. Khaparde and Namdev Nimgade were standing against each other for the position of joint secretary. But they went around and campaigned together. While meeting girl students they used to say jokingly, "My dear, vote for the one you fancy."

Thus, Untouchable students formed the All-India Scheduled Caste Student Federation after the 1942 conference, and branches were started in Madras, Bengal, Uttar Pradesh (then the United Provinces), and Mumbai (Bombay).

It was decided to hold a conference of the students. D. K. Ramteke became principal secretary of the welcoming committee, and V. D. Chahade was elected president. O. Mahipati of Madras, D. S. Motghare, Harbaji Gondane, Bengal's Vishram, two girls, Kausalya Nadeshwar and Shanta Shabharkar, and others were members of the executive committee. They invited Babasaheb to preside over the conference, but as he was immersed in other work he could not attend. He sent Jogendranath Mandal of Bengal in his place.

The conference took place on 25 and 26 October 1946 at the big field of the Kasturchand Park. Thousands of students were present for the welcoming ceremony of Mandal. Discussions went on for three days on student issues. For the first time, our own organization to fight on behalf of our own problems had been created. Immeasurable enthusiasm appeared on students' faces.

On behalf of the student organization, a campaign was held every year to give awards to students who had passed their B.A., M.A., matriculation, and similar examinations. The ceremony was held in April or May at the Indora municipality's Lal Primary School.

In those days, textbooks didn't change very much from year to year. Most of the books for one year were also good for the next year. Since most students in the community were from poor families, I brought the boys together and said, "We should give our books to each other. The higher-standard students should give their books to those behind them. If we do that, many of our expenses will be saved." Everyone liked the idea, and what is called today a book box was prepared. The students who had passed seventh got books from those who had passed eighth and gave their books to other students, and so on.

In the community existed a passion for sports. Pandurang Varade and Dharamdas Patil were together in the same class at Patwardhan High School. Their specialty was that both were adept in all games. Neither the cricket, football, nor hockey teams of Patwardhan could be complete without them.

They were similarly accomplished in *hututu* and *khokho*. However, the all-around championship was given that year to the son of B. G. Kher (later the Brahman Chief Minister of Bombay Province) in spite of his being absent from all the games. Patil and Varade were omitted. All Dalit students were infuriated at this injustice. The teachers in the gathering tried to explain to them how important Kher was in politics. Bapat Master promised that the award would be given them in the following year; later both did get the championship.

Patil and Varade gained admission to the agricultural college after matric. There was no scope for sports in that college. Among those to whom they had taught batting and bowling, some students appeared on the provincial team. Motiram Nagarkar of the science college later played football on the state team and was a winner up to the final round. Just as the great Chambhar cricketeer P. Balu was in Mumbai, so Patil, Varade and Nagarkar were popular among students as athletes in Nagpur.

I was thought of as a steady batsman, though I never hit the ball very hard. To tell the truth, I had no strength in my hands. Besides, my elbow was twisted; therefore, I had no strength in my shoulder or elbow to throw the ball. *Hututu, khokho*, football, hockey, and cricket were the sports played in our Maharpura, and I took part in them. However, I never gained proficiency in any.

One great difference in my daily schedule happened during college. I woke up at four or five in the morning, would go to the public toilets, wash my face, and then go jogging on Jail Road. I would run up to Ajni and come back. There were *nimb* trees on the way. Chewing their leaves, I would return to the house.

Around that time, Janardan Swami began yoga classes in the veranda of the handicraft school. He would spread a sack of jute and tie a rope to the upper story. With that rope he would teach the upside-down yoga positions. These days, after coming to Mumbai, I've gotten a lot of benefit from that yoga. One gets more than exercise from yoga. It prevents the body from unnecessarily getting fat. It keeps daily meals limited. The body has no desire for unrealistic eating. The body remains light and the skin healthy.

In doing yoga, however, no matter how much it was said that the body should not become too stressed, still I put stress on it. The result was later to be seen. Yoga experts are normally irascible because the tendons of their neck become stressed. I eventually became aware that there was too much irritability in my nature. During the time I was doing yoga it seems that my mental balance got spoiled for a while.

# Chapter 15

## POLITICS AND PIGEONS

In 1942 the freedom struggle reached its height with the Quit India movement. Picketing closed down colleges and schools; police patrols increased. The boys of our Maharpura left for school even though they could see many boys from other areas turning back from the road. The whole community knew Ambedkar's policy of avoiding Congress campaigns. Everyone went fearlessly to his own task.

When I reached the school, around eight to ten boys were present in every class. "Those who don't want to come should not leave their houses," proclaimed Khedkar Master, and began to teach. Nobody paid any attention to the turmoil outside. The master sat teaching for forty-five minutes. There were only eight boys present, but he lectured as if the whole class were in front of him. The sons of the rich and of high officials were present. There were Mahar boys in some classes. They slipped in through some corner of the courtyard, trying to ignore the uproar.

Teams of student demonstrators gathered outside to close down the school. Nobody entered the compound, but they obstructed those who came from outside. Even so, classes continued inside. Finally, stones were thrown from outside. Windows broke and glass fell inside. We hid under benches. The police came. A scramble began, and we remained sitting inside the school for the whole day.

The power of the Quit India movement grew. Textile mills closed down, morning processions took place, and young volunteers organized marches, where participants sang such patriotic songs as "This is my India, an unbroken continent!" As the agitation grew, burning and looting began. Demonstrators took control of the road between Variety Chowk and Gandhi Bridge. The main shops on that road were those of Bohras and Khojas, that is, Muslim merchants. Because the Muslim community was separatist, the looters focused on them.

The agitators roamed on the roads in front of our community. In those days, no caste tension existed. The feeling was that each community should have its own movement. The whole of Maharpura was quiet. The turmoil in the city continued to increase. Mahal, Itwara, Gajakhet, Bhankheda, Budhvara, and all parts of eastern Nagpur were in tumult. The hymns of Tukodji Maharaj were part of the Congress campaign. His rattling mountain voice had the capacity to arouse people. His songs were composed in simple popular Marathi and unfaltering Hindustani. He would go himself with his companions and wander through the villages to hold campaigns. Thousands of people crowded to hear his songs and hymns.

> I say, God is not a feeling in the mind, God is in bread;
> God is not built from stones,
> God is in the hunger of the starving.

The effects of these songs of Tukodji could not have been accomplished by a hundred speeches. He ignited all of Vidarbha. In the majority Hindu areas of Nagpur—especially where there were Weaver, Oilpresser, Gardener, and Farmer caste people—turmoil rose. The Brahman community next to ours was quiet. The Sangh members there also remained aloof from the movement.

And the chaos continued to increase. It became impossible for the police to maintain peace. The government called the military from Kamathi. A curfew was imposed on all disturbed areas, including one in place all day and all night for the middle roads. Since our community was not disturbed, there was no military presence, and hence no fear. Outside the community, you had to cross the road to go to the public toilets. People began to sit out chatting in front of the temple. When the police came, they would disperse. When the police left, people would again gather. They made the excuse of going to the toilet. They would sit in the corner of a foundation of a new building being constructed outside.

Because Kamathi was the center of the Mahar regiment, it was Mahar soldiers who had the task of establishing peace. In Ganjakhet square they had to fire to disperse a crowd that was rioting. This square got the name of Bullet Square. When the military established its presence there, no one walked, even accidentally, on the road to Somwar market.

However, Sampat from our community could not be kept in the house. He left to loot a liquor shop. When the soldiers fired on those who were looting shops, Sampat was hit. Fortunately, the bullet entered his foot and he escaped death. The soldiers were instructed to aim below the belt when firing.

Though in the beginning I would get to school on time, later I started neglecting things. I began to keep company with the truant boys of the community.

Since the boys played marbles together, I also started to collect marbles and play. Some boys gambled while playing marbles. Then I would just watch. Or I would get a few coins from somewhere, sit and play, and lose them. The other boys used to think it great fun that anyone studying in ninth should lose at marbles!

This is how I became friends with Sukhdev. He would help me when I played with the others. He could hit the line exactly with his marbles. He would play on my behalf and give me one or two pennies. Whenever the Dal teacher saw me sitting in some lane playing marbles, he would get angry and I would run away.

Sukhdev had a passion for raising pigeons. He lived with his mother and father in a low earthen house. He father would go to the station to work as a porter. His mother was employed in the mill. Once women and men had gone to work in the afternoon, the neighborhood felt empty. We had to keep ourselves amused.

Sukhya had a little toy house like a cupboard of wooden planks with square holes where pigeons lived. They had to be continuously protected from cats, mongooses, and other predators. Sukya had given them various names. Red-eyed pigeons were *jungli* pigeons. To domesticate them, he plucked their wings. By the time the new feathers came in, they had grown accustomed to the house. Then they would go slowly from one house to another, and fly soaring near the house. But until the entire wing grew back, a close watch had to be kept on them.

Sukhya would take me to the field by the railway tracks. From there he would throw a pair of pigeons high into the sky, and by the time we returned to Sukhya's home the birds would be sitting in their holes. In the morning and evening some pairs would make a quick dash high up into the sky. For one or two hours they would fly about, and then return to the house at exactly the time decided.

Every once in a while a pigeon would go wandering off. He would see some other crowd of pigeons. He would go into their flock, and get bewildered at seeing all the strange faces there. The owner of those pigeons would be lying in wait. He would throw out some grain and call the stray pigeon. If the bird leaped away, an experienced pair would be sent after him. They would turn him around and bring him back.

All of this used to be thought of as a sport. The sport was to capture another's pigeons and bring them to one's own flock and tame them. Some of Sukhdev's pigeons would remain out for eight or more days but return home even after that. Taking two pigeons on an arm and going far away, releasing them, taking the eggs laid by the pigeons, making nests in the house and keeping watch until they hatched, seeing the chicks break out of the eggs, examining whether they were male or female . . . we hardly noticed how hours and hours, days and days went by. And what of school and of home! I would take my slate and books and leave my house, and after wandering for a while here and there, I would spend the days at Sukhdev's house watching the pigeons play.

One day a pair—both colored blue as the sky—climbed higher and higher, soaring above the neighborhood, until they reached the white and black clouds overhead. After two hours of gamboling they were ready to return, when a falcon started after them. The two pigeons plunged from the sky. They turned towards their flock. But all they saw were pigeons they didn't know. They once again leaped up, searching for their own flock, which was not to be seen. After circling and circling they grew tired. The falcon, on the watch, took a straight plunge from high above and grabbed and carried away the female of the pair. Then we understood the destructive possibilities of unrestricted freedom. The second pigeon came whirling back to the house. For many days he lived a life of loneliness, but later he took another mate from the flock.

# Chapter 16

## CLIMAX

Just as the climactic moment of a play comes in the middle section, so the Scheduled Caste Federation reached its moment of decision in 1946.

In Nagpur, the Dalit movement had been a Mahar movement. Chambhars (Leatherworkers) and Mangs (Ropemakers, also called Matangs) took part only as individuals. A Matang gentleman named Behade was on the executive committee of the Scheduled Caste Federation. Ramratan Janorkar of the Bhangi (Sweeper) community dedicated his life to the Ambedkar movement and also became a Buddhist. The Buddhist community in turn took him as one of theirs and made him the mayor of the Nagpur corporation.

If you go from Gandhi Bridge to Variety Square one shoe store stands in the row of shops with a photo of Ambedkar hung for all to see. This shop, owned by Mahadevrao Chakole, a Chambhar gentleman, was right next to our neighborhood. Since it was on the road going to the station, we began to feel an easy oneness with the Chakole family. When Babasaheb came to Nagpur he would inquire about him. It is said that he once visited the Chakole house. At a time when most of the Chambhars in Nagpur were in Congress, a man like Chakole was in the Ambedkar movement. Naturally we praised his courage for this.

By 1946 Nagpur city was buzzing with movements. Not a day went by without meetings, rallies, gatherings. That was the year that Hindu–Mahar riots bloodied the atmosphere. The Ravishankar Shukla Congress ministry had been established in the Central Provinces and Berar. Because Hindus dominated the police and other departments, whenever there arose the slightest sign of a riot, Mahar youth were put under house arrest. The battle drums of the satyagraha campaign against the Pune Pact sponsored by the Federation had not yet subsided. The thunder of "Long live Ambedkar! Bhim Raj in a short while!" from the hundreds of satyagrahis taken in police vans along Jail Road could still almost be heard from afar. The disciples of Ambedkar had created a tremendous self-confidence in the Dalit community. For that matter, other communities also were awed by the Dalits.

The office of the Scheduled Caste Federation for CP-Berar was on the first floor of a two-story house on the main road behind the Buti School. Dasharath Laxman Patil was the president, and Revaramji Kavade was secretary. The president of the city branch was Panjabrao Shambharkar. Ganpat Shambharkar was the scout master and captain of the Dal.

Arguing that there should be a journal of the movement, Shri N. K. Tirpude began a weekly called *Arun* (Dawn). Tirpude, Bhaurao Borkar, and other activists, working under the leadership of Raosaheb Thavare, kept the Independent Labour Party separate from the Federation, arguing that there should be an independent workers' organization. Because of this, the Federation leaders began to suspect deliberate splits. It was the beginning of a storm that ended only when Raosaheb Thavare and his group left the Federation and joined Congress.

Wrestling grounds existed in every community in Nagpur. All these grounds had their trainers, wrestling masters who were like bastions protecting the walls of the fortress of their neighborhoods. In Indora, four Ramas were famous. There was Boney Rama, an activist of the Bolshevik Party. After the 1946 rioting, when Chief Minister Ravishankar Shukla came to Indora for an enquiry into the violence, Boney Rama's bold younger brother, a member of the Nagpur municipal corporation, grabbed the minister's hat from his head and then gave it back to him, saying, "Shuklaji, here is your hat. Guard it well!" We thought this was a brave threat.

The second Rama, who looked like coal and so was nicknamed Black Rama, was Rama Santu Vasnik.

The third Rama was Brawling Rama, and the most famous of all the Ramas was Rogue Rama—Rama Rodge. He was the father of the activist Shrimati Chandrikabai Ramteke. He raised Chandrikabai from infancy to be robust and fearless like her father. Once, while she was coming home from school in the evening with her friends, some Romeo deliberately gave her a slap while going by on a bicycle. Chandrikabai and her friends grabbed him. Even with blustering efforts he could not get away from the grasp of her wrist. Shortly the youth of Indora gathered there and taught him a lesson in politeness.

In 1946 the government proclaimed elections. At that time the Scheduled Caste Federation was the only party opposing the Congress in Nagpur. Other parties existed in name only. One woman representative was to be elected. The SCF candidate was Radhabai Kamble, the workers' leader, who lived in Bardi.

Radhabai was adept in standing before thousands of people and delivering sledgehammer speeches like other leaders. Once while she was giving a speech, she declared in the heat of enthusiasm, "We will win our rights whatever happens. If they don't give them to us we will grab them, take them by force, snatch them away."

For the workers' seat Sakharam Meshram was the Scheduled Caste Federation candidate. Rambhau Ruikar had been given the ticket for Congress. For the seat reserved for Untouchables Congress had put up Hemchandra Khandekar, while the Federation had put up Sitaram Hadke. Since he said "Jay Bhim" to show his loyalty to Ambedkar, the Congress goons had given him a beating. However, neither Khandekar nor anyone wearing Congress caps had the guts to campaign in the Dalit neighborhoods. The Ambedkarite community had boycotted "Harijans," completely barring them from dining or intermarrying with others. Many Congressite Mahars had to remain bachelors their whole life because of that.

Meetings were held everywhere. Most of the Mahar community were mill workers. If there was a strike in the mills, these Untouchable workers would leave Nagpur to search for work, so with the tactic of winning the elections this way by getting his main opponents out of the way, Ruikar called for a strike. The Federation leaders decided to defeat this call. Rekharam Kavade, Sitaram Hadke, Dasharath Patil, and all the activists girded their loins. Discussions began throughout the communities.

The small garden of the Pacpavali was at that time used as an open field. It used to be called the Yadavrao Gaikwad Field. It was decided to have a procession starting from there on 15 January 1946. People gathered from all over Nagpur. Batches came from Bhankheda Pacpavali, Indora, and Bardi. The units of the Samata Sainik Dal gathered from places as far as Camelward, Dharampeth, Inamwada, Bardi, Dhantoli, and Pottertown. After the flag salute of the Dal, the troops left in disciplined ranks of four. When the parade of the Dal reached Ganjakhet, thousands of people, men and women, began to walk behind it.

> *Ambedkar kaun hai? Dalitanka Raja hai!*
> *Leke rahenge, leke rahenge, ham apne hak leke rahenge!*
>
> Who is Ambedkar? King of Dalits!
> We will take our rights, we will take our rights!

With such a thunder striking awe throughout Nagpur, the parade went through Gandhibag, Mahal, New Shukravari, and Bardi and finally dispersed at Kasturchand Park. Before a huge gathering Raosaheb Thavare, Radhabai

Kamble, Revaram Kavade, and other leaders gave speeches. People returned to their houses filled with enthusiasm.

Ruikar then proclaimed the workers' strike. His goons went forth for battle, catching workers by ones and twos and beating them up. But the Ambedkarites decided to resist. The men went to work in gangs of twenty to twenty-five. The women determined to go to work in an organized manner. Every Mahar woman took with her a packet of chili powder, a potent weapon of stinging red fire, tied up in the end of her sari.

Defense squads were formed from neighborhood to neighborhood. Training classes began in stick fighting and the use of cudgels. Girls also were taught. Trainers, gangsters, bandits, teachers, youths—all became one. The resolve to give a respond to atrocities grew firm. Some youth patrolled during the night.

The election atmosphere in Nagpur became heated. A huge poster was pasted at Timki, proclaiming, "*Maharonke khun ke holi khelenge!*" (We will play *holi* with the blood of Mahars!). Due to the sentiment asserting "Congress rule is our rule," and with the newspapers systematically spreading the emotional propaganda that Ambedkar's party opposed Independence, the Hindus decided to teach a lesson to the Mahars. People of Weaver, Farmer, and Writer castes from the Hindu communities stopped Mahar youth and beat them up when they could be caught alone. But no attacker had the courage to attack a group openly.

The Hindu trainers had been keeping their eyes on the Mahar wrestlers. Similarly, the Mahar wrestlers took whatever opportunity they could to keep up with the news of the Hindu wrestlers. There was a famous Hindu wrestler named Pochamma living at Gaddi Godam Square. One day a Mahar–Hindu brawl started there, near a toddy shop. Wrestler Pochamma took the opportunity of attacking Ghanshyam Wrestler, and before Ghanshyam was aware of it, Pochamma had grabbed him with one hand and stabbed him in the waist with a knife held in the other. Fearing that Ghanshyam would die, Mango Wrestler and Raghunath Narale took their knives, and just as Shivaji had stabbed Afzal Khan, they split open Pochamma's stomach. Pochamma died. Mango and Raghunath were arrested. Ghanshyam went into hiding. Unable to find him, the police harassed his friends and family. Nisar Ali, a Muslim lawyer who always helped the Mahars in legal matters as part of the friendly relationship between Mahars and Muslims, advised Ghanshyam to appear in court. Ghanshyam came before the magistrate in disguise. The police in the court failed to recognize Ghanshyam until he stood up before them and told them his name.

While the case played out in court, the lawyers of the Mahar community and the activists stood behind their heroes. They collected money. By the time all the accused were released for lack of sufficient evidence, the atmosphere had to a large degree cooled off. After the election, though, quarrels on trivial issues continued to flare up and a big riot developed. On 3 May 1946, the Weavers and Farmers united and decided to attack. Five thousand thugs, with cudgels, spears, and swords in hand, left for Golibar Square with the aim of attacking the Mahar settlement at Indora. At that time there was no sign of any government in Nagpur. The police were as if in hiding. Most of them were on duty at the voting centers.

As the goons entered Pacpavali, the bands of Mahar youth took their own spears and swords and emerged from Bhankheda, Pavpavali, and Military Park. A deadly battle began. Harischand Sakhare, Ghanshyam Wrestler, Tulshiram Wrestler, and many other young men fought with little regard for their own life. The line of the Hindu goons edged ahead. A field lay in front of the Pacpavali police station, empty except for some low thickets. Realizing that the attack was coming on Indora, the four Ramas and five or six other athletes came together and stood at the crossing near Kamathi Road and one by one began to swing their swords. Seeing this manifestation of their readiness to fight, the Hindu goons coming towards them began to feel uncertain. They had also got the illusion that many people waited behind them, ready to attack, and they began to move backward, step by step.

The goons who had entered Pacpavali to beat up people started to run wildly when they saw their companions retreating. Sampat Ramteke and Husain Gajbhiye had been fighting for a long time. Witnessing their courage, the Hindu goons retreated. Sampat and Husain came after them. Just as their blows were about to fall on the goons before them, they stumbled in the drainage canal. The fleeing Bajiraos came back, and within a second both had become martyrs. While they were being beaten, the cries of "Jay Bhim! Victory to Ambedkar!" coming from their mouths reached many nearby houses.

After these events, a curfew was imposed. Everyone was forbidden to leave his house. The police began a search, entering house after house. But no curfew was imposed on the attacking community, only for the Ambedkarites. The Mahar youth went underground. The aged and senior people who stayed in their houses were taken under arrest. Finally, the young girls, the married women, and the very old women and men who remained in their homes made some effort to come out, and the police began to fire on them. Ramdas Dongare, a young Federation activist, was fired upon the moment he left for the toilet; he lost his life. The news of the rioting spread to every nook and corner of Nagpur. All the neighborhoods of Ambedkarites went on the alert.

The police began a close search of every house in Pacpavali. In one house, seeing two young girls, the police said, "We will inspect the house." Two young Ambedkar girls with their life at stake and no men in the house—still they decided to face the situation. Two police and two women. The police showed no sign of leaving. The women said, "There is no one in the house." The police said, "Come up on the roof." Without any choice, the women climbed up. After about fifteen to twenty minutes they came back down. They tied their things together and departed. After realizing that those two policemen had not returned by evening, the police authorities began a search. Their corpses were found in a disordered state on the roof of that small house. An autopsy was done. It turned out that both deaths had occurred because their testicles had been crushed!

In Colonel Park there were Hindu neighborhoods all around. Twenty-five to fifty Mahar houses lay on one side, but all the youth of that neighborhood were companions of Domaji Deshmukh Ustad, a Hindu wrestler. They told Doma Ustad that Hindu–Mahar quarrels should not spread into their neighborhood. "We have helped you in your fights. But if there is any stone-throwing at our community here, then beware. We will do whatever has to be done." Doma Trainer listened to them.

In Shaniwar near the Cotton Market, there were about twenty Mahar houses. All the families there were well-to-do. They locked up their houses and sought refuge with relatives in other neighborhoods.

The Pottertown neighborhood was split into two sections by a road. Nearby lay a neighborhood famous for the kind of crime Doma Trainer had fought against in Colonel Park, and so this neighborhood had a feud going for generations with Colonel Park people. However, all the Hindus united against the Mahars, and three or four thousand goons came running to Pottertown with weapons and torches in their hands.

Fago Ustad always kept his cudgel at close hand. That day he sat playing a flute. People began to flee one by one, saying, "Run, run!" Small boys and girls hid in neighbors' houses. Fago Ustad thought for a minute. In front of him were fifteen or twenty youth with swords. Behind them, numerous thugs were standing ready with torches. Fago Ustad yelled his challenge—"Kids, get ready!"— and without waiting for anyone else he took his four-foot-long battle ax and attacked the sea before him. Just as Fago Ustad's stick began to whirl, so the swords of the goons began to fall one by one. Seeing the fiery form of Fago Ustad, the crowd took a backward step and turned to set fire to one or two houses. Inspired by Fago's courage, the Mahars of Pottertown came running from their houses.

Mahars continued to go to work in the mills. In our neighborhood, around fifty youths took sticks in their hands and sallied forth. Just behind them, led by Radhabai Kamble, many women with chili powder tied in the folds of their saris came out. Beyond the Brahman and Marwari houses outside of the community was the Oilpressers' ward. But they did not have the courage to obstruct us.

The factory area was separated from the square of the Cotton Market. The place where Mahatma Phule Market stands now was empty at that time. Beyond that lay the boundary of the mills. Once they crossed the Cotton Market Square, people were safe!

I and my childhood friend Balkrishna Gajbhiye were running behind the workers and youths. Balya was young in age but very daring. We were watching everything. People were walking by two stone archways. Opening the door of those parapets, fifteen to twenty Hindu goons suddenly came running with sticks. Varade, Gajbhiye, and everyone else were ready for them. One by one they each whirled their sticks; Balya and I threw stones from a distance. And seeing all this, the Hindu goons scattered. Some youths received a few blows, but the women safely reached the mills.

By the time of the elections, a sort of war atmosphere had spread in all the Mahar neighborhoods. "Factories" were set up in every community to make weapons. In our neighborhood, Godbole's house was a center where spears, cudgels, and swords were made, not only for our community but also for other neighborhoods. Abhiman Deshbhratar, a moneylender with a house spread out like a mansion, let his home be used for secret meetings. All the wrestlers, youth, old and wise men in the community came together and discussions began. Who should patrol the neighborhood, who should stay where, what to do—all these issues were decided.

In front of Merchant Abhiman's house was an extended veranda. The boys and girls of the community were called there, where Ustad Daji gave them training in wrestling and stick fighting. The cudgels and sticks began to spin. When the young boys' class began, I learned a few of these techniques, but I could not assimilate very much of this knowledge.

Young men patrolled the whole night. Rumors kept arising that tonight an attack would come from the neighboring Weavers' community. The youth would sit at the place where the attack was expected with their weapons ready. However, up to the end, there was no attack. Only Ganpat Gajbhiye was stabbed when returning from work.

The drums of the 1946 election began to sound. The names of the Ambedkarite voters had been entered in the lists of voting centers in the wrong neighborhoods. The Sadar votes were listed in Cameltown; Indora votes were in Mahalwar; this happened everywhere. Even then voters were brought out from every house. The youth took the voters and went in bands to the voting centers to cast their votes. At Indora the Hindu goons caused a tumult at the voting booths. The police fired a round. Ramdas Dongare, a young activist of the Samata Sainik Dal, fell victim to a bullet.

On voting day, when it was learned that Indora had been attacked, many people of the community gathered. Youth of Inamwada, Shanivari, Dhantoli, and other neighborhoods came together, and around five hundred people departed for Indora. I heard the story of that battle, after nearly a year, from Waman Rangari, who had taken part. He came one night to the Tar, the field in front of our settlement.

"Waman, where have you been?"

"It's a long story; you wouldn't understand it. Aren't you still a kid?"

"Yes, but look, you are our trainer! Without you, who will teach us strategy?"

Saying, "Okay, sit down," he gathered several schoolboys and sat with us on the Tar. The crowd wandering on the roads had quieted down. When the moon came into the sky and its clear, quiet light spread over all, there was no one to be seen even far away in the corners of the field. For many nights we had sat in that place or fallen asleep chatting under our blankets. Stories could be heard being told in neighboring houses. That day we listened to Waman tell his experiences. We responded just as everyone is supposed to do when a good epic is told, and he began.

"We started out from Bardi. The people of Shanivari and Dhantoli had gathered there. We got the men from Inamwada. After that we collected those from Model Mill *chawl* and from Colonel Park and went ahead. We numbered around five hundred. By the time we reached Nawabpura, about a thousand had gathered, and we went forward chanting, 'Long live Ambedkar! Bhim rule in a few days!'

"Our voters had been put on the voting lists of other communities. That was done deliberately. The people of Cameltown were in Nawadpura, and the Nawadpurites in Cameltown. Because of that we had to escort everyone to their voting booths. By the time we had helped all these voters and reached Bhankheda, only about ten or twelve of us were left. There the people of the Military Park entered from Karhadkarpeth and forced their way in with axes. We shouted slogans. They shouted, 'Jay Bhim!' The people of all our neighborhoods know each other!

"We saw that a big procession of four to five thousand Hindus was going towards Military Park. We got the message that they had come into the neighborhoods near the police station. All of us entered the Military Park neighborhood from the railway tracks and compound. There we saw only women from house to house. The men had gone long distances to vote. Weapons were ready in the houses. The women gave us those swords and daggers. Taking these, we ran, and then all fled. Narayan Kirad got a sword cut. After that we hid for thirty days. A woman with a fifteen-day-old baby brought me food and gave me support.

"After that I came to Bardi and stayed with Radhabai Kamble. From there I came to the Model Mill quarters, where a thug named Atkya recognized me.

He had seen me at Military Park. Our building was next to Colonel Park. Taking twenty to twenty-five goons from there, Atkya was planning to come to beat me up. But his talk was overheard by a woman fruitseller named Baru. She came to the house in the evening when I was sleeping.

"'Waman, get up! Atkya is coming with some people. Run!' she yelled. I got up and ran out in no time. Beside us was a big canal. I jumped over that canal and went into Colonel Park. There I met Janba Kamble. He said, 'This neighborhood is next to Hindus. It is not safe. You run and go to Cameltown.'

"After that I reached Cameltown. There I stayed for three or four months."

Even after Waman's story was finished, we could not sleep. For a long time thoughts kept running through my mind. Everywhere was stability. Police whistles could be heard. Wouldn't the police come to arrest Waman? I was looking far in the distance. The railway engines were chugging along on the tracks, and in their whistles the police whistles had long since been absorbed.

I looked to my side. Waman was snoring without a care in the world!

# Chapter 17

# WRATH

In 1942, the Congress had begun its Quit India movement against the British. At that time Babasaheb Ambedkar clarified the policy of the Dalit movement. The Hindus wanted independence for the country only to gain power for themselves. Babasaheb's position was simply that the Hindus and the British government should make clear, before independence, what our share in this independence would be. The Congress refused to take part in the viceroy's ministry. Their policy of opposing the British at the time they were fighting fascism in World War II was unacceptable to many. But the attitude that "Congress and Gandhi mean the country" was being spread everywhere. Because of this all the newspapers in India were depicting Ambedkar as a traitor. Meanwhile the Hindu Mahasabha was also giving support to the British, ripping holes in Mahatma Gandhi's position. Savarkar and Ambedkar were telling Hindus to enter the British army. The Rashtriya Swayamsevak Sangh (RSS), too, following Savarkar's policy, was helping the British in recruitment and in the war. Jinnah and the Muslim League were demanding an independent country. Still, no one said that these parties or leaders were traitors!

A Cabinet Mission was held after the 1946 elections to determine the future of India. The failure of the Scheduled Castes Federation in the election meant that Ambedkar's demands for recognition of Scheduled Caste needs went unheeded. To raise the issue of separate electorates for Untouchables in independent India, Ambedkar proclaimed a satyagraha in front of all the legislative assemblies in India to condemn the Pune Pact. In Nagpur this satyagraha was undertaken in a grand way. It began at noon on 3 September 1946 before the assembly. The police had encircled the assembly on all sides. The satyagrahis made lines of four and came before the assembly in small groups. Like voting booths, the satyagrahis' booths were five hundred feet away from the spot of arrest. All the satyagrahis who came from Bardi were registered in the Federation office behind the Buti School. These satyagrahis went from near Patwardhan School to the Nagpur University gate, and there they were arrested. The police filled the vans and took them to jail. The vans went near the Patwardhan School. When from the vans the satyagrahis loudly shouted, "Victory to Ambedkar!" people in the road from Variety Square to the jail were filled with awe. Many from our community left their jobs to go to jail. Thousands of women took their small children to join the satyagraha.

At that time Dwarkaprasad Mishra was home minister. There is a story about an earlier incident that shows how Ambedkarite activists felt about him. A Communist activist of the Writer caste named Bhai Jaywant lived in our neighborhood. He was the president of the Independent Labour Party. He was given authority by Babasaheb to campaign in the 1937 election. Bhai Jaywant was a clever organizer and a forceful speaker. While he was in jail during a jail-filling campaign of the Communist party, Pandit Mishra had come to survey the jails. When Jaywant was brought for questioning, he threw the coffee cup that he had been given to drink in Mishra's face. This was a subject of praise among the Ambedkarite activists. Bhai Jaywant would gather the small children and take them around in a truck with the red flag. If the people of the community had any problems, they would go to Jaywant for advice.

Pandit Dwarkaprasad Mishra was famous for crafty politics. According to his orders, the arrested activists were not put in jail by the police department. Instead they were driven far off and released at a distance of eight to ten miles. These satyagrahis, left in open fields at eight or nine at night, reached their houses by walking until the early hours of the morning. Until the end of the assembly session such things happened daily. Even so the numbers of satyagrahis grew day by day.

On the final day of the session, all the satyagrahis were put in the central jail of Nagpur. Because they had not expected to go to jail, they had not made any preparations. The news began to reach the community that these satyagrahis were being harassed in jail. They were kept inside the jail like animals. A barrack with facilities for one hundred prisoners held three to four hundred satyagrahis crowded inside. Some families in the community tried to send food, but it was not accepted. From the second day onwards complaints were heard that the satyagrahis had begun to suffer bloody stools and vomiting. They were fed half-cooked rice of extremely inferior quality and watery lentil soup smelling of bad oil. In protest they held a food satyagraha inside the jail, from 19 to 26 September 1946. The jail police made a *lathi* charge on them. Many women and men were wounded. For several days there was a little improvement. However, the jail experience was an issue of discussion for many days in the community.

In our neighborhood there was a fruit seller named Godubai who used the excuse of selling fruit to gain entry into the assembly area and then, evading the police, managed to get into the assembly hall. There she threw leaflets and shouted "Long live Ambedkar!"

The policy of the Federation was that students should not take part in politics. However, we helped in such tasks as distributing leaflets.

In those days there were no factions within the SCF. All the leaders came together to support the cases of the satyagrahis.


After Mahatma Gandhi's assassination in 1948 by a Maharashtrian Brahman, not only was a ban imposed on the Rashitriya Swayamsevak Sangh, to which the assassin had belonged, but on all other semimilitant organizations as well, including our Samata Sainik Dal. Many activists burned the files of *Bahishkrit Bharat, Janata, Dalit Bandhu,* and other Ambedkarite journals kept in their houses. If these were found the police would harass them. The atmosphere had just begun to settle down after the Hindu–Mahar riots ended in 1946. With Mahatma Gandhi's death, the atmosphere throughout Nagpur became agitated once more. The non-Brahman Hindu communities became agitated against Brahmans. The Narkesari press was burned. Production of the *Tarun Bharat* daily, with chiefly Brahman leadership, was stopped for some time. Bhausaheb Madkholkar's editorials were the ornaments of this *Tarun Bharat*. With artistic elegance, he wrote articles on social, political, and various other subjects. Many bought *Tarun Bharat* just to read Madkholkar's articles on Mondays. Now, *Tarun Bharat* was burned and closed down, but only for a brief time. It came out again with renewed force almost at once. The whole strength of the Rashtriya Swayamsevak Sangh was behind it.

The only current paper of the Dalits, the *Janata*, came from Mumbai. In Nagpur, around 1946, there was also a weekly named *Dawn* under the leadership of N. K. Tirpude, which ran for around two years. Raosaheb Thavare returned from the Congress into the Scheduled Caste Federation, but the only result was that factions started among the Federation activists. Complaints went up to Dr. Ambedkar. He accepted the word of the old activists, and Thavare Saheb left the Federation with a very big group, including Tirpude and Bhaurao Borkar, who were leading organizers, one in politics and one taking care of the workers' organization. Later, all of these entered Congress. Congress's Hemachandra Khandekar died in Delhi and Bhaurao Borkar in a plane accident. It was said that since they opposed Ambedkar no one was ready to even give them water. From this it can be seen how staunch was the harshness of the Ambedkarites and the hatred of the Congress's "Harijan" policy. While *Dawn* was running, Narayan Hari Kumbhare, Dinkar M. Khairkar, and other youths began a monthly named *Siddharth. Dawn* and *Siddharth* were different types of journals, but just as the difference between the Ambedkarite activists and Thavare's group grew, so the two papers were drawn into that quarrel.

Some people of the Thavare party lived in our community. However, their number was minimal. The anti-Ambedkarites were called "Harijans," "ragpickers," and other insulting names. Connections with Harijan families were broken. Their girls were not asked for in marriage. They were not invited for marriage festivals. They were excluded from feasts at the time of naming ceremonies, housewarmings, and other celebrations. If by mistake anyone had been invited, they were insulted and thrown out at the time of the event itself, or else the host would be considered polluted. If the hand of some Harijan girl had been asked for in marriage by a boy, there would be an effort to stop the marriage, and if it took place they would be boycotted. If anyone among the Harijans died no one would go to touch his body or wash it. Once when a group of Congress Harijans appeared together at the railway station, Mahars, who were numerous among the railway workers, came together and gave all of them a beating.

In our community, Haribhau Dongare was a handsome youth, light-skinned, round-faced, with catlike eyes. He acted in plays, and later he became an attorney under Varma Vakil. His first young wife died. After that he began to work in Thavare's party. This finished him; no one would permit him to marry their daughter. He had to remain unmarried for his whole life. I have seen how harsh such a social boycott can be. N. R. Shende, who always wore khadi coat and pajama, would come to our neighborhood from time to time. He was understood to be in the Thavare party. The boys in the community called him "Harijan." If he came, he would sit for a little while and then leave. He never visited the Dal branch or gained the trust of the Ambedkarite activists. As long as I was in college, N. R. Shende was understood to be a Brahmanized Harijan writer. Later he never kept any connection with the Buddhist community.

Three or four of us had a passion for wandering together in the evening in Maharaj Park, after the Dal meeting had finished. It was when we had gone as usual, one evening, that we heard the news of Mahatma Gandhi's murder. Everyone's mind almost unconsciously sank into depression. In the sky clouds had begun to gather. The roads appeared empty. If some great man dies nature reflects the despondency. When Babasaheb Ambedkar died, nature shed tears. That day also, everywhere, automatically, despondency spread. We had never felt much sympathy for Gandhi; we understood Ambedkar's opposition to him. Even so we were conscious that he was a great man. And as we went to Maharaj Park, the thought passed through our minds again and again, "What if it is a Dalit who has killed Gandhi? If that comes out how will we face it?" Various questions filled our minds. That day we returned to the house with a gloomy spirit.

Then came the news, "The man who fired was a Hindu." And then he was discovered to be a Maharashtrian Brahman.

# Chapter 18

## CULTURAL TRANSFORMATION

Babasaheb Ambedkar's movement had a tremendous effect on the cultural life of the community. From time immemorial numerous sadhus, Muslim fakirs, and beggars had come to the neighborhood. Mahars had had the habit of religious giving from ancient times. The heads of the Mahanubhav sect would come and stay in the house of our landlady. This poor, aged widow would never let these men go without giving them food.

In the heat of the afternoon, the loud cry of "sifters, baskets, buy some, buy some" would resound through the neighborhood, and a band of four to six Ropemaker women would begin to wander through the town. Though they used to have a stock of a few baskets, begging alms was their real occupation. For four to six pennies these women would make toy sifters or baskets of bamboo or husk for little girls. In between, one of the women would give voice to, "Devamaya [Godmother], give a little bread and food, Devamaya." These women could not speak without calling any woman "mother" and any man "brother."

Every woman had on her hips, back, or head some small kid sleeping peacefully in a basket. If a woman in the community suffered from a pain or ache, these Mang woman would give her a massage. If children cried too much, the women would feed them opium. The thanks they gave for alms was beyond imagination:

> Oh star-faced sari-wearer, fair-faced Gauribai,
> Your husband should be a dwarf,
> Your brother should come to take you back, Devamaya.

They would say a lot of such things. But the women of the community were not satisfied with just this. Young girls would gather around them and urge

107

them to tell of "the fight of two rivals." Then they would sing in their melodious voices,

> The husband of one woman eats bread and jam,
> The husband of two women sits hungry,
> He goes and sits alone, one pulls his hair, one slaps his cheek.

After much detailed description, she draws her conclusion. Her song finishes with a picture of how a woman can be a queen with one husband:

> Sister-in-law is made a pan for cleaning wheat,
> Father-in-law is made reins for tying the bullocks
> Husband is made a parrot, O Mother, to babble sweet stories.

Then the imploring of "Devamaya" would again be heard.

An old man also used to come, and yell out, "Cotton floss dolls, four for a penny." These toys were softer than combed cotton, and small children liked them very much. Fakirs who said, "Bless you if you give money, bless you if you don't" also came to the community. Wandering and crying out, "Mortars and pestles, get mortars and pestles," women of the Stonebreaker caste would come riding on donkeys to sell mortars and pestles for the kitchen. Mothers of children who wouldn't drink milk would also buy a couple pennies worth of donkey's milk. Since it is very sweet, it had to be drunk right after milking, otherwise it would spoil.

One day a blind man and his lame sighted wife came to beg alms. The two sang together a hymn about Babasaheb Ambedkar in fine, thin voices. Once the words "Bhimrao Ambedkar" came out of their mouths, women and children came out from all the nearby houses and began to listen. While they listened, they filled the couple's begging bags with grain. From then on this pair did the rounds of our neighborhood for many days.

At the beginning Gondadis, or traditional singing troupes, used to come. For the whole night they would entertain us by spinning out some legend. I can still remember dimly the story of Doral, a girl with forty brothers who are all transformed into birds by a witch. These brothers go with her everywhere. Only she wanders night and day in the forests and fields in search of her brothers. The Gondadis would describe that tale of compassion in lively detail, and finally people would collect a bag of grain and give it to them.

After the Gondadis, the Ambedkar play troupes and balladeers came; hymn-singing groups also sang songs about Babasaheb. The springtime of poets and singers came after the founding of the Scheduled Caste Federation in 1942. The drama troupe of Uddhav was famous throughout the whole Marathi-speaking region of the Central Provinces. No women took part in drama troupes at that time, so Uddhav Ramteke played women's roles from the age of sixteen on. He was fair and graceful to look at, and after putting on makeup, no one could recognize him as a man.

In Uddhav's plays, Natthu Shende and Atmaram Dhok would play the humorous parts. Govardhan Gaurkhede of our community played the main role. Manik Patil and Shankar Ramteke took other parts. In that play troupe, two plays, *Shaving, or the Widow's Humiliation* and *Conversion,* were very popular. The performances took place on the veranda in front of the Vitthal-Rukmini temple. All around were the houses of white-collar Brahmans. There were many widowed women there. They used to come to see the *Shaving* play and at points would break out in tears. In that play the Master Shankar Ramteke played the harmonium and a Ropemaker boy named Ganesh Bavane was the tabla expert.

In the play, Yami is a Brahman widow. Her father decides that her head should be shaved. Ramteke himself played Yami's part. Ganya the barber comes to do the shaving. When he arrives, Yami tells him, "Ganya, go, go away, why have you come here?"

Ganya: "To remove your hair."

Yami: "Who told you to do that?"

Ganya: "Your father sent me."

Yami: "I will not be shaved, I tell you truly, I am determined."

After that Yami's father comes. She debates with him and cites the scriptures. Even so, the father doesn't listen and leaves, giving Ganya the order to cut her hair. Then Ganya and Yami join together and run away, go to the city, and get married!

The comedy *Conversion* was also very effective. One village watchman, an Untouchable, continuously cries out, "Give me water, give me water, I'm dying of thirst!" When he tries to drink the water from a nearby well, two Brahmans come and give him a beating. His wife goes to perform prayers in a temple, and the priest there tries to rape her. Then he even begins to think of suicide. However, he learns of Babasaheb's conversion call and becomes determined to change his religion.

Stories that ordinary people could understand according to their own lights were shown on the stage, and the teaching of social reform came to the lanes and footpaths. The players dramatized many stories on education and giving up begging and superstitions.

These drama groups were called from village to village by the Satyashodhak village headmen of that time. One *patil* called them for dinner with the intention of examining them. He told a Ropemaker to make all the arrangements in his house for the troupe. He felt that they would not eat in that house since Mahars usually considered Ropemakers even lower Untouchables. However, these players did not respect caste distinctions. Therefore when everyone ate and they emerged from the house laughing and joking, he felt it was a marvel. The Ambedkari dramatists acted according to their word.

In our community around 1940, Laxmanrao Kavade celebrated Rama's birthday for ten days. The ballad group of Vishvanathbuva Khobragade would come for that festival. This man was a very renowned balladeer. Hundreds of people would come for long distances to hear his sermon and songs. He had established a Das Bhajan Mandal. Meghnath Ramteke and Devman Dhengare were his companions in that group. The three used to compose poems. Their songs played on people's lips.

They would include in the ballads stories from the Puranas and the epics, playing on the names of the character Bhim in the *Mahabharata* and the short form of Bhimrao Ramji Ambedkar's name, "Bhim."

> Oh toilers, oh Dalits, who is your protector?
> The wealth of Indra was in the ocean,
> He got it back through churning,
> It became ours by right.
> They are saying let us loot it all!
> Just as the Kauravas, hearing the roar of Bhim,
> Hid crying like Jambuk—
> Das thinks
> Truth has taken the form of Bhim.

All the poems of this group would put "Das" as their name interwoven in the poem. These singers composed and sang Hindi as well as Marathi songs. Haribhau Ramteke was in that ballad troupe. While he was singing, even the listeners of other troupes would get up and come to him. Haribhau was light-skinned, handsome, and his body was graceful from wrestling. His speech was also pure. When Raghuji Raja Bhosle heard his *kirtans*, he sat listening attentively. Finally he asked Haribhau his caste. Haribhau proudly said, "I am a Mahar." Raghuji patted him on the back.

One Hindi *qawwali* of the Das Mandal spread far and wide:

> From the moment that the glance of Bhim fell upon the poor
> From that day our strength also grew
> To win freedom Gandhi and Jinnah met each other
> They did not ask Ambedkar, nor were they going to ask,
> Pandit Jawahar Nehru also tried a new trick
> When Bhim learned the secret his eyes were opened,
> The tyrannical Hindu people wanted to destroy us,
> Hearing the voice of Bhim they lost their zest,
> Pandit Jawahar Nehru himself fell silent

The moment that the glance of Bhim fell upon the poor
From that day our strength grew and grew.

The Das Mandal sang *qawwalis* along with their *bhajans*. In those days there were many poets among us, powerful poets and singers who created inspiration among the people. However there were three men whose names came to the lips of young and old alike. These were Patitpavan Das, Ramdas Ramteke Master, and Attubaba Ballamvale or Spearman. Patitpavan Das was originally from Wardha. He had run a journal by the name of *Patitpavan*. He was the general secretary of the Nashik temple satyagraha from 1930–1935. His two wives sold cloth for blouses from handcarts to maintain him. Patitpavan's surname was Dev. He was free from the compulsions of daily life and continued to do public service his whole life. There are a few collections of his poetry available today.

Like Patitpavan, Attababa also lived like a mendicant. He was originally from the Hinganghat area. However, he came to Nagpur and settled in our community. His surname was Wasnik. He wandered on foot, spreading the teaching of Babasaheb from village to village. He carried a long spear with jangling bells in his hand. He would move the spear, make a noise with the iron bangles on his arms and with that accompaniment sing his own songs. These songs were called Songs of the Torch. They were in Hindi-Urdu and very effective. Even today they can be heard on people's tongues. Attababa would sing, in a very weighty and hoarse voice,

> The nation is without unity, like vultures they harass us,
> Those whom God created are worse off than dogs.
> Some great man capable of understanding could grasp it—
> The organization of those who can unite is powerful.
> Those who honor truth as religion are one throughout the world,
> But Mahatmas have made numerous sects of them
> And so there is a tug-of-war, each pulling to his own side,
> Whoever's unity is strongest has the hitching post!

Like Attababa, Ramdas Ramteke Master was a poet who wandered from place to place singing his songs for social awakening. He lived in Dhantoli. His specialty was a ballad named "The Ballad of Jay Bhim" (Victory to Ambedkar). Wherever there was a *Satyanarayan puja* or a death ceremony or some other *puja,* this master would be called. He would tell traditional stories and then give a speech on the Ambedkarite movement. When the Hindu-Mahar riots happened in 1946, he spread the story of the courage of the four "Ramas" of Indora. Ramteke Master made a ballad of their meritoriousness.

*Qawwali* programs began to surpass the ballads in popularity among the Mahar communities in the Nagpur area. The style of singing was mainly that of the Muslim community, but the Mahars of Nagpur made it their own, and many became *qawwals*. Hindi, the language of *qawwali*, was as widely known as Marathi. In Bhandara district it was used everywhere as a spoken language. In those days, once the monsoon was finished, the programs of the *qawwalis* would begin. These *qawwali* programs would go on from midnight till seven or eight in the morning. In the beginning one *qawwal* would come to sing. Later there would be a competition between two *qawwals*. I would sit with other boys for the whole night at the *qawwali* programs in the community.

The people of the Das group would sing:

> This is the voice of the Das, they will not fall behind
> We will not lie gasping on our beds,
> Dalits will come forward for freedom.
> Coming forward they gain victory, they will not fall behind.

In the duet there was a competition between the Das party and the Sher Khan Vasnik party of Indora. The *qawwalis* of Sher Khan were very aggressive and caused the mind to tremble.

> When the voice comes out of the heart
> Do not let it go unused.
> When you roll up your sleeves,
> When you take the sword out of its sheath
> When you go forth and strike at the enemy
> Do not let it go unused.

Sher Khan himself used to sing. Ramchandra Bhave Ropemaker of Dhanoli, Nitale Master, and Laxman Kolhatkar of our community were in his *qawwali* party. Laxman was called Laxman Fitter because he worked at cycle fitting. He would play the harmonium and drums in a rare manner. His voice was faint, but sweet.

After Independence, Sher Khan sang in a *qawwali*,

> This is not freedom but destruction,
> The world has been fractured by the fight of those two.
> For fear of the League they agreed to Pakistan,
> And caused the fragmentation of the country.

Thousands of big and small poets wrote verses on the personality of Babasaheb Ambedkar. Just as the "saint poets" of medieval times sang in praise of God, so Bhim was hailed:

> Oh my king Bhimraj, protect our honor with your hands;
> See, see how our life is in difficulty

Surrounded by tyrants from four directions.
This rowboat is caught in a whirlpool;
How will we take it to the other shore?
Who will hear our cries besides you?
See, see how our life is in difficulty!

Just as in this rough spoken Hindi, songs were also composed in Urdu. This composition showing unending faith in Babasaheb was done by Ganvir of Indora:

May the world change, may the land change,
May even blood from my body change,
But my Bhim will not change.

See how Manohar Nagarale has described Babasaheb:

He is the beloved of our hearts, the crown on our heads,
He lives and will live tomorrow, our Ambedkar.
There will be words of gold and his name will remain
Whenever our history is written.

In these poetry parties Mahars, Ropemakers, Sweepers, Muslims, and people of all castes were included. In everyone's mind an unbroken faith in Ambedkar was created. One Muslim poet wrote a very memorable verse on Babasaheb:

Whenever we faced difficulties in the time of darkness
We remembered the wisdom of your eyes.

There were two *qawwals* of the Sweeper community. Among them, Horilal Mehtar was a nationalist *qawwal* while Ratan Mehtar sang songs about Babasaheb. The lines in his most popular song were:

The procession of Bhim is marching through India,
We have awakened, the victory is ours!

The events of the Ambedkarite movement were reflected in poetry. When the satyagraha against the Pune Pact took place in 1946 and thousands of people were kept in the Nagpur jail including Raosaheb Thavare and other leaders, Indora's Ganvir sang,

The battle of the satyagrahis, O young fighters of India!
When the jail doors opened for your coming
There the lentils and bread you got were mixed with grass.
When blood flowed in your urine and the heart was crying out,
Thavare Saheb fell sick and he was a strong man,
When the jail doors opened for your coming.

When Sampat Vasnik and Husain Gajbhiye were killed fighting during the Hindu–Mahar struggle at the time of the 1946 elections, Baburao Meshram wrote a long poem. The beginning lines went as follows:

> These warriors Sampat and Husain,
> They were arrows of Dalits, they who have been killed
> Shouting the slogan of "Jay Bhim."

In connection with the riots so many Mahar *qawwals* sang,

> When these things happened, "Jay Bhim" was our slogan.
> We killed their young men, one by one.

These songs were such as to create courage in the community. Giving a call to Dalits, they said,

> Rise, all Dalits, from among Hindus.
> Your sleeping fortunes have awakened now.
> Bhim is number one in writing the Constitution.
> They have not won, we have not been defeated.

Ramdas Dongare fell victim to firing at the time of the elections in Indora. At that time the poet trumpeted,

> Ramdas did not lose his heroism in the battle.
> When the bullet struck his chest, he shouted the name of Bhim.

While Gopichand Wrestler was going to the pavilion some thugs attacked him and he was killed, an event commemorated in verse:

> Gopichand died in the field of battle.
> His name was printed in the journal of Bhim.

Everyone felt pride in having his name joined to that of Bhim. They felt that if a life was dedicated for the community then it would be meaningful. The poets said,

> Time is running moment by moment,
> At every moment, keep taking the name of Bhim.

These singers were young men who would experience an upsurge of rage about atrocities and the battle for our rights. They were not striving to publish books of poetry. They went from neighborhood to neighborhood, village to village to raise consciousness through their songs.

Once, when a meeting of the Congress working committee was being held at Wardha, the Scheduled Caste Federation took out a huge protest march to draw attention to our political rights. Thousands of Untouchables from Nagpur went to join it. Many youth went by bicycle. The session was to begin at 11 A.M. Pandit Nehru came to Nagpur in the morning and left for Wardha by car. Near Somalwada on the road a nine-year-old boy named Manohar riding a bicycle got caught beneath his car. Nehru stopped the car, took him inside, and took him to the hospital in Wardha. However by that time he had died. If this news had not been suppressed at Wardha, it would have taken no time for the atmosphere to become stormy. A song was written about this Manohar.

These songwriters took up various styles of music. From Rajasthan, Madhya Pradesh, and Punjab there is a type of folk song called *alauddal* that sings of heroism. In our community Lahanu Gaurkhede used to recite *alauddal*. One poet wrote of Fago Ustad's heroism in this way:

> Weaving and dancing Fago, slashing his sword;
> Some should take a cudgel, some a stone, some a dagger in their hands,
> Great fighters are Jay Bhimwale, the people of Ambedkar!

In the postindependence period Nagorao Qawwal emerged. He was so popular in Vidarbha that if anyone mentioned his *qawwali*, thousands of people would spend the whole night listening. His voice was sweet and dignified and his compositions were heartrending.

> Ask our country, Hindustan, about our situation.
> Ask the powerful Shivaji how we fought!

It is also noteworthy that there was a Muslim named Mastan who composed songs for this singer.

After 1950, Govind Mashalikar, Tara Chand, and many other *qawwals* began to come from Mumbai to Nagpur. Among those, I very much liked Mashalikar. He used to sing songs composed by Shridhar Hoval:

> Bhim Mother, Bhim Mother, to Dalits a mother, to calves a cow,
> Let them moo repeatedly, and be caressed,
> Hold the seventy million children to your heart,
> Like baby birds under the wing, don't let them remain exposed,
> Take care of them, be concerned for them,
> Without this the sleep of happiness will not come to you.

See how expressive is one composition of Shridhar Hoval, written after Ambedkar's death:

> This field was tilled by Bhim, here grass and weeds will not grow;
> Even if the seeds of dissension are harvested, here they will not sprout;
> Better for the organization to be widowed than live a feeble married life.
> We will not leave the lion's gymnasium to study the way of sheep!

One poet named Vitthalnath used to come from Mumbai before 1945. He would take a troupe of *qawwals* and wander from village to village. One of his memories remains strongly in my mind. After wandering for one or two months in the villages, when this poet returned home, his wife said to him, "Do you have any concern for your house and home or not? There is not even a piece of bread for these four children to eat. How will we maintain ourselves?"

Vitthalnath's instant reply in song throws light on his loyalty:

> Life's companion, I am your lord and master but I am the servant of Dalits.
> We'll look after our daily life, the business of Dalits comes first.
> Your nagging is not good, why do you need jewelry?
> Wear the beautiful amulet of Bhim's name around your neck.
> Have these four kids of your house become a burden to you?
> See how Mother Bhim pulls the cart of ninety million children,
> Be of service and be loyal to the caste.
> Oh my companion, Vitthalnath should not be seen as a traitor to the caste.

Around Nagpur the compositions remained mixed with Hindi-Urdu. The Urdu language is very effective in creating enthusiasm among the people. Manohar Nagarale in Bhankhed won people's attention with his *qawwalis* and singing from 1942 onwards. Since his primary and middle-school education was in Urdu, he gave speeches in pure Urdu and easily composed songs in it. While he was a volunteer of the Samata Sainik Dal, he got the chance of singing a song before Babasaheb. The two-line poem he sang became a proverb that spread from house to house: "The boy who died for freedom was victorious, / Hold high the standard of the Independent Labour Party!"

After that Nagarale kept on singing songs. Some verses that he composed after the death of Babasaheb testify to the power of his genius:

> Whatever we had to be told was said by Ambedkar.
> His teachings are finished, his speaking finished, his commands finished.
> But don't let your mind be deceived that we are adrift and destroyed—
> Ambedkar has lifted us up, liberated us.
> Don't lose your strength in sorrow, keep the wisdom that is life,
> There is no benefit in futile sobbing, remember who you are;
> Don't give scope to treachery, backbiting, infighting,
> These are such insignificant things, but be wary of them.

Such were the Ambedkarite poets of the time. These poets molded the mentality of the community. Only a few singers of hundreds remain in my memory. The names of so many others have been swept away in the stream of time.

Today, poets flourish like grass during monsoons. But poets who rise in revolt against the atrocities on Dalits and go forth to awaken the mind of society do not appear. Though there are a few writers who take account of the history of the Ambedkarite revolution, still the writers who run factories of poetry and churn out songs on the name of Ambedkar to fill their stomachs are not even ready to acknowledge their debt to the earlier ones. In Pahadganj, the oil market of Delhi, Hakim Kishan Shay's daughter Kumari Devi Nandkumar published around 1940 or 1941 an Urdu book on Ambedkar. The name of that book was *Pistol with a Hundred Rounds*. The stanza at the beginning of that book is noteworthy: "Why do you keep on asking about the feet that have gone on that path? There are so many, not even their footprints have remained."

I would stay out the whole night for *qawwal* programs. On the way from Bardi to Inamwada near Zhatat Road, an iron bridge crosses the Nag River near Dhantoli; to reach the programs I had to walk under it. This place was entirely covered by thorny bushes. Bodies were buried there. Even during the day people avoided going there. I would go through it at night. I felt that if ghosts do exist, they must live in such a place, so I sat once for a whole night to see if I could experience their presence. At night I couldn't sleep until three or four in the morning. I kept my eyes half opened, just so much as a tall tree lets in spots of light through its shadows. However, no such thing as a ghost appeared to me. Attababa Spearman used to roam throughout the night in burial grounds. He would say, "I have been wandering for so many years in the cemetery. I have not seen any ghosts. Ghosts are not outside of us; they are in our minds." I was so mad over *qawwali* that I would listen to them in the morning and come back and sit immediately for a school examination. Since the *qawwali* programs came at the time of Ambedkar *jayanti* in April, which was also the period of examinations, I would forgo sleep, sitting and listening to the singing throughout the night and taking examinations during the day. There is no other medium more popular and effective than the *qawwali* for people's awakening.

As education spread within the community, its cultural consciousness began to be transformed. People demanded that the *qawwali* singers do social songs. But then, as the type of composition changed, the effectiveness of the songs diminished. The new generation finished off the *qawwali* as a type of song, and the community lost one effective means of propaganda.

# Chapter 19

## AN UNSPOILED PICTURE

Mother was now established in the mill. Many people worked there from the Mahar community. Nilkant Ramteke was a supervisor and also an organizer of the union. If I went with Mother to the mill, I would go and sit by him. He would cross-examine me on my studies. The mill workers' organization, in various ways, worked for the people.

Mother would come home a bit late from the mill. Until she came, my sister Malti would bring water and do other tasks. When Mother came she would do the cooking and would make spicy rich food while chatting with her neighbors. After eating she would take some *supari* out of a box and chew it. She chewed *supari* until the time of her death.

I used to sleep in a corner of the veranda with my feet beside the hearth and my head in a different corner. It was such a tiny house. A six-by-six-foot room, and in front a four-by-four veranda. When Mother came to this tiny area to sprinkle water on the ground and light the hearth, I would get up. She would start her tasks at 4:30. It must have taken her forty-five minutes to reach the mill. At 7:30 the doors of the mill were shut. By six, the women of the community would be giving their last instructions to their children and neighbors: "Look, don't wander around uselessly"; "Now, child, go to your aunt and do your homework"; "Oh, woman, keep an eye on my house." There were mothers who went to work leaving their small boys and girls in the care of some trustworthy neighbor, and there were the aged teachers, uncles, and elders who kept watch over the emptied neighborhood.

Due to Mother's work schedule, I got used to getting up before dawn, and this habit has remained with me lifelong. We would finish the half-done cooking that Mother had left. Of course, I would only light the stove; Malti did the rest of the work. However, lighting this hearth was the most difficult work.

From our blowing on the coal of the wet wood, again and again, much smoke would come, but the fire would not light. And then I would be gasping from the smoke that went into my nose and eyes. For years that smoke made me cry. My eyes became permanently yellow from it. However, some who saw my light eyes thought they were like a Konkanastha Brahman's!

In 1949 I dedicated myself to college. That year, for the first time, I put on long pants. Up through high school there were many like me who wore shorts. Only I couldn't get sandals for many days. In college boys wore long pants and most girls wore saris. In my time, not even one or two girls wore skirts.

The first day was considered to be very important. The college, previously known as Morris College, was now called the Mahavidyalaya. It had a romantic reputation throughout the province. Even with a free atmosphere there was a kind of discipline among the youth. There was no such thing as ragging. On the first day the principal told us, "Now you have come to college. You have complete freedom. From now on the teachers will give you guidance, they will not just lecture you."

Mahar students in the college were few in number, but organized. They would take part in all the events and happenings of the college. There was competition to win their confidence for elections. There was a foursome of Mahar students named Ate, Mate, Bele, Bansod. If there was any complaint about someone harassing a Mahar girl, this quartet would always teach him a lesson. Many Mahar students were older; some were married. Students of other Untouchable communities were rare.

There were B.A. examinations and Inter after two years. Students went automatically from the first to the second class. Only their attendance was recorded. Because of this no one did very much studying the first year.

English was a compulsory subject. Therefore we got acquainted with all the boys and girls in our class. In Marathi classes, girls were double the number of boys. In citizenship and economics, girls and boys were equal. Boys and girls did not wander freely together as they do today. If you wanted to meet or speak to anyone, you called to a girl in the common room and said something like, "Oh, hello, would you give me your notes for economics?"

If, after a class, a boy encountered a girl and began to talk to her, leaning slightly against the wall, it would be enough for the band of boys standing around nearby. The chant would begin, "Talk goes on secretly, secretly, the first meeting, it's the first meeting," and there would be loud laughter and clapping.

We had two incomparable teachers named Mishra and Guha for English. Mishra was six feet tall and corpulent and would make his entrance in a coat and pants. The students had all studied in Marathi up to that time. No one even looked up for fear the teacher would ask them something. Only a few girls from rich families could speak adequate English.

Once Mishra began, he would keep circling like a tank. "What is a sense of hearing? Hey, you, get up," he would shout in English. But if a student was dumbstruck to begin with, what would he say? Then came a second question: "What is a sense of seeing?" He kept this up in an attempt to drag out an answer. Even then the students didn't speak. Then he would get angry. "My dog can speak better English than you. You better go and open a pan shop."

Guha would never get angry at anyone. He would lecture for an hour and then leave. I began to sit in Guha's class. But from time to time I enjoyed sitting in Mishra's class. Only the Madrasi, Bengali, and some Hindi-speaking students would answer his questions. The Marathi students could not understand English at all.

The Marathi class, however, was a happy experience. Our teacher, B. S. Pandit, had a mild voice and would linger on descriptions of vice or love and painlessly capture the students' minds.

One day just before Pandit came into the class a student wrote on the board, "Love is nothing but the meeting of two hearts." Mr. Pandit came in. Looking at the board he read it out loud and in his usual style said, "What kind of meaning have you been taking? Say rather 'cheating of two hearts'! False coins, vows, promises, aren't they the same?" Again giggling throughout the class.

By the time of matric, rationalism had taken hold of my mind due to the Ambedkarite movement. However, in college we learned how to criticize religious ideas through studying Lokahitawadi's *Shatpatre* and Agarkar's essays. V. B. Kolte and Madhav Gopal Deshmukh were my Marathi teachers in college from the first year up through the M.A.

Kolte was a lover of discipline. He could not stand anyone making noise in class, and he had no love for those who did not study. But he did not have to make any special efforts to impose discipline. His style of teaching was so engrossing that the students would sit listening, filled with enchantment. Once I became so enamored of one of his lectures that I sat with my head nodding. After the class finished he called me, "Don't nod your head over any subject without agreeing with it." No one casually stayed away from his lectures.

While teaching Chiplunkar's essays he would expound on Chiplunkar's criticism of Mahatma Jotirao Phule. Only in those days there was no Phule literature available. Therefore we could not get Phule's own thought to read.

Agarkar's reformist ideas had a strong effect on my mind. "The Season of Five People" or "The Foolishness of the Wise or Our Care of Corpses" and other Agarkar essays gave a turn to my thinking and use of language. The way the Brahman Lokahitawadi cursed Brahman practices was helpful to us in our mockery of religion.

Kolte would give us an awareness of the ordeal of the social reformers. In those days I felt Agarkar and Lokahitawadi to be great men. Later, when I read Ambedkar's analysis of social reform, I recognized the limitations of Agarkar. I no longer felt it to be strange that Agarkar did not leave his home and join the work of Phule going on in those days. My understanding is that the stage of social reform in Agarkar's thinking was limited to the ideological reform of the Brahman community. He did not have sufficient mental courage to join Phule's broad and active social reformism. Even so, Agarkar has a great place among those intellectuals whose thinking shaped a generation.

Dr. Kolte taught us Chakradhar's *Lilacharitra*. He also would take great joy in teaching Moropant's *Kekavali*. He would explain the meaning and elucidate the rhyming, alliteration, metaphors, and other figures of speech. If the bell rang while he was teaching a certain verse, he would start the next day exactly from the place he'd finished the day before. He had an eye fixed on the use of Marathi words in all fields of writing. After I got a job that was helpful, for not only the petitions for leave but also court decisions and reports were written in Marathi and Hindi. In college, for the very first time, I understood the significance of the word "Acharya" (Sanskrit for "teacher") due to him. Professor Kolte also had a big role in strengthening my rationalist ideas.

We had to study many writers and poets in the college syllabus. But some among those left a permanent stamp on the mind. A collection of eleven essays by contemporary essayists called *Ekadashi* was included in our syllabus. One of these, "Ideals are God," by Waman Malhar Joshi, left a big imprint on my mind. For that matter, I felt that Joshi's "Sushila's God," "Indu Was Black, Sarla Was Innocent," and other writings were somehow or another congenial. In *Ekadashi*, S. M. Mate has one light essay, "The Cock Crows," in which he has very beautifully sketched how a poor Untouchable peasant in a village reacts after hearing that Babasaheb Ambedkar is to make a speech in a nearby village. With this one exception, the picture of Ambedkar's movement appeared nowhere in literature. Though we had to study the poetry of Madhav Julian, Vinayak, and other poets, it is only the poetry that joins itself to our mental situation that remains with us for life.

In Narayan Waman Tilak's "The Flower of the Forest," the lines "Without darkness even the light of the sun is dim, without sorrow the idea of happiness seems in vain" even today give inspiration to the mind. I would read only a line of Kusumagraj's and it would become fixed in my mind. Whenever I felt the need it would come out. I used to feel like reciting his "Song of Pride of

Columbus" or "The Love Song of the Earth" more than his famous "Victory Slogan of Revolution!"

> Boundless are our ideals, boundless is our hope,
> Like a far shore calling such a small person.

or

> Can ideals, dreams, hope be fulfilled at any time?
> We, like madmen, pray to idols that will be shattered.
> Disentangle, my love, your moonlight hands from this loving embrace;
> Beyond the horizon are waiting the messengers of the day.

The core of these poems of Kusumagraj would touch the heart of every person who was, like me, a dreamer of broken dreams, a passionate nurturer of ideals. However, I also thought of doing an imitation of the lines given above: A thief comes from outside to meet his beloved, knowing that the police are after him. He sees his beloved making chapatis, embraces her and says,

> Disentangle, my love, your doughy hands from this loving embrace;
> Beyond the walls await the messengers of the state.

An English professor named Hukins taught Thomas Hardy's novel *Return of the Native*. The roles in this novel revolve around a specific region of England. The atmosphere of this region determines the life and nature of those characters. The form of composition of that novel impressed itself on my mind. I became conscious that my life also was shaped by the community and people around me. In those days, I kept on thinking that I should write a novel and create a picture of the Ambedkarite movement in it.

I got employment in the office of the Deputy Accountant General, Post and Telegraph, after the supplementary B.A. examination. I left it in 1955 to register for my M.A. The question was whether to take politics, economics, or Marathi. I was of a mind to become a Marathi professor. So I applied for Marathi. In Marathi renowned teachers like Kolte, M. G. Deshmukh, A. V. Deshmukh, S. D. Pendse, and B. S. Pandit were there to teach us.

At the M.A. level my daily program changed. I wanted to get high marks, so I studied night and day. I studied my Marathi homework and did yoga. For the whole day I would read. At four o'clock I would sleep at Uncle Hari's house. At eight in the evening I would rise and have a little dinner and then study the whole night. For that year I had to keep a schedule of sleeping in the evening and then studying. Even then, in the first year's examination I could solve only three and a half out of five questions in the allotted time.

I took the second-year M.A. exams three years later, while employed, as an external student. I had thought I would get second class for the M.A. examinations. However, I received third rank in the results. When the report card came there was a second rank mark. This was sufficient merit to get a job as a professor. However, I wanted a degree. So I corresponded with the university about getting a rank according to the report card. After much correspondence the university informed me that "Your report card is mistaken." They sent a corrected second report card and gave me a third rank. That was how my dream of becoming a professor got spoiled.

# Chapter 20

## THE WELFARE OF THE WORLD

So many young men and women, children, and elderly people used to come from nearby areas to take an evening walk on the green grass of Maharaj Park. At this time, in the 1940s, a gentleman of around forty in a clean white shirt and pants could be seen distributing leaflets. These leaflets bore the title "The Vitthal of Pandhari is Buddha."

At first we didn't pay him much attention. But we began to meet him often, and I started reading his leaflets. As our connection grew I began to visit his home. The name of this gentleman was Anant Ramchandra Kulkarni, a Brahman.

From the time of my childhood on, Kulkarni propagated Buddhism. His intention was not to convert people to the religion, but rather to give Hindus an understanding of the ideas of the Buddha.

Kulkarni was the Nagpur secretary of the Calcutta-based Mahabodhi society. Its president was Bhavani Shankar Niyogi, the chief justice of the CP-Berar high court. The branch, though, had no office. Kulkarni was the one who managed its work.

It was Wamanrao Godbole who brought us the news that Babasaheb was going to convert to Buddhism even before 1950. Kulkarni also began to get an idea about this from the newspapers. After that he began to meet with the branches of the Samata Sainik Dal. From time to time Wamanrao told him to come to teach the thought of the Buddha.

Wamanrao Godbole, Keshavrao Patil, and other Dal leaders decided to hold a class every Sunday to give people an understanding of Buddhism. A big building known as Dhanvate Chambers owned by Baburao Dhanvate stands in front of the *vasti*. Above the third floor is a spacious open hall. This place would be useful and convenient for the Sunday meeting, but we didn't know how to get the space. Besides, there was the question of rent!

Dhanvate had a manager living in Nagjibhai Town near the *vasti*. I went to him myself and told him our difficulties. He had known me to some extent before. He used to go to Pralhad Mhali's shop for a shave, and I would be lounging there morning and evening. The manager gave us the space for free, and we began to hold a class every Sunday on the Buddhist religion. I myself went to Niyogi's bungalow in Ambazari every Sunday to bring him, sometimes on a friend's bicycle with a double seat, sometimes on foot. If I arrived one or two hours early, Niyogi would have me listen to his erudite preaching. At those times his sermons would leave my mind astonished. Niyogi was not simply a retired chief justice; he had also been the chairman of the Madhya Pradesh Public Service Commission. He had made a colossal study of all religions. He was influenced by Gandhi's philosophy, and had participated in the freedom movement. It appears from some published leaflets that he had also given his contribution to Untouchables' conferences from 1920 onwards. Whenever I met this learned man of high post he would feed me the nectar of the wisdom about the history of Buddhism as if he were teaching a student. Until 1955, as long as I was in Nagpur, and after that for many years whenever I went to Nagpur, I would make a point of going to visit Niyogi. Niyogi lived for over a hundred years.

Kulkarni had collected many valuable books on Buddhism. He had a small library. These books were kept in an open space under the stairs going to the second floor of Dhanvate Chambers. That small library had B. C. Law's history of the Pali language, Harisingh Gaur's *Spirit of Buddhism*, the books of Mr. and Mrs. Rhys David, and around two hundred other important books. Besides that there were many rare magazines with beautiful pictures of the Buddha. Seeing my love for books, Kulkarni made me the keeper of the keys for the library, and I had greedily read all of them by the time I had finished college.

Those books were later included in the Siddharth Bhagyoday Library, and in only one year, just as other libraries had gone to rack and ruin, so it happened with those books. They were all scattered just as leaves are blown away in a storm.

On 14 October 1956, Kulkarni seemed to accept the Buddhist religion along with Niyogi and of course Dr. Ambedkar. But now the Kulkarni was not the same Kulkarni who had so loyally propagated Buddhism before. He was only a supporter of Buddhism, and still a Hindu.

As every year, in that year also it was decided to celebrate Ambedkar *jayanti*. I had seen the rehearsals of plays in college gatherings. I got it in my mind that a drama should be performed in our community also. Prabhakar Jivane could play flute, drums, and other instruments. Wamanrao Godbole said, "Do a play about Buddha," and we began our preparations.

A big book, *Buddhalilasar,* by Dharmanad Kosambi, was in Kulkarni's library. After reading this Prabhakar Jivane and I began to sit writing until twelve or one at night. I had already read Shankarrao Dev's *For Bhagwan Buddha,* based on the life of the Chinese pilgrim Hiuen Tsang. From this the title *The Welfare of the World* was suggested, and we completed our writing of the drama.

Who would make the costumes and draperies from the Buddhist period for this play? Harishchandra Jangam had done women's roles in many plays; in addition he knew everything about makeup. One day we asked him, and he told us, laughing, "I'm ready anytime. You make all the preparations."

Jangam was a barber by caste. However, he was not so talkative as the others. This man of few words was light-skinned, with a small, shapely face, so it is no wonder that in every play he was given the women's role. Besides, no girl in our community in the 1950s was ready to take part in a play. All the actors in our play were students. I was eager to see what we could learn from Jangam. Jangam came out of the shop with us. We sat on the top of the well near the temple and talked. Jangam gave us suggestions about what needed to be brought for makeup.

We based *Welfare of the World* on Buddha's life. This was our first attempt at writing plays. Since this play was to be performed in the community, we thought the beginning should be dramatic and inspiring. So I had an idea. Five *bhikshus* are looking towards the sky. One says to another, "Look, see in the sky a new star is shining. Today the Buddha will be born on this earth. Let us go there."

Of course, it was an attempt to link the story of Jesus Christ's birth to that of the Buddha. But on stage this event was so impressive that people remained absorbed in the play for three hours. The Buddha's sight of an old man, a sick man, a corpse, and a sannyasi, leading to the renunciation of his home, was shown in tableau form, which the audience liked very much. We used the Buddha's debates with Vashisth Bharadvaj and others. The boys rehearsed so much that each could remember the lines of the others. Wrestler Tulshidas was given the role of Angulimal. At the time our idea was that Angulimal was a kind of demon, and when he played the part the audience became overcome with laughter. I got the part of the Brahman Bharadvaj. But I could not manage to wear a dhoti. Harishchandra Jangam, who had helped us so much with makeup, helped me. Bhavani Shankar Niyogi and Kulkarni sat for the full rehearsal. At the end of the performance, Niyogi said, "Moon, you have beautifully composed this play. Do another performance with tickets in Maharaj Park hall."

But I couldn't manage that. Only Prabhakar Jivane maintained the inspiration of our drama and held other performances in different communities. In addition he wrote other plays and performed them.

Before doing the drama, the volunteers of the Dal collected everything needed for the play. The curtain that had to be placed before the stage, drapes— all had to be rented. Wamanrao said, "Bring some cloth, we'll make it our- selves"; and Godbole himself sewed all the curtains. This curtain proved useful for many years for the club.

I have one more memory about the theater. It must have been around the time of Ambedkar *jayanti* in 1951. In 1950, after the performance of *Welfare of the World,* enthusiasm mounted among the boys to perform another play. We thought that the play should be social or connected with social issues. But I had no spare time to write another play. I was to sit for the university inter exam.

About that time the play *Victory Monument of Koregaon* was published in *Vividhrut* weekly. A penetrating description is given in this play about how Mahar soldiers defeated Bapu Gokhale, the *peshwa's* commander, in 1818. The audience is amused to see how the English governor Elphinstone speaks Marathi with an English accent on the stage. This play also became very well known at Ambedkar *jayantis.*

My friend Jayant Vairagade got the part of Ghashiram Kotwal in this play. At that time my study about the *peshwa* period, where the *kotwal* was a high of- ficial, was very minimal. To us a *kotwal* meant a low-level village watchman. Be- cause of that we told him to wear the torn clothes of a *kotwal.* However, before entering "Ghashiram" sat down and said, "Only if you give me a new shirt will I play the part." We tried to explain to him. But he was not ready. Finally we had to give him a clean white shirt and send him on stage.

I wrote and prepared one more short play. Its name was *Birthday.* In real- ity, basically I didn't write it at all. This play was published in a book in the form of a dialogue between brother and sister. We made some changes in the dia- logue and in the name of Babasaheb's birthday we performed the play. In it there were parts for three girls and three boys. We convinced the parents of three girls from the community who were in middle school to let them be in the play. The play was four days away when the father of one girl said, "I won't let my daughter come." This man was a wrestler and a rogue. Who would ex- plain to him? Finally the dialogue of the girl was divided among the other two girls and the full play had to be rewritten and was done well.

Every year Ambedkar *jayanti* used to be celebrated for ten days. This cel- ebration was done by the volunteers of the Dal with the help of people of the community. We began the custom of offering lectures at the beginning of many programs. The understanding earlier was that only Dalit leaders should be called for speeches. In the Bardi *jayanti,* for the first time, non-Dalit Marathi professors began to be invited, and huge crowds came to hear the lectures. Up to that time there was not one professor in the Dalit communities.

I myself invited M. G. Deshmukh, Professor Kolte, A. N. Deshpande, and others. Dr. Deshmukh once said, around 1954, "Moon, is there a biography of Ambedkar to read?" Just at that time a part of Khairmode's biography had been published. I gave this to him. And on that topic he made a very nice speech. The Sangh's Dattopant Thengadi, the Communist party's Bhai Bardhan, and others also gave speeches on the *jayanti* celebrations.

# Chapter 21

## FOR WHAT? FOR BOOKS!

There was a *panch* supervisory committee for the Vitthal-Rukmini temple. It did little aside from gossiping and chatting. The temple had become so run-down that even to repair it would be difficult. Seeing the organizing work of the Dal, some suggested delegating the work of the temple trust to the Dal. However, the members of the temple committee would not give up their pretensions. Finally all the youth came together. A meeting was held, and it was decided to give the work of the temple committee to a new group. Supervisor Kavadu Khobragade was made the first chairperson of the new committee. Keshavrao Patil, who had been the first to pass the law examination in the community, headed the working committee. Some people in the community brought a legal case against the new arrangements, but the new committee finally won it.

Keshavrao Patil was about Wamanrao Godbole's age. He was an official in the law department of the Central Province's government. He, Wamanrao, and some people with understanding sat down to consider the constitution of the trust, and formed a new permanent committee for the Vitthal-Rukmini Temple Trust. Its constitution was prepared, and new members were registered. In that constitution was included a provision for two kinds of bodies: a working committee and an advisory committee. To ensure a check on both of them, a structure of elections and delegated authority was set up. Activities occurred according to the constitution for many years. I was a member of the first working committee. Seeing the good work of the new youth, the old members of the temple *panch* accepted their retirement. The new winds that began to blow in the community were those of the new, educated generation.

On behalf of the new Vitthal-Rukmini Temple Trust, much construction was begun in 1950 around the temple. Gymnasium areas were also built. Many youth who before had gone to the Khate Gokhale Gymnasium now did their exercises in that area. The temple trust committee started taking the place of the Bhagyodaya Club, which had become inactive. Sports like cricket, football, and hockey were started on behalf of the trust. These teams began to play matches against various big and small groups. We never thought of sitting; we never fell sick. I never spent even five minutes in the house. One program or another was always going on.

The temple had a spacious ground that is still there today. The trust gave me the responsibility of building a library in that area.

I used to go by the Monday market while going to the Patwardhan school. At that time the whole area behind Rajaram Library was vacant. From there to Patwardhan school was a row of used-book stores. Books were not as abundant then as today. But it was easy to find books we liked. I hardly ever had spare cash in my hands. However, after mother got her job in the mill, she would give a rupee or two for buying vegetables. I used to take a few coins from that amount and buy books with the money. Once I saw a book with the pages falling out, so I bargained. This was Khandekar's *White Clouds*, which I got for four annas. Hudson's book, *Introduction to the Study of Literature*, which was required for college, I bought for half a rupee. I bought books of stories in that way. And gradually my space in the hut grew cramped. Once it was decided to build a library on behalf of the Vitthal-Rukmini Temple Trust, I began to demand books from many people. Our uncle Hari Patil owned nearly two hundred books; he donated all of them. I created a twelve hundred–book library and gave it to the trust. I donated some of my own rare books. Among them was the important book *Ancient Universities*, by N. C. Kelkar. Daily newspapers, magazines, and weeklies began to come to the library. Their expense was covered by some senior employed members of the Dal.

Later I was employed at the General Post and Telegraph. Then I would buy at least one book a month for the temple trust library. At that time I was possessed by books! Sane Guruji was a writer I liked very much. I would buy his *Sweet Stories* and many other storybooks and novels and give them to the library. A. R. Kulkarni gave me his own book collection, and after three to four years, around 1954, I included that in the library. I was part of the committee for four to five years. But later the committee was reestablished. New people were elected. And slowly all the activity got scattered. The old Samata Sainik Dal's discipline vanished with their volunteers.

The Dal's volunteers lost the next election to the temple trust committee. Seeing that there was no scope there, some of us established the B.R.A. (Bhimrao Ramji Ambedkar) club and kept the cricket and football games going. There was a debate in one meeting of the temple trust committee whether to

*Vasant and Meenakshi Moon in the doorway of the library built on top of their Nagpur house in the 1970s. The mosaic is from a painting in the Ajanta Buddhist caves. Moon's collection of books and documents has been used by many scholars. Photo by Eleanor Zelliot, 1975.*

call it by the name of "Bhagyodaya." I urged them to name it the Siddharth Club. Finally the compromise name of Siddhartha-Bhagyodaya Sports Club was chosen. Even today one can see its signboard in the Bardi Temple Trust Committee Room.

Buddhism had exerted some kind of influence on the Dal activists for a long time. While I was in seventh standard the Dal presented me with Dharmanand Kosambi's *Lord Buddha* in Marathi as a prize. After the new temple trust committee was founded, a four-foot statue of Lord Buddha was placed in a square glass box in the meeting room just outside the inner room of the temple. Those who went into the temple would do *puja* to Vitthal. However, they started doing *puja* to Buddha upon coming out. Later on, aside from Narayan Watchman, no man or woman in the community did *puja* to Vitthal.

The B.R.A. club had no meeting place. The Varade clan had their houses on the main road in front of the temple. Among them was one Dal volunteer, Dinanath Varade, who had a room. We started to meet in that room. Since not much equipment could be kept in that ten-by-ten-foot room, the cricket equipment had to be left with someone else.

By 1942 we had given up our celebration of nearly all the Hindu festivals. There were two trends of thinking even about Diwali. Some said we could light lamps and set off firecrackers but not do *puja*, while others would argue for not doing anything. One evening, when I reached our club's room as usual, I saw some of my companions ready to do Lakshmipuja. I asked, "What is this?"

"Today is Lakshmipuja [worship of wealth]."

"Up to today we don't have any money, so where has this Lakshmi gone?"

"So what? If you don't want to do the *puja* yourself, don't do it."

I angrily left.

Around that time the Vitthal-Rukmini Temple Trust Committee was slowly going to rack and ruin. One day I saw a gentleman named Namdevrao Nagdevete from Chandrapur district coming out of the temple trust library. He was carrying a stack of newspapers in his hand. When I inquired, I learned they were issues of the *Janata*. Those issues which I had made such strenuous efforts to collect were being sold for waste.

While I had been on the first executive committee of the temple trust, I gave my resignation later because I didn't agree with their method of working. But I continued to work with companions on the committee. When I got employment, I used to send contributions for newspaper subscriptions to the temple trust committee. I continued sending these subscriptions for many days after I became Deputy County Commissioner in 1955. One important event happened around 1952. The remains of two important disciples of Lord Buddha, Sariputra and Moggalayan, were given by the British government to India. These bones had been discovered by Alexander Cunningham when he excavated two stupas at Sanchi. They had been kept in the British Museum. They were going to be installed again at Sanchi in November 1952. Prime Minister Jawaharlal Nehru himself was going to do the installation.

Wamanrao Godbole and the volunteers of the Samata Sainik Dal were to be present at this occasion. The Dal no longer existed in a formal sense. But there still existed enough sense of identity among the youth. Nearly fifteen of us reached Sanchi. Since Wamanrao had previously written for accommodations, we were put up in a small tent.

Babasaheb was not given any special invitation. He did not come. Everyone was disgusted. Only P. N. Rajbhoj was present, and he was given a chance to speak. Sanchi is forty miles from Bhopal. You have to go from Bhopal by railway, getting off at Bhilsa station. As we got off, we saw many Hindu priests lolling around. They tried to extract money for taking people to see statues of Buddha at their houses in Bhilsa. We also went to see the statues but did not give money.

That night in Sanchi it was bitterly cold. I had taken only one sweater. When I opened my case in the evening, I saw that the sweater had disappeared. There was no question of anyone coming in from outside the tent. I asked everyone but got no response. At night we lit a small fire and warmed ourselves by it. After a long time I lay down on the mat. Even the cold on my clothes would not go away. For the whole night I was shivering. At dawn the cold reached its climax. If one is mentally determined to act as if the body does not feel cold, then, no matter how cold it is, there is not so much trouble. I was making such an attempt not to feel the cold. But my body refused to listen. Around early morning I got a little sleep.

We stayed at the camp for three days. We saw a lot of Sanchi and returned. The whole group shared my distress that my sweater had disappeared. Everyone knew my economic condition. For many days, our trip to Sanchi was our main topic of discussion. After three or four days a friend of mine brought a message. "Vasanta, your sweater is with an old man. You go and ask for it." They gave me his name. But I didn't go.

The sight of that huge stupa at Sanchi left a great impression on my mind. At the college, all the students had learned of our trip. I also started telling people here and there about the stupa. Pundalik Sunghate and I were very close friends. My English was rough, but Pundalik had a good command of the language. His handwriting was also elegant. In college or out of it, we two were always together. Because of that, we got hailed by a student named Mate in our college as "Sariputra-Moggalayan."

After our return from Sanchi, a new spirit began to throb in the community. Every year Ambedkar *jayanti* was celebrated for ten days. This year it was decided to also celebrate Buddha *jayanti*. A huge procession on Buddha *jayanti* was organized, and Buddha's birthday was honored for the first time in Bardi. A drum merchant donated a statue of Buddha to put in the temple grounds. This statue was of cement. Some people in the community filed a case in court saying that a statue of Buddha should not be set in the Vitthal temple. Chavan, who was at one time an activist of the Independent Labor Party, began to work with this opposition group. However, the petition was rejected. It is unnecessary to add that the ceremony of Buddha *jayanti* begun by the Bardi people spread to other communities.

Pundalik and I had entered college at the same time. When classes finished in the afternoon, we both left Nagpur College. There is a lane, hardly even an alley, between Government Press and Morris College. We would go down that alley to the university library. There we would take out books, reading them sometimes in the university or sometimes going to sit in the Maharaj park.

There were two years of Inter after matric and then two years allowed to make the B.A. Pundalik and I passed Inter. Pundalik got the most marks of any Untouchable student, and won the Behere Award. After Inter, Pundalik wanted to complete B.A. (Honors), which took three years. But only selected students got permission. And when Sinha, the principal, interviewed Pundalik, he told him in bad English, "How do you Scheduled Caste people aspire for Honors? You be a graduate and just do your M.A."

When Pundalik came out of the principal's room and met me, he told me about this. The scorching blast of caste hatred left a scar on our minds. There was no question but that Pundalik was intelligent and that he had the command of English required for Honors.

# Chapter 22

## I BEGIN TO WRITE

I had an unbounded passion for reading. I had read somewhere that Bernard Shaw used to read eighty pages every day. Because of this I also cultivated the habit of fast reading, and I used to examine myself to see how fast and how many pages I could read.

In those days, no matter what efforts I made I would grow very bored when writing. Instead, I would lose myself in the joy of reading. I used to sit and spend two hours every evening reading all the papers in the temple trust committee's room.

In middle school, while I was in eighth grade, probably around 1945 to 1946, the Chokhamela hostel students published a handwritten monthly magazine. Students would produce such magazines through their colleges and schools. They would be decorated with lucid handwriting, pictures, poems, and stories. In the Mahar community, something like a competition was introduced to bring out such magazines. I dimly remember writing a fictionalized article on the childhood of Ambedkar in the Chokhamela hostel magazine. That must have been my first effort at writing.

In those days, for that matter, there were no facilities to give scope to Untouchable boys in writing. As the Ambedkarite movement began to win renown, leaders such as Sankharam Meshram, N. H. Kumbhare, Hardas Avale, N. K. Tirpude, and Bhaurao Borkar were creative writers among the youth. However, they complained that their articles were not published in *Tarun Bharat* or in the Nagpur daily, *Maharashtra*. The movement of handwritten "magazines" started among the students as a result. These would come out once a year.

Later I did publish some writing, and this is how it came about. New elections had just been declared according to the Constitution of India. For this first election, Babasaheb Ambedkar made a campaign tour throughout India. He came to Nagpur, and at a huge public meeting he made a stormy speech. When Babasaheb stood up to speak in Military Park on a stage designed like a lotus, people had the image of a Buddha standing on that lotus. Once the speech began, people would not allow even a bit of shifting around. The Samata Sainik Dal kept complete order. R. R. Patil was the main person responsible for this system. Volunteers came from every Mahar neighborhood. Previously, up to 1948, the units of the Dal had daily activities. By this time this was true only of a few areas. Even so, hundreds of volunteers would come on time and see to the arrangements. The police were completely kept out.

The Congress newspapers unleashed a barrage of criticism against Ambedkar on the occasion of that election. Raosaheb Thavare had gone into Congress. Many other Dalit leaders with him had left Ambedkar's party. However, there was no sign of factionalism among the common people.

Raosaheb Thavare published around that time a small sixteen-page booklet titled *Dr. Ambedkar's Politics.* There he made the statement that "Ambedkar will have to live on crumbs thrown to him by the Congress." The statement made my temper flare. Nobody took the trouble of answering such booklets. Any reply would have to be published at my own expense. I was in Inter at that time. I wrote a response reviewing every point made in that booklet. I showed it to such senior leaders as Keshavrao Patil and Wamanrao Godbole. They liked it and told me to publish it. Wamanrao himself gave two hundred rupees towards the expense of the book, and in this way a small booklet, *Beware Mercenary Propaganda*, my first literary offspring, came to birth in 1950. The book was published in a press on Ghat Road.

Even after a book is published, the question of how to distribute it is always a problem for writers and publishers. Though I had my circle of friends, still there was the question of where to sell the book. The Hindu owners of bookstores did not stock such books. Just at this time, a *hututu* march took place in January at Kamathi. I took my books and stood on the road shouting, "Two annas, two annas"—and so began to sell them. Some boys from Kamathi also helped. However, I also made an effort to go to various neighborhoods during *jayanti* and sell the book. It took a long time to sell one thousand copies.

Along with the movement of the Dal in the community, I took part in various programs in college. I always roamed around with Chandrasekhar Dharmadhikari and V. P. Salve, who have recently retired as judges of the high court. The Marathi and Hindi groups were constantly opposed to each other in college gatherings and elections. In the second-year gathering, a rich boy named Porakh gave a trophy to the college labeled "Best Volunteer," which was awarded to me. However, my mind had become so used to doing every kind of work without expectation of reward that I avoided going up to the stage to receive the award.

In college the Hindi and Marathi boys competed to win the votes of the Dalit boys, who always voted as a bloc. They would unite, have a meeting, and decide how to vote. If some Dalit boy was running for vice president or general secretary, there was a great scope for compromise. At that time the practice of distributing money for votes did not exist.

# Chapter 23

## THE END OF OMAR KHAYYAM

I sometimes went to Calcutta during summer vacations. My half-sister Anu-tai's husband, Mahadevrao, was a head cook in the restaurant car of the mail train. He supervised all the waiters and other cooks in the dining car. One year, he sent a message to Mother that said, "Send Vasant. We'll have him in Calcutta for the summer vacation." So I boarded the train.

My father lived with Mahadevrao and Anutai. In Nagpur, a prohibition law had been passed after Independence, but not in Calcutta. Father had a passion for drink. He could not survive without drinking alcohol. However, as long as he was conscious he would tell all kinds of stories. It is said that from the Malti-Mahadev folk tales he had chosen my sister's name, Malti, and my name, Vasant. He would carry on a business of looking through the almanac to help people select an auspicious time for weddings and naming ceremonies, and he also told fortunes. These priestly activities of Father's also spread to Mahadevrao's railway quarters, in the Sangragacchi Parganas seventy miles from Calcutta. He had an abundance of invitations to conduct Satyanarayan *pujas*. But when he got the chance to drink, his purity completely vanished.

I was in college. Communication with my father had been almost broken since my childhood. Mother never invoked his memory. From the time she got employed in the mill she had become independent economically. We did not think about our father. Because of that, I had no awe or respect for him in my mind.

I went to visit him in Calcutta one summer. One day, a boy came running to the house. "Where is Mamaji?" he asked; my brother-in-law called my father Mamaji; so did the neighbors. He was lying down inside. When he realized that someone was calling him from outside, he immediately came out and said, "What, Gajja, what work is there?"

"My mother has called you."

"For what?"

"The baby won't take milk, she said."

I went with him to Gajja's house. A young woman was sitting with a child on her lap. Seeing Father, she began to speak in Hindi. "Mamaji, my child here doesn't drink enough milk. Many lumps have developed in my breast." If a baby wouldn't drink milk or if a woman had too much milk, she would get lumps in her breast. To prevent these lumps, these days plastic suction devices are used to express the milk. But there was no such thing then. Women called in indigenous doctors, *vaidyas*.

Father told her to bring some water in a pitcher. He soaked a small comb in that and began to mutter chants. After a little while he ran the comb over her breast just as one combs hair. In about ten or fifteen minutes, after some more chanting, the baby began to nurse. The young mother tried to give Father some money, but he didn't take it.

I felt this was a marvel at the time. I was especially curious about the mantras he had chanted. He could also chant mantras to extract scorpions' poison. Once I asked him about it. He gave me something in writing, but he also said, "Oh Vasanta, the patient feels there is some magic in the mantra. We use words they don't understand. They look at us with wonder. It is like doing some kind of magic on their minds. Their attention is distracted from the pain and they get some ease." Father made some effort to give a rational explanation for my educated mind. How much faith he had in his own explanation is difficult to say.

However, when I arrived in Calcutta in the summer of 1954, Father was bedridden. He had diarrhea night and day. His stools were bloody. Even with medicines the bleeding did not stop. Anutai had to change his clothes night and day.

I asked, "What happened?"

"What can I say, Vasanta?" Anu said. "Baba has the craze for drinking, as you know. He drank one day and while coming home he fell on a stone in the canal. The neighbors brought him to the house, and since then there's been diarrhea and blood. The doctor says he may have suffered a blow to his intestines."

For fifteen days Father lay senseless. One morning he called Mahadev, "Son-in-law, come here."

Replying, "Sir," Mahadev came.

"Look, now I can't go on living, I'm completely exhausted. Now I want to go."

"No, Mamaji, you can't go so soon from here, tell us your final wishes!" Mahadevrao said.

Baba opened his sunken eyes a little bit. Hollows had sunk in everywhere on his face. He gave a sign to Mahadev to bring his ear a bit closer, and in a voice that could be heard loudly he said into his ear, "I don't have many desires left. Only, let me drink two spoonfuls of brandy."

Mahadev took a bottle of brandy from the cupboard. He poured a little liquid into a big tablespoon and slowly gave it to Father to drink. After drinking one or two spoonfuls, Father let out his last breath.

All of our relatives considered it a marvel that Father's death had taken place in front of me. They said that death did not come before his son's hand had touched him. Vasant's father was so fortunate that his son had held his father in his arms!

I myself felt nothing about my father's death. Anutai made a show of crying. Mahadevrao did all the rites, and in the evening the ceremony of taking him to the nearby cremation ground was done. Since I was present, the torch was given to me. Taking this rude torch, I began to run around the corpse. However, due to the wind coming from the opposite direction, all the fire was blown towards me. I was quickly rescued. Otherwise I would have been seared in the fire.

On the third day the rite of taking the ashes to the river was observed, and this time a religious crisis confronted me. A barber was called. My sister said to me, "Dada, you'll have to be shaven. You'll have to have a tonsure."

I said, "What tonsure? I don't feel that my father's soul won't go to heaven if I have my hair." This was an Agarkarite answer. Mahadevrao was not particular about religious duties, customs, or ceremonies. He explained to his wife, "Oh, let it go, what will go wrong if he doesn't do it?"

I had just studied Agarkar's essays in college. They had left a great impression on my mind. Especially the arguments presented in "The Foolishness of the Wise, or Our Care of Corpses" were on the tip of my tongue. I gave a clear refusal and sent the barber home.

That day Anutai fasted. I got the Hindi-Urdu novels of the revolutionary progressive writer Kushavaha Kant from Mahadevrao and sat reading them under a tree. Anutai fasted for three days. She had also become stubborn. Finally, Mahadevrao convinced her.

"Why should Vasant feel anything about his father? Has Mamaji done anything for him? When Mamaji sold the house, did he give him one penny?"

On the fourth day Anutai gave up her fasting and in the end I did not have my head shaved. For eight or ten days I stayed there, and then returned to Nagpur. No one in Nagpur had heard the news.

I never used to spend much time with any relatives. Because of that, there was no question of telling anyone else. I went to my house and told my mother, "Mother, Baba has died."

"Oh? When?"

"It's been eight days."

She fell silent. She broke her bangles on a tree in front of the door. She wiped the *kumkum* off her forehead. She tore the black string off her throat and threw it away and went to work. She neither gave any lamentation nor observed mourning about her husband's death. In those days, if anyone in a house died the women of the house would cry and wail loudly. Nothing like that happened. I explained to the neighbors. Then the story spread everywhere.

With the death of her husband, the burden of the *kumkum* on her forehead was lifted. The black thread around her neck and the bangles on her hand had ensnared her. Now she had been completely liberated.

# Chapter 24

## RISING MOON

In 1953 we decided to put out a handwritten magazine in the community. I was given the task of collecting articles, while Ramdas Tirpude was assigned the job of design. Ram was a perfected painter. He would draw freehand with crayons or pencils on *watman* paper. Babasaheb Ambedkar's face could not be drawn easily by artists. For some reason, artists found it difficult to draw a good likeness of Ambedkar. Ram, on the other hand, could draw his face very minutely. At that time there was not one artist in Nagpur who could draw Babasaheb's face like Ram.

Ram's house was near mine. During vacation I would go to him and sit looking at his pictures for hours. He very often used watercolors. However, he would draw Babasaheb's face in crayon pencils. With a dark purple color he would make minute and fine jottings. Taking a published photo of Babasaheb, he would draw a graph of crossed lines and after deciding on the size would fill in Ambedkar's face. Seeing Ram Tirpude's artistry created in me a love for painting, and I began to collect books of art. In 1954 when I was employed for a while, I studied painting in Dikhale's art classes.

Handwritten magazines were published in many communities like ours. In Dharampeth, a Dnyanodaya Association had been established that published *Dnyanodaya* as an annual for many years. Researchers like Ratnakir Banvir and painters like Chandrakant Mugale built up a collection of Ambedkar's photos and other art in that association. One or another Marathi writer would be invited for the publication ceremony of *Dnyanodaya* every year, which we regularly attended. The literary tradition was continued later in Bhankhed, Pacpavile, Indora, and Colonel Park.

The boys in our community had no tradition of writing. However, after we decided to put out a magazine, many made the effort. Boys from eighth standard up wrote articles. I refined them. I myself wrote various articles, poems, and stories for the magazine. I used different names such as Madhup or Shashi. From friends in college I obtained sketches and articles that I included.

The name of the magazine was *Shuklendu* (Rising Moon). Just as the moon grows steadily, I expressed the hope as editor that the magazine would grow. I wrote, "There are so many latent writers like these in the community who have not had the scope to give the light of their wisdom to society. *Shuklendu* will continue to bring these writers into the field of literature." Encouraging the newly educated, bringing the ignorant into the light, fostering the writing of students from the lowest classes to create a class of writers from them—this was the aim of the handwritten journal.

The issue was extremely attractive. On the background of a picture of Buddha, Tirpude had drawn Babasaheb Ambedkar's face in fine lines. Underneath that was a dedication to Babasaheb. Twenty-four writers appeared in that issue. Some poems, some short plays, quotations from great writers—all sorts of different things appeared in the issue. Theoretical articles were the greatest in number.

I mentioned in the editorial the activities that had been carried out by the Sitabardi Sports Club, formed in August 1953 after the work of the B.R.A. (Bhimrao Ramji Ambedkar) Club had languished. In those two and a half months we had taken around sixty old and young people from the community on a trip to the lovely surroundings of the Telankhedi pond area. We had also begun a program of distributing free milk to children in the community. In those days, 250-pound bags of milk powder came to India from UNESCO. We became one of the social service organizations distributing the milk. When we followed the recommended measure of one glass of powder to eight glasses of water, we observed that the children could not digest it. So we increased the proportion of water.

Among the articles in the handwritten journal one was especially splendid. Mrs. Sushila Gajbhiye, who was studying in the second year at Nagpur College, wrote an article called "The Epidemic" in which she unleashed a severe criticism in harsh language against the educated white-collar class of Untouchables who hide their caste and live separately from the rest of the community. I sent that article to *Janata* and got it published. The author didn't keep up her writing after this. However, this article is so realistic that it is applicable even today to Dalit social conditions.

I had one poem, three small verses, two light articles, a play–monologue, and one theoretical article included in the journal. A total of thirty-six selections appeared in the 134-page issue. Included were an English article by a high-level employed person and five Hindi articles by students. Among these five, two were written on Lord Buddha's concepts of compassion and nonattachment. In the Marathi section, Pundalik Sughate had written a very studied article on the Buddha's life. One of my essays, "When Will the Demon of Subcasteism Come to an End?" was written on current problems.

The happiness that comes from collecting writing from students to include in the magazine and writing much of it by hand, and then having the publication ceremony, is beyond the imagination of those who publish magazines today. On 7 November 1953 an audience seated on mats on the dark tiles of

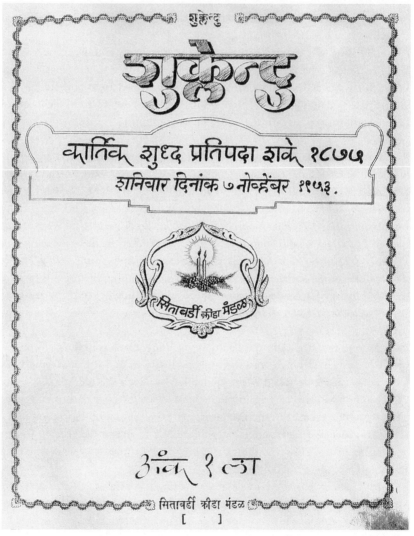

*Illustration for* Shuklendu, *the handwritten magazine created by Moon and others, dated November 1956. Copy courtesy of Vasant Moon.*

the Vitthal Temple Trust attended the inauguration of the magazine by a Brahman Marathi professor, A. N. Deshpande. It is important to mention here the comments made by Deshpande, because it is the understanding of many writers that Dalit literature begins only after 1960. The creation of literature is an ongoing process. Deshpande's interjection is so remarkable that it seems to tell the future story of Dalit literature, even though he used the despised word "Harijan." Deshpande wrote, "This issue is a pointer of awakening about the creation of literature for Harijan brothers and sisters. If our Harijan brothers study thoroughly high-quality literature in Marathi and other languages, and

*Ram Tirpude's drawing of the face of Dr. Ambedkar superimposed on the profile of the Buddha. Copy courtesy of Vasant Moon.*

express their joys and sorrows, their dilemmas, in truly living vibrant form in stories, novels, plays, essays, and other literature, then they can enrich Marathi literature."

Such lecture programs went on in one place or another throughout Nagpur's Dalit communities. Most Marathi professors came to lecture in our community on the occasion of Ambedkar *jayanti*. The temple trust committee delegated to me the work of bringing them. Every Sunday, Dr. Bhavani Shankar Niyogi and A. R. Kulkarni would deliver lectures on Buddhism on the top floor of Dhanvate Chambers. I would also from time to time invite some writer coming from Mumbai to the small hall of the temple trust committee. Around that time Professor S. J. Mate's lecture was held at Nagpur College. Mate was famous for his writing and speaking style. His ninety-minute lecture, filled with Marathi jokes, proved so effective that it remained in our memory for a long time.

I brought Mate for a lecture in the temple committee room. At that time his daughter, who was with him, also gave a speech on women's problems. "It should be kept in mind that the questions of dowry and spinsterhood that have been created in the Brahman community today will terrify the Dalit community also in the next fifty years," was the theme of her lecture. I made a report of this speech and sent it to the *Maharashtra* daily. At that time, it was the understanding of us youth that *Maharashtra* and *Tarun Bharat* were indifferent to the Dalit movement. Their tendency was never to publish Ambedkar's speeches but rather to give full publicity to the statements and actions of his Congress Harijan opponents. Even so, we sent them the news.

Two days later, when *Maharashtra* gave full publicity to this story, the people of the community felt it to be a miracle. Pralhad the barber and Pundalik Kavade of the neighborhood bought the most newspapers. They told us that the report in *Maharashtra* was also published eight days later in the *Navshakti* in Mumbai.

At that time Ram Tirpude was told to make a picture to give to Ambedkar as a present. Working night and day, Ram finished it. For three days I watched him labor. I had just received my scholarship money. It must have been around 301 rupees, but a frame was needed for the picture, so I contributed 25 rupees and immediately got the frame made. It was decided to give it to Babasaheb when he came to the temple trust committee room.

One day Wamanrao brought the news that Babasaheb was going to arrive around three that afternoon. The Scheduled Caste Federation activists prepared a garland for his welcome. The news had spread everywhere, and hundreds of people had crowded around the temple trust by two o'clock. It was afternoon, and the heat was somewhat fierce; even so, people were enthusiastic to see Babasaheb.

Around 3:30 Babasaheb showed up with his wife, Maisaheb, in a car. When the car reached the temple area and Babasaheb opened the door to get out, people began to push and shove. Some youth made a protective ring around him, but the crush of people reached him anyway. Babasaheb got angry at all the chaotic attention and told the driver to drive away. The old Ford returned with him to Mount Hotel.

The next morning all of us went to meet Babasaheb at the Mount Hotel. I took my handwritten magazine and Ram Tirpude took his picture. After waiting for some time on the veranda, Wamanrao took us inside. Babasaheb was sitting on a cane chair reading the *Times*. Maisaheb was sitting next to him on the left. Entering, Wamanrao went and sat at his feet. Some of us touched his feet, some only did *namaskar*. I did a *namaskar* and stood in front of him. There were not many chairs. Babasaheb was wearing a delicately textured Bengali shirt of white material and pajamas. I had seen him on several occasions before, but never had enjoyed the chance to see him so close.

Wamanrao introduced us, telling Babasaheb everyone's name. Then we gave Babasaheb the black-and-white portrait so lovingly done. Looking at it, he inquired about Ram. He gave Ram's picture to the local leaders, who mounted it in the office of the Scheduled Castes Federation. (Later, when the owner of the office filed a lawsuit claiming unpaid rent, the picture fell neglected in a pile of confiscated goods in the courtyard. Because of the insistence of some activists it was released and brought back.)

Everyone was quiet for a moment. Then I held the magazine up and gave it to Babasaheb. He read through the entire issue and asked, "Who wrote this article on the Buddha?"

"My friend Pundalik Sughate has written it. He's in my class," I said.

"What is going on regarding Buddhism?"

"In our community, we have begun a class on the Buddhist religion. Dr. Niyogi comes to explain Buddhism to us," I said. Babasaheb, giving me a glance, said, "Who? Dr. Niyogi? The one who was a high-court judge? Remember, he's also a Brahman." Maisaheb was sitting nearby listening. Then Babasaheb said, "At first those who accepted Buddhism were Brahmans. Still, later on it was the Brahmans who corrupted the basic principles of Buddhism; this should not be forgotten." I continued asking Babasaheb questions, and he went on talking to us as one teaches students. Of these questions, two remain clearly in my mind. I asked, "Babasaheb, Buddhism does not believe in the soul, but if this is so how can there be rebirth? Everyone asks us this question, yet I can't understand it."

"Listen, one candle can light another candle, can't it? Doesn't the spark go from one to another? Rebirth is the same way. Without being extinguished, the spark from the candle arises in another place, this is what is called rebirth. Look, no one dies, sees heavens, and then gets reborn."

At the time I could understand the explanation of Babasaheb only a little. Only after reading his *The Buddha and His Dhamma* could I understand his whole philosophy. I asked him a second question. "We have many old traditions among ourselves. The rituals of marriage are from earlier times. After accepting the Buddhist religion, are we going to have a new marriage ceremony?"

"Oh, whether you put a paper hat on your head or on your knees, does it make any difference? Yes, even so, for the common people, some rituals are necessary." Babasaheb was giving answers while skimming through the magazine. In those days there was no such thing as fear in my mind. Even before such a great man as Babasaheb I had no fear. Our friends mutely listened to my questions and Babasaheb's explanations. Babasaheb once again held up the pages of the magazine and asked, "Who has written this article?"

"That is my article," I said, and he saw that my name was written there. He was referring to "When Will the Demon of Subcasteism Come to an End?"

"Well, boys, what are you doing about that?" he pointedly asked everyone, and I answered, "Babasaheb, we don't respect subcastes in our Dal. People of all subcastes are in our organization."

After a long time we got the magazine back with Babasaheb's written comments: "Excellent. Well worthy of emulation." After this the magazine went from house to house for reading, then disappeared for years. It was only in 1992 that Ram Tirpude gave the issue back to me, and I found again the comment that had been like a tonic of encouragement to us all.

# Chapter 25

## THE VOWS OF RELIGION

After 1950 the winds of conversion began to blow. Around 1954 Babasaheb publicly proclaimed that the conversion ceremony would take place in Mumbai. Wamanrao Godbole and all of us had the strong desire that the honor should belong to Nagpur. Godbole's study of Buddhism was deep and detailed. He had brought a very important book from Mumbai titled *The Life of Buddha,* by E. J. Thomas. In the book a very minute analysis was written of the Buddha's *mahaparinirvan,* which completed the Buddha's final journey. A detailed description was given of where Lord Buddha went after leaving Vaishali. After that, at Kushinara, the Buddha's bodily death took place. There is a description of a shower of flowers on his body. Taking account of all the daily routine of that trip, the Buddhist scholar Fleet came to the conclusion that Buddha's death must have taken place in October. The types of flowers included in that shower bloom in September and October, and he narrowed the date down to October 13. Wamanrao obtained this information from E. J. Thomas's book.

Using this information for support, Wamanrao wrote a letter to Babasaheb Ambedkar that mentioned two things. He told Babasaheb, "There is no way of telling on what basis you chose Mumbai. It has no place in the history of Buddhism. If the choice had been made for one among the holy places of Buddhism, we would have had no objection. So you should reconsider your decision and chose Nagpur. There is a mention in one book of a tooth of the Buddha's being in Nagpur.

"The other point is that, though you haven't chosen the date, we feel that you should have the conversion on 14 October 1956."

In May of 1956, under the leadership of Wamanrao, the twenty-five hundredth birth anniversary of Buddha had been celebrated by the Madhya Pradesh government in a very big way. The Buddha's statue was carried in a large cart in procession. Elephants were brought in for the procession. Huge banners were floated, and the procession, accompanied by singing and playing, moved completely peacefully through the whole of Nagpur. Wamanrao organized the entire procession with the help of Bardi's Maharpura activists.

After Babasaheb agreed to hold the ceremony in Nagpur and fixed the date, Wamanrao rented a room on the ground floor of Kothari Mansion in the Vasant Talkies lane of Bardi and organized his office there. All the correspondence regarding the conversion ceremony was conducted from this room. The place selected by Wamanrao was a plot of fourteen acres near the Vaccine Institute at Shradhanand Peth, which has since been known as the Diksha Bhumi, place of conversion. During the planning I made a trip every Sunday from Saunsar, where I was employed at the time, and stayed in the conversion office. Wamanrao was drawing up the entire plan and implementing it himself. There was a group of youth from Bardi under his direction. The work of correspondence was given to a gentleman named Manik Domaji Panchbhai. Everyone tended to his assigned task with discipline. Because of his dedication, Panchbhai did not even see the arrangements set up at the Dikhsa Bhoomi until the very last day. The mixture of duty and loyalty was natural to Panchbhai.

It would be impossible to relate here all the events regarding conversion that took place, and I don't think it necessary to do so. I will only mention the events I had some connection with.

One day, when I inquired about Wamanrao at the office I learned that he had gone to Delhi. A telegram from Revaram Kavade had arrived from Delhi

*The Buddhist office of Wamanrao Godbole in Nagpur, 1964. The Buddhist flag flies above the entrance. Photo by Eleanor Zelliot.*

saying that Wamanrao should immediately meet with Babasaheb. The note also indicated that the conversion preparations should be stopped. As he left for Delhi, Wamanrao said that there was no necessity to stop the preparations; the work should be continued as before.

Wamanrao returned in two days. He told us the news of the events that had happened. When Wamanrao reached Delhi he first met with Kavade, who told him, "Babu Hardas Avale and Akant Mate have given their own place to Babasaheb. That means they are intending to change the site of the conversion ceremony." Wamanrao was silent. He couldn't believe that Babasaheb would be ready to change the place for such a reason and also without asking him.

When Babasaheb called Wamanrao to him, he first asked Avale to explain why the site should be changed.

"The place where conversion is to take place is surrounded by Sangh people," said Avale. He added, "Shri Mate of our community has five acres of land near our people's settlement in Joginagar and is ready to give this free of charge for the conversion ceremony."

"All right, what else?"

Avale was silent for a second, then he said, "Wamanrao held a *puja* of the place for the conversion ceremony. This *puja* was done at the hands of the Brahman Shri Bhavani Shankar Niyogi."

Babasaheb thundered, "What, is this true?"

Wamanrao immediately answered, "We did *puja* for the Diksha Bhumi but it was at the hands of one of our Buddhists. Shri Laxmanrao Kavade, who has just taken the vow of a *shramaner*, did a program of *bhumipuja*. Shri Niyogi came walking by. Out of curiosity he stopped to see and joined in the ceremony. There was no kind of *puja* at his hands."

"All right. What about the place?"

"We have made complete preparations. There is no other convenient place in Nagpur so spacious. It is a plot of fourteen acres. We have made complete arrangements for your protection."

"I am not at all worried about my life. All right, I'll tell you my decision later." Babasaheb sat calmly.

The evening of the same day Babasaheb went with Maisaheb for a car ride. The full fury of monsoons had begun. Suddenly, the driver lost control of the steering wheel and the car dashed against an electricity pole. Maisaheb grabbed Babasaheb just as he was going to be thrown out of the car. Babasaheb was troubled. He thought he had been saved from death. The moment he returned to the veranda, he asked, "Where is Waman?" When Wamanrao came forward, Babasaheb said, "Go; you should return to Nagpur. Where the arrangements have been made will be where the conversion ceremony is done. I have no more concern for my life."

The preparations for the conversion ceremony continued on a war footing. The Federation's activists, however, were displeased with Wamanrao. All the political leaders came together to demand a part in the work. A meeting took place with Wamanrao, and twenty-five to thirty different committees were established. Receipt books were given to the committees. Work responsibility was distributed. But in actuality the work was done by a few selected individuals.

On the ninth and tenth of October, 1956, at eight at night, about a hundred people gathered at that huge expanse of land in Shraddhanand Peth. This was wasteland, and a small jungle of thorny bushes had spread there. Our group began the work of tearing up those bushes by the light of a petromax. Youth from Sitabardi's Maharpura, Dharampeth, Colonel Park and nearby settlements took part in the activity. Along with Wamanrao, Prahlad Medhe, and others, I helped in the work of cleaning that rough field.

Babasaheb arrived from Delhi by airplane on the morning of the eleventh. He was put up in a first-floor room in a special hotel in Bardi. From his room to the outside entrance a guard of the Colonel Park Samata Sainik Dal in ordinary white clothes stood by for his protection. Pralhad Medhe was given leadership of these volunteers. But since the hotel was in front of our *vasti,* all of Maharpura kept a close watch on it.

I was running around night and day to help with the arrangements for the conversion. On all four nights, from the tenth to the thirteenth, I did not sleep. Various rumors were coming to our ears, even rumors of threats to Wamanrao's life. But we didn't pay much attention.

Two tasks of the conversion ceremony had been given to me. We all realized that hundreds of thousands of people would come for the conversion. Some political leaders thought that a fee of one rupee should be charged for entrance to the pavilion, and this suggestion was even brought to Babasaheb. However, Wamanrao silenced them with the question of whether we should ban those who had no money. Wamanrao had left twenty-five registers with me so that the names of those taking conversion should be written down. I was given the responsibility of getting the name, age, caste, and religion of those coming along, together with their signatures. I distributed this work among Dal activists positioned just inside every gate in the pavilion.

The second task was to oversee the organization of the entire surroundings. A full fence stood around the area, with big gates on all four sides. I took care that not a single tradesman's stall should be set up next to those gates. The tar road of Shraddhanand Peth went in front of the field. Permission was given to set up stalls on the other side of that. One shop owner of my acquaintance kept coming continuously for two days urging me to let him set up a stall beside the main gate. But I gave no response.

The conversion field was very rough. We had wanted the city government to complete such work as leveling it and preparing conveniences for water and toilets. Now we could see that this work was being done night and day by Sadanand Phuljhele, who was at that time the deputy mayor of Nagpur.

It is necessary to note one important event that took place on the day of the conversion ceremony, the *dhamma diksha*. We had been told that Babasaheb Ambedkar would come to the stage at nine A.M. I was looking after all the arrangements on the *diksha* field. I distributed boys from all branches of the Samata Sainik Dal among the people and went towards the stage. Cudgel-bearing volunteers appeared on all four sides of the stage. They had been sent there by one of the political leaders. However, we had decided that only the volunteers of Colonel Park who were in the service of Babasaheb at the Sham Hotel should be placed near the stage. Since I was the one who had selected the Colonel Park volunteers, I asked where they had gone, and then I saw them standing off to the side. I took aside the other volunteers who were near the stage and shifted them, telling them I was giving them duty someplace else, and gave the responsibility for the stage to Pralhad Medhe of Colonel Park and his volunteers.

My attention then went to the stage. There I saw steel folding chairs. Revaram Kavade was standing on the stage. I asked him, "Guruji, are these chairs for Babasaheb to sit on?"

"No, some big chairs are coming in the city government's truck. Sadanand Phuljhele is bringing them."

"Yes, but it's now a quarter to nine. When are they coming?"

"They must be coming now. Where else will chairs be found at the last moment?"

Saying, "All right, I'll see," I took a volunteer standing nearby with me. I went out of the field by the main gate and saw a house just at the side of the main road. The owner of the house was sitting on an easy chair on his veranda. I entered the compound and saluted him.

"Speak, what is it?" he said. I appealed to him to lend us the easy chairs. From his manner of speaking I felt he must be a Muslim. He said, "You can gladly take them! But don't forget to return them!"

Saying, "*Yaqinan!*" (All right!) I and the volunteer each lifted one chair to our heads. These old teak chairs were heavy. Still, carrying them on our heads, we went running and panting up to the stage. We put the chairs on the stage, and just at that moment Babasaheb entered the stage from the back. The whole surrounding area was filled with the thunder of "Long live Babasaheb Ambedkar!" Pandit Revaram Kavade said to me, "Who told you to do this?" I said, "I felt that Babasaheb could not sit on a steel folding chair."

Everyone was wary of some threat to Babasaheb's life during the conversion ceremony. We took the Buddhist conversion oaths while the program was going on; meanwhile we were attentive to all four sides. The stage from which Babasaheb gave the *diksha* measured about thirty by fifty feet. From the stage to about fifty feet in front was a compound of wooden planks, and beyond that a half circle of twenty feet in diameter was left empty, and beyond that were the arrangements for the seating of the people. Men were positioned to the right and women to the left of the stage. This distance had been decided keeping in mind the range of a pistol.

During the second day's program, before Babasaheb's speech was to begin, an old lady with a bundle tried to push through the crowd. With some suspicion we grabbed her. There might even have been a bomb in the bundle, we thought. She implored, "Oh let me see my Baba; I'm going to die now!" After examining her bundle we let her sit alone in the very front before the stage.

After performing the conversion, Babasaheb left by the way he had come in. This path was a secret road made so that no one could see Babasaheb's car between the stage and the entrance to the field from Ramdas Peth. We benefited from Wamanrao's resourcefulness about all matters.

Once Babasaheb came down from the stage, I myself returned the chairs of that Muslim. I was tired from top to toe after three days of sleeplessness.

*Dr. Ambedkar and Maisaheb Ambedkar holding an image of the Buddha at the time of the conversion in Nagpur, 14 October 1956. The face behind them is that of Yashwant Ambedkar, his only surviving son. The teak chair so important in Moon's memory can be partially seen. Photo courtesy of Vasant Moon.*

The Buddhist stupa built on the Diksha Bhumi, the grounds where Ambedkar's 1956 Buddhist conversion took place. The model for the stupa is at Sanchi, the Buddhist site visited by Moon as a youth. Photo by Eleanor Zelliot, 1999.

Hirekhan Master's house was close by. I went to a room there and fell on the ground. I hardly knew when sleep came.

When I awoke the dark of night had spread. Then I ate.

I remember one special thing about Babasaheb's *diksha*. He had written the twenty-two vows in his own hand, writing each vow in large letters on a separate piece of paper. Without putting on his glasses, Babasaheb read out these vows. We felt that probably Babasaheb must have wanted to take the *dhamma diksha* without glasses of any color, that is without preconceptions.

At the time of the conversion ceremony Babasaheb had to use a cane. When Babasaheb asked for a cane, a bundle of canes was brought from a shop. From those he chose a splendid eight-noduled cane, so we heard.

When the Bardi group returned home, only one subject of discussion came up in the entire neighborhood. Everyone was whispering, "Who did it? Who did it?" When I asked, "Did what?" someone said, "All the idols in our Vitthal-Rukmini temple have disappeared."

We had thought that this would happen. Everyone knew whose work this was. Wamanrao's brother Premchandra Godbole, who was very daring, had taken away those idols in the middle of the night with one or two companions. However it was not possible for Narayan Watchman to forget his duty. He made a report to the police station. Who knows how he learned it, or whether it was simply a guess, but he said to search in the well near the temple. The idols were found there. They were once again set in the inner room of the temple.

Three or four months after the program I went once more to see the conversion grounds. The whole area had fallen desolate. But I still remembered the white-clothed mass of people, and I remembered all at once how I had to look for that chair, which was purified by the hand of Babasaheb taking *dhamma diksha*. It is a historical chair. I went to the bungalow near the conversion grounds, and when I inquired, was told, "The man who used to live here has gone to Madhya Pradesh."

"Do you have his address?"

"No. We don't know anything."

I returned home in a morose mood.

# Chapter 26

## FALLING STAR

I took up various jobs after matric. For a while I worked in the office of the Deputy Accountant General, Post and Telegraph. In that office worked a deputy accountant named Chari who was very sympathetic to Untouchable boys. He allowed Untouchable employees to carry on their education while employed there. Mahar boys were very dogged about education. They would show up at work, finish the day's tasks in a short time, hang their coats on a chair, and go to the college to register their attendance. Many Mahar boys who worked there studied for higher education and graduated while holding down a job.

I must have worked there for about ten months. Other employees cut work to attend classes. I didn't need to do so for my law studies. It was not difficult to attend the law class until nine in the morning and then take care of my job. But my intention was to obtain an M.A. in Marathi, and that class met in the afternoon. I decided it was necessary to get permission from the office to attend afternoon classes, and I filed an application. But who would give anyone permission to be free of work? The application was rejected. Mother's pay from the mill was only so-so, but I earned at least 110 rupees a month from my job, so our economic situation at home had become a little more stable. However, the idea of getting an M.A. would not leave my mind. If I resigned my job to continue my studies, then Mother would have to continue bearing the burden of mill work. When I asked her, she said, "Do what you think is best. As long as I have my hands and feet there's no anxiety." I experienced a great deal of mental tension in making a definite decision. Finally, giving a month's notice, I left my job and applied to the college to complete an M.A. in Marathi.

Around that time, an advertisement appeared for a position as deputy county commissioner. On the very the last day for filing the application, Pundalik Sunghate helped me get my form filled out, and we took it to the public-service commission. I was called in for an interview and ultimately selected.

The position of deputy county commissioner was considered a very important one among the "executive" officials. The question of M.A. versus employment still loomed in my mind; however, the wise people in the community told me, "This is an important position; you go immediately." I didn't have the slightest idea of what a deputy county commissioner was or what to do about it. Sadubhau, a friend whose older brother held a position as county commissioner, came to my house and gave me detailed information about the position. He selected a "hold-all" bag—a briefcase—for me to carry. He told me to get a coat, shoes, and hat so that I could look like a "saheb." The old people in the community said, "Don't even take tea in Brahmans' houses. Bageshwar Commissioner was put in danger by doing that."

Saunsar, where I had been assigned, was a town in the Chhindwara district next to Nagpur. I knew no one there. I departed from Nagpur on 23 April 1955 at 7:30 in the morning. I reached the bus stop around ten o'clock. Sadubhau had suggested that I shouldn't carry my own baggage. A porter took my hold-all and household goods on his head and I left for the Government Rest House. The bus stand was near the county office. As I met journalists, lawyers, and the like going to their offices, I had an experience that I had never had before. Seeing me with coat and hat and thinking that some new saheb had arrived, many people bowed to greet me. I was twenty-three years old. It was my first time wearing a hat and coat. Even elderly people greeted me with deference. I liked it very much. I was enjoying the new experience of "sahebness."

Just before the conversion ceremony, I was transferred to Pusad in the Yeotmal district. Because of the reorganization of states on a linguistic basis, Marathi-speakers were all transferred from their posts in Madhya Pradesh to the Marathi-speaking areas of Bombay.

While I was in Pusad, fifty-three days after the fourteenth of October, the date of the conversion ceremony, Babasaheb passed away. On the seventh of December, at 1:30 in the afternoon, I left the county office. About a hundred yards ahead was the government residence of Range Forest Officer Uddhavrao Sant. I always went there to chat with him. Sant was related to my mother. His older brother, Janardhan Sant, was an activist of the Dalit Student Federation and had established a boys' hostel at Chandrapur. With all this background he was good company for discussion. Before I reached Sant's house, Mohol Guruji came searching for me on the road. He could hardly utter a word. With a huge effort he said, "Saheb, have you heard?"

"What?"

"Very bad news. It is said that the radio has reported that Babasaheb has expired."

"No!" I couldn't believe my ears.

We went to the house of Nanasaheb Wankhede, the retired deputy county commissioner. (One of his sons, Dr. M. N. Wankhede, later became the president of the Maharashtra Public Service Commission.) Nanasaheb was an extremely warm person, but he lived completely apart from the community. He didn't care to mix with me even as a deputy commissioner. Looking at my bookcase one day he said, "Moonsaheb, don't you value your employment?"

"Yes, why?" I asked.

"Then what is this? Why do you keep books about Babasaheb, Buddhism, and all that? And aren't you always talking about these topics? One day the CID [Central Intelligence Department] people will swoop down on you, and all these books will be confiscated."

Because I was new in employment I thought that even officials might be banned from keeping such books. I had read that when revolutionaries' houses were searched, books were the first things confiscated. So I wrote the name of my cousin in each of the two hundred or so books I owned. With all this, I felt stifled by the atmosphere in Pusad.

However, when I told Nanasaheb the news of Babasaheb's death, he broke into tears. We sat talking for some time. By this time the news had spread through town. People crowded before Vishwasrao Kamble's house, and women came wailing out of their houses.

I returned to the office and wrote out a petition for leave. In it I stated, "I have just learned the news of the death of Dr. Babasaheb Ambedkar. I feel many times the sorrow I felt at the death of my father. I want to go to his funeral procession in Mumbai. So please approve the leave." The leave was approved.

Most of the trains to Mumbai departed from Malkapur. I saw people sitting on the roof of every train. The Vidarbha Express arrived around dawn. Pushing through the crowd, somehow or another I entered and left for the first trip in my life to Mumbai.

There was no such thing as sleep on this journey. Passengers were boarding at every station. I saw no one I knew. We reached Igatpuri on the afternoon of the second day. I didn't know what time in the evening the train reached Dadar in Mumbai. But at that moment, a gentleman came and sat by my side. He asked my name, and said, "I'm a ticket collector at Mumbai. I have just finished my duties. My name is Nirbhavane." The news of Babasaheb's death had spread grief everywhere; men and women in every settlement were wailing and lamenting, so Nirbhavane told me. No hearth had been lit for cooking in any house. After our acquaintance had grown to familiarity, when I told Nirbhavane, "I am coming for the first time to Mumbai; I don't know where to stay," he urged me to come to his house on Naigaon Cross Road.

That night we reached his home at nine or ten. After taking a little dinner we came to the cremation ground at Dadar to find only the funeral pyre burning. Most people had left. We paid our respects and returned to his home. Earlier in the year, hundreds of people had come from Mumbai for the *diksha* ceremony in Nagpur, and facilities and food had sprung up throughout the city. This time similar arrangements were made in all the Buddhist communities of Mumbai for those who had come from outside.

I spent three or four days with Nirbhavane in Mumbai. Bimal Roy's film *The Buddha* was showing at the Metro. It was a good film, but I felt that by showing Gandhiji's picture at the end, it could not achieve real artistry.

As we moved about among various bands of people, we heard everywhere that Babasaheb's death was not natural; he had been murdered. Mindhe Patil was publishing an eight-page paper, titled *Marhata*. The paper contained sensational news about an attempt at poisoning Babasaheb, how his beloved dog was killed, and the like. People flocked to read it. Mainly, though, people were very enthusiastic about the editorials in Acharya Atre's *Maratha,* a highly respected Mumbai newspaper. Atre paid his respects to Ambedkar with a thirteen-day series of articles.

People described to us the gathering before the funeral pyre of Babasaheb. The mass of people was so huge that the boundary between people and the sea had nearly vanished. When the words "Baba has gone" fell from Acharya Atre's mouth, the whole mass erupted. For some minutes only crying could be heard everywhere.

I attended gatherings on the morning and evening of the third day. In the evening meeting, memorial speeches were delivered. At that event, Acharya Atre's powerful speaking fell so strongly on the minds of the listeners that for some time they forgot their sorrow and merged their grief into a sea of laughter. Even when sorrowing, Atre could make humorous remarks.

I met Wamanrao Godbole on the fourth day. He was involved in an effort to obtain Babasaheb's ashes. We decided to return to Nagpur together. Within one or two days we caught the train back. There were many people on the train. In the carriage, the urn with the ashes had been placed to one side. When I told Godbole I had been able to get Dhananjay's Keer's biography of Ambedkar in Mumbai, he took the photos out of the book and placed them on the urn as a death offering.

The news that Babasaheb's ashes were on the train traveled before us. At every station hundreds of people crowded to see the urn. The sight of people crying uncontrollably was enough to move the heart. Thousands of people had thronged to see the urn at Nagpur, and when we emerged from the train, carrying it with us, a wild shout of lamentation came from this mass of people.

The chanting of Buddhist texts by the son of Manik Panchbhai (referred to in chapter 25) in a Nagpur vihar in 1975. Photo by Eleanor Zelliot.

During the trip I stored all of the sights calmly in my mind. While viewing the funeral pyre in Mumbai I maintained a calm and cool manner, keeping the words of the Buddha fixed in my mind: "This body will be destroyed; death is inevitable." However, hearing the cry from the masses in Nagpur, my heart trembled. Without my being aware of it, tears began to fall from my eyes, and I began to cry along with everyone else.

In the evening, a huge procession left from the Indora area. Winding through the whole of Nagpur it dispersed at the conversion ground. The procession had begun as the sun was sinking into the west. Everyone held candles. In ranks of four and as disciplined as soldiers, thousands of people walked one after another. Small children, women and men, old people, everyone went along in that procession without shouting slogans and with peaceful minds.

Only one day before, the people in the procession might have felt a little fear while going past settlements of Hindus, but that day they moved ahead fearlessly, as if with a torch in their hands and with the solemn chant of "*Buddham saranam gacchami;* I go for protection to the Buddha." The Nagpurites were trying to extinguish the fire of sorrow.

I returned to my duties at Pusad and wrote an article from my notes. It was called "Baba and Death," and was published by Dharamdash Meshram, the editor of *Yeotmal Lokmat*. The tears and upsurge of feeling I saw were given expression in this small booklet.

# Chapter 27

## TYING THE KNOT

After I entered the working world it was natural that everyone would start thinking of marriage for me. However, I didn't give my consent to any match. I wanted a girl who had studied at least up to matric. But in those days the number of such girls was minuscule. If a girl was nice to look at, her marriage was arranged when she was in seventh or eighth grade. I had made one firm decision. In 1954 Babasaheb had asked, "Who has written this article about the burning away of subcasteism?" I had said, "In our Dal we don't observe subcastes." I determined that at least I would marry outside the subcaste.

In 1956, as a result of the conversion, even uneducated men and women started saying that there should be nothing wrong with giving their daughters in marriage outside the subcaste. Once the time came, though, the educated boys and their parents would back down.

In the Mahar community, going to see the girl was a ceremony. Generally the expectation was that the girl should be nice to look at, modest, and blameless in character. However, one more accomplishment was expected. Many families continued to ask that she be able to make *mandes*. If *mandes* were served at the introduction event, then the girl was considered excellent.

Making *mandes*, a very thin chapati, is an art of cooking in the Mahar community that is dying away. This kind of bread is made on an overturned, heated earthen pot. Men in the community might or might not drink liquor, but they always delivered a hard beating to their wives. While kneading the dough for the *mandes*, women would take out their grievances on their husbands by pounding the dough. In a full pan of flour, the dough is prepared like sweet coagulated milk, not too thick, not too thin. Then the dough is formed into a ball, taken in both hands, lifted up as high as the head, and slammed down hard on the pan. Again and again a little water is worked into the dough and it is slammed down. As the particles of dough come together, the bubbles in it express the anger of the dough by popping out noisily. To see if the kneaded dough is truly ready, a small chapati is thrown on the griddle. If a proper dough has not been made, it will break in the hand. If there is too much or too little salt, the consistency of the dough will not be right. Only if the consistency is proper will a nearly transparent chapati, like the thin paper of a kite, result. Not just any wheat will do. You must use a certain *howra* wheat. And care must be taken that the flame of the fire is neither too high nor too low. If a little oil is smeared on the hands, then the dough will not stick. A small ball of dough is taken in the hand, the left hand is wiped on the right wrist, and the dough is thrown on the pot with the right hand in such a way that this small piece covers half the pot. By the time it is cooked a second ball is ready in the hand. You might be served "handkerchief chapatis" in hotels, but they don't have the taste of these thin chapatis or *mandes*.

The girl's mother would think it fortunate if the guests who had come to see her daughter could see such *mandes*. Along with the *mandes*, of course, mutton or chicken was necessary. It should be spicy enough so that the guests gasped for breath when they soaked a piece of *mande* in the gravy and ate it. If village mangos were available, then the sweet, thin juice of mangoes was served with these thin chapatis. The dexterity of making such *mandes* was taught by mother to daughter as a tradition. New daughters-in-law were not eager to learn these old arts, since they were so laborious. One had to sit for hours in front of the fire. But many women thought it a blessing to sit in the Nagpur heat in the evenings on the back verandas and make and serve hot *mandes*. Then the father of the girl would say to the guests, "Tell me, is my daughter's cooking good or isn't it? The *mandes* are made by her own hand. Our Lakshmi has trained her completely."

*Mandes* were a traditional art of Mahars. Around 1938 the freedom fighter Savarkar came to Nagpur. People decided to make a mutton dinner for him. The arrangements were made in the Bhide Girls' School. It was difficult to find anyone outside of Maharpura to cook for so many people, so it was the Mahar women of our community who made mutton for Savarkar. Whenever Dr. Babasaheb Ambedkar came to Nagpur he would eat mutton and *mandes*. Once, in 1930, Babasaheb called Yogesh Varade's mother, Sagunabai, and told her, holding out the *mandes*, "Through these almost transparent *mandes* your face can be seen. Such a beautiful art is in your hands." He himself gave her money to buy material for a blouse (a traditional gift of respect for women). Many of the women who served Savarkar and Ambedkar dinner would tell of these memories.

One day Bhanudas Varade of our Dal said to me, "Why are you looking to others to find a wife? There's a girl near my house."

I said, "Where?"

He said, "Come on, I'll show you."

We went on cycles to the community at Khalami Line. There, Madhavrao Sontakke, from Dhantoli, lived in a rented house. He worked as supervisor in the office of the deputy accountant general of post and telegraph. He was of a calm mentality and guileless nature. We reached his house around three in the afternoon. No one was home at the time except his daughter Meenakshi. Since she had a little fever she came out with swollen eyes and disheveled hair. Bhanudas Varade was her brother-in-law. Saying, "Come in, sit down," she brought a chair forward. I sat formally on a chair but suddenly fell when the legs broke. Even so, the pair of us stayed for a while and left after inquiring about Meenakshi's mother and father.

After that, Varade did the work of carrying messages. Meenakshi's father, Madhavrao, approved the match. I sent my agreement. The engagement ceremony was planned. Just then some muttering came to my ear. Sontakke was not of my subcaste. Because of that, some of his relatives didn't like this engagement. One of my classmates showed him another match and said, "Look, Mamaji, aren't there boys in our caste? The boys that we are bringing are not inferior! This one is employed and he's suitable for your daughter." Madhavrao had no concern for caste and subcaste. He said, "Everyone likes this Moon boy. We have given our consent. There will be no change."

I had no faith in the matching of horoscopes to see if a couple was well suited. And due to the firm decision of Madhavrao, the schemes of his relatives fell apart. I did not have many relatives to invite. Since I was deciding everything myself, there was no question of anyone negotiating on my behalf. The two of us decided how to reduce wedding costs, and these expenses were divided. The date of the wedding was fixed according to the time I could get leave.

Our wedding was held in the afternoon of 14 May 1958, at Bhagani Mandal in Nagpur. In the Vidarbha Mahar community no custom existed of a dowry or of an exchange of money. Madhavrao was said to be progressive by the standards of those days. Though he would impose discipline on the girls in the house, after the engagement, he permitted us the opportunity for discussion together. I asked Meenakshi, "Will any jewelry be necessary?" The husband traditionally gave jewelry to the bride.

She said, "You should do what was done for my big sister." Her big sister was Dr. Namdevrao Nimgade's wife. He was studying in America for a Ph.D. in "soil science," and the whole family lived there.

I said, "What exactly does that mean?"

She said, "A total of four bangles, a *mangalsutra* [wedding necklace], and earrings, and shawls and saris as usual."

At that time gold cost 21 rupees per tola. Including four bangles at three tolas each, a two-tola *mangalsutra,* and the earrings, the expense for jewelry must have amounted to seven or eight hundred rupees. Both parties were sharing the expenses of the wedding, which, including jewelry, came to about twenty-five hundred rupees, of which I would have to bear half. From my wife's family I received a white coat and rings weighing five grams total. Previously there had been a movement in the community not to spend over fifty rupees on a weddings, but as prices rose expenses rose. We had about three thousand people for dinner. All the cooking was done by our relatives, women and men. The boys of the community did the serving.

However, my bankbook showed that I had saved only about five hundred rupees. At that time I was deputy county commissioner in Darvha of the Yeotmal district. There, a rich Muslim landlord named Mahmad Khan was my friend. I borrowed five hundred rupees from him, which proved very helpful.

After marriage, no change took place in my habits. Expenses continued; work also continued. Meenakshi slowly became adjusted to my nature. Though she had had no experience in social work previously, she understood my concerns, and one day she took up writing, and has continued ever since. She works night and day at stories, articles, and poems. Now she single-handedly edits and publishes a women's magazine in Marathi called *Maitrani,* or Womanfriend. Her determination and hard work and progress are surprising. During Mother's bad health she and the children cared for her night and day. This trait of helpfulness has spread among all the children.

*Wedding photograph of Vasant and Meenakshi Moon. Photo courtesy of Vasant Moon.*

*The oldest daughter of the Moons, Anjali Salve, and her son, the Moon's first grandchild, who is now in medical school. Photo by Eleanor Zelliot.*

Three of my daughters—Anjali, Bharati, and Arati—were married, respectively, to Dr. Chandrakant Salve, Dr. Prakash Vakode, and Dr. Anant Sokal. My daughter Dr. Sushma married Praful and opened a clinic at Amraoti, and my son, Milind, who works in a bank, started married life with Ujwala Davare. That all my children and sons-in-law are Ambedkarite loyalists with feeling for the community and its movements brings me more than a little satisfaction. They were taught the life-giving essence of Buddhism from childhood.

After the Buddhist conversion ceremony, Hindu wedding rituals were rejected. People decided not to take anything from the old wedding ceremony. The new festivities had not yet been decided, but even then the new converts threw away their old customs and rituals along with the idols of gods and goddesses, just as worn-out clothes are thrown away. They performed wedding ceremonies by chanting the three refuges (*trisharana*) and the five principles (*panchshila*) and the Buddha's *puja* as found in Babasaheb's book, *The Buddha and His Dhamma*.

One day Wamanrao Godbole's youngest sister's wedding was decided. The groom was a deputy county commissioner, Lalchand Wasnik, from our circle of friends. When the wedding party came from Gondiya, the people of Maharpura went to welcome it. There they saw the groom completely decked out in the old style, with a dagger in his hand, a yellow paper crown with tassels on his head, daubed with yellow turmeric, and a bracelet of yellow cloth on his wrists. The Mahapura youth tried to explain Buddhist principles and told him to take off the ornaments. However, the husband and his relatives considered themselves "Harijans." They were not ready to listen. They continued ahead as they were. By the time they had reached the stage in the tent, many attempts had been made to convince them. This brought up a question about Wamanrao Godbole, the same one who had arranged the conversion ceremony! Wamanrao was a man of principle. On one hand was the future of his sister, and on the other the issue of following principle. Finally the husband's yellow crown was snatched off his head and thrown away. The Bardi folk had upheld Wamanrao's honor. This became a subject of discussion throughout Nagpur.

People in official positions used to balk even about putting up Ambedkar's photo. Considering the times, it is no wonder that my wedding, the first major wedding on a Buddhist basis and joining two people from different subcastes, became a subject for admiration.

Truly, I entered the second stage of my life after conversion.

# Chapter 28

## THE SPINNING TOP

When I began work in 1953 as deputy county commissioner at Sausar in Madhya Pradesh, Mother was working in the folding department at Model Mill. Three to four months after getting employment I said to her, "You can leave your job." However, she didn't quit then.

Then the mill workers, including Mother, went on strike. Vasantrao Sathe was the mill workers' leader in Nagpur. While the strike was going on, Mother bundled up some things, came to Sausar, and said to me, "Now you have a job. What need is there for me to work?" After the strike finished she went to the mill to collect her back pay. However, she didn't get very much money. She had no regrets about leaving work.

Mother now began a life of ease. At first she herself cooked and served the meals. She wouldn't allow the household employees to meddle in the cooking. She didn't keep a maidservant to wash clothes or dishes. She felt happy doing this work herself. Then, after we had children, her time was spent playing with her grandchildren. I was transferred from time to time. Because of that, my daughters stayed with her in the house I had built in Nagpur.

Her time was spent taking care of the house in Nagpur. She would sit for the whole day at the front door. Sometimes she went out to visit relatives, but she never stayed anywhere for long. On the other hand, many relatives would come to see her.

One day she began to feel very shaky. Her chest began to hurt. She went outside. There was a medical college about a hundred yards from the house. It was evening. She walked alone towards the clinic. On the way she saw a nurse and said, "Lady, help me to the clinic." The nurse led her to the outpatient ward. There she asked for Dr. Kishore Bhatkar.

That nurse gave her a lot of help. Then Dr. Kishore came. Kishore and his friends always used to come to our house, so Mother knew everyone's name.

The doctor examined her and admitted her. He said that she had suffered a heart attack. This was around 1980.

After she got better we brought her to Mumbai, where we lived, where she underwent a detailed examination. The cardiologist said, "The heart has been damaged. If she lives one or two years she will be lucky." There was no complicating disease such as diabetes or high blood pressure. Her seventieth year had begun.

She became absorbed in my children. She forgot her illness. Slowly her health began to improve. However, with her age her sight went dim. One eye was operated on. She began to see a little and started watching TV. However this eye also began to go dark. Even then she could not sit quietly. She went on telling the maid where to put what, how to keep things. She always kept a minute watch on the household. If my wife was out of town, Mother herself would cook and serve. However, soon she began to say, "Oh, Bapu, I can't see very well."

"Then why are you doing the cooking?"

She would laugh and say, "If I can't leave it alone, then what can I do about that?"

From time to time she recited the poems she had learned in school. She would tell the story of the fox and crow:

> I saw a crow sitting on a tree
> With a piece of bread in his mouth.
> Then the fox came and said,
> "Oh crow, sing me a song,
> My heart will be at peace because of your song."

Then she would give a lively description of how the crow sings and how the bread drops out of its mouth and falls to the ground, and the grandchildren would be delighted.

However, she had one favorite song that she always hummed:

> Once there was a crow, so, so black.
> The crow says, "I'm black, but this heron appears so pure white,"
> Then he thought and quickly bought a penny's worth of soap....

The crow tries to become white like the heron, but he is unable to. Instead, by scrubbing and scrubbing his body, he bleeds to death. I always wondered why this particular poem should remain constantly on Mother's mind. Its meaning seems to be that no matter what attempts are made by those who are low by birth, they cannot become high; suppose that *was* its meaning? It was better that Mother did not understand this symbolism.

I had never seen Mother do any *puja*. She never fasted. If anyone was fasting, she would say, "What is in that fast? How many days have we spent in fasting? Now I won't do any fasting, Baba. Enough. If we remain pure it's enough. There's no need for fasting."

During my school days I roamed around all the time and would fail the three-month and six-month exams. Mother would get worried. I would pass only the yearly examination. When examination day came close, Mother would say, "Oh, Bapu, go fall at Maruti's feet." There was a temple of Maruti on the Sitabardi hill. I would go there, take *darshan* and return. Every once in a while I would ask Mother, "If I don't study, will Maruti see that I pass?" "Oh, of course you have to study. That is understood." I would go to the temple to satisfy Mother. I stopped that practice only in college.

Mother never went to any temple. In the morning on occasion she would do a *namaskar* to the sun. So that there would be a sweet atmosphere in the house, she lit incense.

After the conversion, while we were still in Nagpur, she bought a small framed picture of the Buddha and began to do *puja* before that. One day I lifted up the picture and looked at it. Beneath it was Babasaheb's book *Buddha Puja Path*. I asked Mother, "Where did you get this book?"

"Some boys were selling it. They gave it to me. I've memorized all of it." I felt it a wonder. That evening she recited the whole of the *trisharan* and *panchshila*. She would do *puja* of the book along with Buddha's picture. Her faith could be seen in the drops of wax from the candle that fell on the book.

One day I returned from town. Mother was sitting in the door of the house. After changing my clothes, I went out to the toilet in back. When I went through the kitchen, I could see all her *puja* material. My attention went to the Buddha's picture and I was suddenly struck by surprise. Next to the Buddha's photo was a small picture of Sai Baba.

I went closer and picked up Sai Baba's picture. My mother was watching. I asked, "How did this picture get here?"

"Oh, Bapu, I went to the market. The women with me each bought a picture. So I said, why not get one too? I bought it and brought it here."

I thought for a little while. Should I hurt Mother's feelings? Would she be upset? Then I made a sudden decision. Facing us there was a tiled house. I hurled the picture of Sai Baba at that house. I said, "You know, in this house we don't do any *puja* besides the Buddha's. Not to Sai Baba or Gajanan Maharaj or whoever."

She said, "It's a good thing you threw it away. I won't bring one home again." After that, she never bought any photo or idol. She never even put up the picture of Lakshmi she used to put up at Diwali.

When I was in college and my sister Malti came of age, Mother began to think about her marriage. There was a possible match in Katol. Calling guests to the house, Mother fixed a date for the engagement according to an auspicious time. At that time the wedding itself was fixed. The boy was a clerk in the post office. Though my sister had only studied to third in school, she was fair to look at and her eyes and nose were good.

While the wedding was being decided, Mother had not even thought about my exams. The date for the wedding was fixed on the advice of the groom's father. The whole wedding ceremony was scheduled at exactly the time of examinations. I sat for the B.A. exam while trying to manage this. The final result was what might have been expected: I failed the B.A. exam. But the seven-hundred–rupee scholarship I had gotten that year from the Indian government helped to pay for my little sister Malti's marriage in the courtyard in front of the temple.

The son-in-law Sopanrao's father and mother were extremely loving and of a religious nature. They did not eat meat. Mother had done her duty in seeing that her daughter got a good household.

After we moved to Mumbai, Mother kept herself continuously active. Many people came to the house. They made inquiries. When we went out we had no worries about the house. Whoever came, she would open the door a bit and ask, "Who is it?" After she recognized someone, she would open the door completely. "Saheb is not at home. What shall I tell him when he comes?" Giving the guest water, she would send him on his way. If I was home, when anyone came and Meenakshi was not there, she would watch quietly. After a little time she would ask, "Should I make tea?" Anyone who came would be treated as an honored guest. If someone came searching for me and wanted to wait a little while, she would invite him to sit down. Such people were usually acquaintances. Seating them on the sofa, she would converse about who was doing what and the like. Until they left, she would keep a close watch. If anyone put a hand on the books left open all over the house she would say, "These are used for work. Please look at them after Saheb comes." She was uneducated—but cultured. She understood the importance of paper. If a postman brought a registered parcel to the door and said, "Mother, give your thumb mark here," she would say, "Give me a pen, I will sign." Then she would sign "Purnabai." She at one time had been able to read the newspaper, but later her reading and even her writing of the letters in her name stopped, because she could no longer see.

By now she was around eighty. Once in a while her legs would swell. Her chest would hurt. If she felt a little extra pain, she would ask for medicine to ease the pain. My son-in-law Dr. Salve, who lived in Ulhasnagar, would visit from time to time on Sunday. He would give Mother a tonic or some pills, which made her feel sleepy.

One night she screamed loudly. We ran to her room and turned on the light. She was frightened. "Four people came to kill me." I realized that her mental balance was worsening. We stayed awake the whole night. Following Dr. Salve's advice she underwent a complete checkup and began to eat less sugar and salt. But until the end of her life, she was not satisfied unless she had plenty of salt and sugar.

One night she said that she felt many lumps in her chest. I was not at home. My daughter Sushma had become a doctor. Meenakshi and Sushma together took Mother to a private hospital. Four days later she had to be moved to Sion Hospital.

Meenakshi and Dr. Sushma went night and day to Sion. All her grandchildren and their spouses began to worry. The lumps in her chest looked life-threatening. Even if she lived, it was clear that she would remain crippled and be continuously troubled. Mother realized this and said, "Bapu, now I won't live. Only, why does it hurt so much?"

I told the doctor, "Mother's death is inevitable. She is older than eighty. She also does not want to live. Simply lessen the pain. Let her die happily."

Various kinds of machines were applied. My son Milind and his friends donated the required blood. However, one after another her limbs slowly became useless. Her nails became white. Then her kidney, her heart, and finally her brain failed. On 19 January 1992, at the stroke of midnight, her breath stopped.

By the time we brought her body to the house, all the relatives had arrived. They each had memories of her love, her hospitality. When we conducted the ceremony in the Sion cremation grounds, all eyes were shedding tears.

Mother always sang one song to me, in her thin voice:

> How the top spins buzzing,
> Who knows how it goes without stopping.

I had no idea as a youngster that some philosophy lay hidden in the spinning of the top. Life, like the top, is in motion. It never stops. Mother's journey had stopped; her body had been absorbed in the unending. However, Mother had given motion to others. She had given a spin to the top, but she did not hold it caged.

Today, if you enter our house, it is as if her invisible form is breathing nearby. Everywhere is the fragrance of her movement. If there is a clatter in the kitchen you feel you should say, "Mother, why are you taking so much

*Eleanor Zelliot with Vasant Moon's Mother, Purnabai, in 1975. Photo by Vasant Moon.*

trouble?" I remember her saying while giving money to the wanderers who came to the door, "Bapu, if water does not stay in the river, why should money remain in our hands?"

Mother saw her son's and daughter's weddings. She arranged her granddaughters' marriages. She saw her great grandsons born. She felt pride in seeing her son as a saheb. She lived a life of contentment, and then she slept.

Oh, friends. This was the second turning point in my life after conversion. Mother's life had been one with our *vasti,* our neighborhood in Nagpur, and with her death, the *vasti* let go of me.

# Chapter 29

## SUMMING UP

Friends, such was the *vasti*.

Here I came into being and grew, from small to big. This community gave me food and gave me the store of experience with which I have made my life's journey. I have been going to back to Nagpur every one or two months since I left. I can never refrain from taking a *darshan* of the *vasti*.

In this autobiography of mine Gangya is present, Balya is present, Pandya is there, Janya is there. You will find such a group in any community. Our community was a reflection of the public life of Nagpur. The Ambedkarite movement existed in every neighborhood. Mill workers, *bidi* rollers, laborers, barbers, wrestlers and trainers, singers and balladeers, hymn-singing Varkaris and chanting Kabirpanthi mendicants, library managers and magazine makers, feast organizers and play producers—all these various types were found in the Nagpuri life of those days. All were merged in the Ambedkarite movement just as all rivers merge into the sea.

The sweet tonic of that community's public activities fed me, nourished the life of social consciousness. Youth like me who left still continued to work, somewhere or another, in every field. This community gave birth to Radhabai Kamble, the first woman workers' leader. It gave us fiery young political leaders like Jogendra Kavade. It gave us founders of BAMCEF, like Devidas Khaparde. Vishwanath Hirekar, who went to England and placed the sorrow of the society before the public, was from here, and so was Yogesh Varhade, who sincerely proclaimed the Dalit question beyond the boundaries of the nation even after becoming established in Canada. The General Secretary of the All-India Samata Sainik Dal, R. R. Patil, became a matric here, and loyal spiritual soldiers like Wamanrao Godbole, who carried out the responsibility of the Dhamma Diksha program to fulfill Babasaheb Ambedkar's desire for conversion, were also of this community.

Friends, such was the *vasti*, small, settled in a quadrangle. Today if you go to the Maharpura of Sitabardi you will not be able to meet the old men or see the earthen houses. Everything has changed. The name of Maharpura has been changed to Anandnagar, "Happy City." Concrete houses have been built everywhere. The surrounding fields have vanished. Where there were *shembda, shindori, nagphani, chincha,* and *chichabilai* trees there is now a cement jungle. The old men have gone and a new generation has come. There are no elders in the community who have to be listened to. Nobody listens to anyone. The community has not remained a community, so everyone says.

Even so I remember it from time to time. I should again become small and go live in some small earthen house in that *vasti*. I should experience the love of neighbors. I should hear again the Buddhist and Ambedkarite songs sung by the new generation and be merged with the soil that nurtured that community.

# CHRONOLOGY

| VASANT MOON'S LIFE: | THE NATION'S AND DR. AMBEDKAR'S BENCHMARKS: |
|---|---|
| | **1853** British annexation of Nagpur, Bhosle's state |
| | **1857** The Indian Rebellion |
| | **1920** First Gandhian nationwide campaign |
| | **1920** First Conference of Depressed Classes called by Ambedkar |
| | **1930** Ambedkar's Depressed Classes Conference in Nagpur |
| **1932** January 22: Birth of Vasant Moon | |
| | **1935** Independent Labour Party formed |
| | **1935** Announcement of need for conversion |
| | **1937** Elections for central and state legislatures |
| | **1942** Scheduled Castes Federation formed |
| | **1942** Indian National Congress "Quit India" Campaign |
| | **1946** Hindu-Mahar riots in Nagpur |
| | **1946** Scheduled Caste Students Conference |

| VASANT MOON'S LIFE: (cont.) | THE NATION'S AND DR. AMBEDKAR'S BENCHMARKS: (cont.) |
|---|---|
|  | **1947** Indian Independence |
|  | **1948** Death of Mohandas K. Gandhi |
| **1955** B.A., Nagpur University |  |
| **1955–1978** Appointments as county commissioner in various counties |  |
|  | **1956** October 14: Buddhist conversion ceremony |
|  | **1956** December 6: Death of Dr. Ambedkar |
|  | **1957** Republican Party founded by Ambedkar's followers according to his plans |
| **1958** M.A., Nagpur University, in Marathi Literature |  |
| **1958** Marriage to Meenakshi Sontakke |  |
| **1978** Seconded to Maharashtra Government to edit *Dr. Babasaheb Ambedkar: Writings and Speeches* in many volumes, now sixteen in number |  |

# GLOSSARY

*acharya.* A spiritual guide or teacher. Also used as a title for a learned man. P. K. Atre (q.v., Biography) was known as Acharya Atre for his broad intellectual contributions to Maharashtrian culture.

**Adivasi.** The "first inhabitants"; a term used for "tribal" peoples who generally lived in hilly areas, were not urbanized, and did not generally worship Hindu gods or follow Hindu practices.

**avatar.** Usually used for one of the reincarnated forms of Vishnu. Here simply used for the appearance of a person in a particular sort of dress.

**Babasaheb.** Literally Father-Master. Affectionate and respectful title given to Ambedkar around 1928. Often shortened to Baba.

*bai.* An informal honorific, as in Purnabai. Also used in address for "woman."

**BAMCEF.** Backward and Minority Communities Employees Federation. Founded by Kanshi Ram, who since has become a national figure as the leader of the Bahujan Samaj Party, BAMCEF is an influential organization of government employees that undertakes social service work.

**Bengalis.** Migrants to Nagpur from Bengal or residents of that area. Note that outsiders are given area names with no reference to caste and that in Bengal, Mahars seem to be caste-free.

*bhajan.* Translated at times as "hymn-singing session," a *bhajan* is more properly a session of singing of the songs of the *bhakti* movement, known in Maharashtra as the *warkari panth.*

**bhakti.** Devotional religion. The *bhakti* movement refers to the historical phenomenon of a series of poet-saints in most areas of India. In the Marathi-speaking area, the movement was known as *warkari panth* and brought thousands of pilgrims to Pandharpur and resulted in temples to the gods of Pandharpur, Vithoba, and Rukmini, becoming widespread throughout the area. The movement began in the thirteenth century, and the pilgrimage continues today.

*bhatji.* Term of address to a Brahman priest.

*bhikshu.* A monk in the Buddhist religion

**Bhim.** Affectionate nickname for Bhimrao Ramji Ambedkar. Also can be a reference to the Bhim of the Mahabharata epic, the strongest of the five brothers.

**Bhoodan Movement.** Gandhian influence was continued by Vinoba Bhave, who after Gandhi's death launched a *bhoodan* (literally "land gift") movement to provide land to the landless.

**Bhosle.** The princely house of Nagpur, which was annexed in 1853 by the British with little reaction. However, the Bhosles and their palace seem to still be of importance. Some family members appear herein as royalty, such as in the procession of Raghuji Raja.

*bidi.* Cheap Indian cigarette; tobacco in a hand-rolled leaf. In spite of the idea that Mahar touch was polluting, Mahars were heavily involved in the *bidi* home industry.

**Brahmans.** Often spelled Brahmins. The ritually highest caste; dominant in religious, educational, and literary matters because of their ancient religious rights and their literacy.

*The Buddha and His Dhamma.* Published posthumously, this book, written in English by Ambedkar, contains his rationalist humanist interpretation of the Buddha's life and teachings. It has been reprinted in the *Dr. Babasaheb Ambedkar:Writings and Speeches* series, edited by Vasant Moon, who has also published a booklet of Pali sources for the volume.

**Buddha *jayanti*.** The celebration of the Buddha's traditional birthday.

**Chaudar tank.** A pool of water in the Brahman sector of Mahad, a city south of Bombay (now Mumbai) that was the site of a 1927 satyagraha (q.v.) to drink water there according to a new Bombay Legislature resolution. When Untouchables were beaten back and the tank was purified, a later conference was held there at which sections of the orthodox Hindu lawbook, the *Manusmriti*, that decreed restrictions and punishments for Shudras were burned. Mahad is held to be the beginning of the mass Ambedkar movement.

*chawl.* Usually a large apartment building of one-room homes, with central water and toilet facilities. Hundreds were built in British days to house the workers flooding into the cities that offered employment in mills or docks.

**Congress.** The Indian National Congress. Founded in1885 as India's first and longest-lasting nationalist movement, the Congress became a political party in the 1937 election. Gandhi was the most important Congress leader, along with Jawaharlal Nehru and Sardar Patel, from 1920 on.

**Dal.** See Samata Sainik Dal.

**Dalit.** Downtrodden, oppressed. Used first by Jotiba Phule in the mid-nineteenth century. The word gained currency as a self-chosen, proud name with the early 1970s development of the Dalit Panthers and Dalit literature. Today it has replaced most other names in the vocabulary of politically aware ex-Untouchables and the press.

*darshan.* To experience a sight of a god, a shrine, a religious person, or even a city that would bring merit or a blessing to the one looking.

*dhobi.* A washerman. Also a caste name.

**dhoti.** Traditional male garment; an unsewn length of cloth wrapped around the lower body.

**Dhyanba–Tukaram.** The chant of *warkaris* on pilgrimage or in *bhajans,* which refers to the founder of the Vithoba cult, Dnyaneshwar, and the most popular saint-poet, Tukaram.

*diksha.* Conversion or ordination. *Dhamma diksha* refers to the conversion to Buddhism of Dr. Ambedkar and his followers.

**Diwali.** A popular fall festival that begins with a *puja* to Lakshmi (the goddess of wealth) for economic well-being. Known as the Festival of Lights in the tradition of lighting the way of Ram, Sita, and Lakshman back to Ayodhya from Lanka.

*durgah.* Muslim tomb, usually that of a Sufi saint or a fakir.

**fakir.** Muslim holy man, usually a wanderer.

**Ganpati.** The elephant-headed god much beloved in Maharashtra; also called Ganesh. The public festival begun by Lokmanya Tilak in the late nineteenth century is one of the central urban religious festivals even today. After a ten-day exhibition and a procession, Ganpati images are immersed in a body of water.

**Gayatri Mantra.** One of the holiest of mantras from the *Rig Veda.* It means: "Let us think on the splendor of the sun so that our minds might be inspired." It was supposed to be uttered only by the three upper classes, not by Shudras or Untouchables.

**ghee.** Clarified butter. Considered an expensive but necessary delicacy in upper-class Hindu homes.

**Gita.** A reference to the Bhagavad Gita, the sermon of Krishna in the Mahabharata that is one of the most important religious texts of contemporary Hinduism. Expositions of the Gita were so important that a "Gita ground" took the name of the text.

**Gurkhas.** Nepalese soldiers in the British army, known for their fighting skill.

*guruji.* A title used for an admired teacher or elder.

**Harijan and Harijan Sevak Sangh.** People or children of God and the organization for service to them. "Harijan" was Gandhi's euphemism for Untouchable, rejected by Ambedkar as patronizing and useless but until recently used by most caste Hindus and the press and some Untouchables.

**Hindi.** The language of Northern India, related to Marathi and spoken widely in the Vidarbha area along with Marathi.

**Holi.** A festival of fun and frolic held at the beginning of spring, involving a *holi* fire and a reversal of many normal roles. Colored water or powder is squirted or thrown around freely.

*hututu.* A traditional game of running and tag, competitive and very popular, played without any equipment.

**ILP.** Independent Labour Party, founded by Ambedkar in 1935. Fifteen of the seventeen candidates for legislative seats in the Bombay Legislature put up by the party in the 1937 election were successful, and included caste Hindus as well as Scheduled Castes. The party was the second-largest opposition to the Indian National Congress in the 1937–1939 Bombay legislature and proposed legislation on labor as well as Scheduled Caste matters.

**Independence.** India became independent of British rule on 15 August 1947.

*Janata.* Ambedkar's very influential newspaper.

**Janmashtami.** The day celebrated as the birthday of the god Krishna.

*jayanti.* In Hinduism, the anniversary of an incarnation of Vishnu, celebrated publicly. Also adapted to non-Hindu celebrations, such as the birthday of the Buddha and the birthday of Ambedkar.

**Kanoba.** A god of the Vidarbha region, considered to be a form of Krishna.

**Kartik.** A month of the Hindu calendar bridging October–November.

**Karve's case.** R. D. Karve's writing on the necessity for population control was considered obscene because of its mention of birth control.

*khokho.* A traditional Indian game, played without equipment.

*kirtan.* The celebration and praising of a god through song and sermon. An important part of bhakti devotion. *Kirtankars* were famous for their singing interspersed with messages.

**Konkanastha.** Meaning "from the Konkan," which is the coastal strip south of Mumbai (Bombay). The term usually refers to Chitpavan Brahmans, a high caste of achievers who originated from the Konkan.

*kulkarni.* The village accountant responsible to the government, almost always a Brahman.

*kumkum.* The red mark on the forehead of married women.

*lathi.* The wooden weapon of the police in India, deadly in a *lathi* charge.

**linga.** The phallic symbol that represents the god Shiva.

**Madhya Pradesh.** The contemporary name for the "middle state" of India. Before States Reorganization after Independence, Central Provinces and Berar was the British state that included portions of present day Madhya Pradesh and Maharashtra.

**Madrasis.** Migrants from the southern state of Madras now called Tamilnadu.

**Maha Bodhi Society.** Founded in Calcutta in the nineteenth century by Anagarika Dharmapala of Ceylon (now Sri Lanka), the Maha Bodhi Society has at times been cordial to the Ambedkar Buddhist movement, but also is suspected of treating Buddhism as a branch of Hinduism.

*Mahabharata.* The great Indian epic, codified between 200 B.C.E. and 200 C.E. The story of the Pandava brothers (including Bhim) and the battle between them and the Kauravas is known to all Indians.

**Mahanubhav.** A bhakti devotional movement of the thirteenth century still active today, but more marginalized than the better-known Pandharpur movement of the *warkaris* devoted to Vitthal. Basically egalitarian, the sect was begun by Chakradhar and has been chiefly studied by V. B. Kolte (a teacher in Moon's narrative) and more recently by Anne Feldhaus.

*mahaparinirvan.* The death or the great departing of the Buddha from his earthly life.

**Mahar Regiment.** At the urging of Dr. Ambedkar, the British government in India created the Mahar Regiment during World War II. Mahars had served in the British army during the eighteenth and nineteenth centuries, before it was reorganized to disqualify Untouchables.

**Maharpura.** Literally, city of the Mahars. The section of a village in which Mahars live is known as the Maharwada. Moon's *vasti* in the Sitabardi area in Nagpur was known as the Maharpura until the conversion to Buddhism.

**Malguzar landlords.** Rent receivers recognized by the British as a landowning class.

**mantra.** A phrase or spell used in meditation or healing.

**Marwaris.** Rajasthani business-class migrants, very important economically in Vidarbha.

**Matamai.** Also known as Mariai in the Marathi-speaking area. The goddess of pestilence, especially smallpox, who is traditionally cared for by Mahars. She is represented by a stone, not an image.

**matriculation.** The examination that must be passed to signify high-school graduation. Marks indicate a first-, second-, or third-class pass or failure.

**Moharram.** A Muslim festival mourning the death of Muhammad's grandson in the battle of Karbala. Many Hindus took part in the procession, and a young boy often wore the stripes of a tiger as he drummed.

**Mumbai.** Marathi name for the city of Bombay, now officially used in all languages.

**Nagpanchmi.** Festival of the snakes, celebrated all over Maharashtra.

*namaskar.* The traditional Hindu greeting with folded hands. Moon's mother greets the sun in this fashion.

**Nandi.** The bull of Shiva, almost always represented in Shaiva temples.

**Nasik satyagraha.** From 1930–1935, Mahars attempted to enter the Kalaram Temple in Nasik or to join the temple procession. Congress opposed this satyagraha for temple entry. Failure to win temple-entry rights preceded Ambedkar's announcement at nearby Yeola in 1935 that he would not die a Hindu.

*pan.* A betel leaf filled with various substances, usually chewed after a meal. *Pan* shops are found everywhere in India.

*panch, panchayat.* A council of leaders, either caste or village, traditionally five (*panch*) in number.

**pandit.** Now an English word meaning an expert or scholar. Traditionally a master of some scholarly or musical body of knowledge. Used for all Kashmiri Brahmans, as in the title of the first Prime Minister of India, Pandit Nehru.

**Parsis.** A group that came from Persia around the eighth century, settled in Gujarat, and in the nineteenth century entered into British businesses and then began their own businesses. Here they appear as mill owners and founders of medical clinics. Since they were Zoroastrian by religion and outside caste, they employed many Mahars in their homes.

*patil.* Village headman. In the more loosely structured caste society of Vidarbha, Mahars could bear the surname Patil; normally it indicates a Maratha.

*peshwa.* A Persian term for prime minister. The de facto ruler of the Maratha Kingdom in the eighteenth century, the last *peshwa* was defeated near Pune by the British in 1818 with an army that included many Mahars.

*puja.* Ritual worship of a god or goddess. Also a ritual that marks a life stage, or in the case of Satyanarayan *puja,* a new venture or a need for an auspicious result of some proposed action.

**Pune Pact.** The 1932 agreement between Ambedkar and Gandhi in which Ambedkar gave up a separate electorate for Untouchables that would have allowed them to elect their own representatives (as the Muslims did) and secured additional reserved places in the legislatures. The pact took place in the Yeravda Jail in Pune, where Gandhi was held, and was signed to prevent Gandhi's death by fasting.

**Puranas.** Collections of stories in Sanskrit, written chiefly in the first millennium C.E., which are the basic source for the stories about the Hindu gods and goddesses.

*qawwali.* A song genre stemming from the religious music of the Sufis, Muslim mystics, but popular throughout north India in all societies. Today, the recordings of the late Nusrat Fateh Ali Khan have made the *qawwali* known in the West. In Moon's time, the *qawwali* form was adapted to songs about Dr. Ambedkar.

**Radha and Krishna.** Radha is the beloved of the god Krishna, an avatar of Vishnu. The pair symbolizes the love of man for the divine but also is depicted as a romantic couple.

**raj.** Rule or reign. Usually used for the British Raj, but here used for the time when Ambedkar's ideals would rule, i.e., Bhim Raj.

*Raja Harischandra.* A legend of royal truthfulness, much told in story and drama.

*rakshasa.* Demons possessed of godly powers; a concept used to frighten children.

**Ram, Sita, Lakshman.** The main characters of the beloved epic *The Ramayana,* in which Ram, the king and an avatar of Vishnu; his brother Lakshman and Ram's wife, Sita, endure exile, Sita's capture, and war, and return triumphantly to Ayodhya.

**Rashtriya Swayamsevak Sangh.** The organization of nationalist volunteers, known as the RSS or simply the Sangh. Founded in Nagpur in 1924 to train young men in nonsectarian, militant, conservative Hinduism. Still important as the ideological foundation of the ruling Bharatiya Janata Party. In Moon's day, the Sangh was inclusive and popular in Nagpur.

**reservations, reserved seats.** India's version of affirmative action. The Government of India Act of 1935 placed some four hundred castes on a list or schedule, and Untouchables, after that known as Scheduled Castes, were then qualified for reserved places in legislatures, educational institutions, and government jobs. Reservations are now extended to groups above the Scheduled Castes known as Other Backward Castes, and in Moon's narrative the Weavers demand such privileges.

**rupee.** The basic Indian unit of currency.

**sadhu.** A commonly used term for a mendicant or holy man.

*samadhi.* A memorial for a holy man. Its use for the resting place of Hardas L. N.'s ashes indicates his exceptional standing in the Mahar, now Buddhist, community.

**Samata Sainik Dal.** The Army of Equality, a group made up primarily of youths and founded by Ambedkar for education and for protection of Depressed Class activities. Often called simply the Dal.

*sambhar.* A gravy of lentils and spices, eaten with rice or other south Indian foods.

**Sanchi.** A complex of first-century B.C.E. stupas with ornamented gates that are classical Buddhist art. Very important as a pilgrimage place for Buddhists internationally.

**sandal/shoe.** Throwing a sandal or shoe at someone or garlanding a statue with shoes is the ultimate insult.

**Sangh.** See Rashtriya Swayamsevak Sangh.

**sannyasi.** A holy man who has taken vows of homelessness.

**Satnami.** A sect of Hinduism which brought together chiefly the Chamars of the Chattisgarh area of central India in a movement for religious purity and social progress.

**satyagraha.** Literally, truth force or grasp. A nonviolent, direct-action, mass technique developed by Gandhi and then used by the Ambedkar movement for water rights, temple entry, and protest of the 1946 omission of separate electorates from the franchise plan just before Independence.

**Satyashodak Samaj.** The radical reform organization of Jotiba Phule in the nineteenth century that still in Moon's day had some organization and influence in Maharashtrian villages.

**SCF.** Scheduled Castes Federation. Ambedkar's second political party, founded in 1942 when it was clear that the all-inclusive Independent Labour Party had little caste Hindu support. The 1942 SCF conference in Nagpur is famous for its inclusion of women and their concerns. The Scheduled Castes Federation lost badly in the 1946 elections.

**Shiva.** One of the most important gods of Hinduism.

*shramaner.* A stage of ordination in Buddhism requiring vows less permanent than those of a *bhikshu.*

**Shudra.** The fourth *varna,* or caste cluster, of classical Hinduism. Supposedly composed of all who serve the higher castes. Aside from Brahmans, all the Marathi-speaking castes referred to in Moon's narrative would technically qualify as Shudras.

**subcaste.** The large Mahar caste, like all large castes, contained endogamous units. Among the Nagpur Mahars, these were Ladvan, Bavane, Barke, Zhade-Bavane, and Somvanshi. Before the Ambedkar movement they were ranked hierarchically, formed the basis for social life, and served as smaller units of identity.

*supari.* A mix of betel with various other substances to make a digestive to be chewed after a meal.

**sweeper.** An English name used here for two groups of Untouchables who basically remove human waste: the Bhangis of north India and the Mehtars of Madhya Pradesh. No Untouchable caste in Maharashtra performed that duty, and so sweepers were imported.

**talkies.** Generic term for movies or films. Still used today.

*tamasha.* Maharashtrian folk theater. Money is thrown to popular actors during the performance.

**Urdu.** A language developed after Muslims from Aghanistan entered India in the thirteenth century. Its syntax is that of Hindi, but its vocabulary borrows from Persian, Turkish, and Arabic. Nagpur was in a Hindi-speaking state before States Reorganization. Most city dwellers speak Hindi as well as Marathi, and some speak Urdu, which is considered a very poetic language.

*ustad.* Master. Here a wrestling trainer. In other contexts, a master musician.

**Vaishakh.** The month bridging April and May in the Hindu calendar.

*varkari.* One who makes the pilgrimage to Pandharur, to the temple of Vitthal and Rukmini, singing the songs of the saint-poets.

**Vidarbha.** The northeastern section of the Marathi-speaking area, culturally separate from three other areas: the coastal strip below Mumbai known as the Konkan; the area around and south of Pune known as the Desh; and the area to the southeast that was under the Nizam of Hyderabad known as Marathwada. Each area has its own culture and mix of castes.

**Vitthal and Rukmini.** The dominant religious sect among the non-Brahmans of the Marathi-speaking area is the *varkari* (pilgrimage) *sampradaya* (tradition), centered on worship of the god Vitthal or Vithoba and his wife Rukmini. A pilgrimage to the chief Vithoba temple in Pandharpur is the central activity of *varkaris,* but the hymns of the many saint-poets of the *sampradaya* are sung all over Maharashtra in *bhajan* sessions. A Mahar, Chokhamela, and his family are among the poet-saints of the sect. One school of thought finds the origin of Vitthal in Buddhism. Vithoba, like other gods and saints, is sometimes given a "mother" status, i.e., Vithai.

# BIOGRAPHICAL NOTES

**Agarkar, Gopal Ganesh.** 1856–1895. Rationalist Brahman thinker and writer, based in Pune but influential in the Vidarbha area.

**Angulimal.** A robber and murderer who was converted by the Buddha. A figure much included in Dalit literature.

**Atre, P. K.** 1898–1969. Brahman writer, editor, playwright, and teacher, known as Acharya Atre. The importance of his support of Ambedkar and Dalit activities can be seen in his being asked to give the funeral oration for Dr. Ambedkar.

**Bajiraos.** A reference to two Brahman *peshwas* (prime ministers), Bajirao I, who ruled the Maratha kingdom from 1720 to 1740, and Bajirao II, who ruled from 1795 until the British defeated his army in 1818. The *peshwa* period was seen as severely restrictive for Untouchables.

**Bal Gandharva.** Theater idol for the first third of the twentieth century. Known for his singing and his female roles. A music festival in Pune yearly celebrates his memory.

**Bansode, Kisan Fagoji.** 1879–1946. Early Mahar leader and educator in the Nagpur area. Founded Mahar conferences, petitioned the British for rights, held the saint-poet Chokhamela important as a past Mahar achievement of creativity and piety. Close to Ambedkar until the conversion announcement of 1935.

**Chakradhar.** Thirteenth-century founder of the Mahanubhav sect of Hinduism, a radical egalitarian movement that soon became marginalized by Brahman disapproval. Important especially in the Vidarbha area. The *Lilacharita* is the life of Chakradhar, one of the first books to be written in the Marathi language.

**Chiplunkar, Vishnu Krishna,** known as **Vishnushastri.** 1850–1882. A conservative Pune Brahman known for his elegant Marathi prose.

**Chokhamela.** A thirteenth-century poet-saint from the Mahar caste in the bhakti (devotional religion) tradition of Maharashtra. He and his wife, sister, brother-in-law, and son all sang hymns (*abhangas*) that are recognized as important in the bhakti tradition. Nineteenth- and twentieth-century Mahar leaders before Ambedkar often used his name to indicate religious worth, of which the Chokhamela Hostel in Nagpur is a symbol. Since the Untouchables could not enter the temple that was the center of the bhakti pilgrimage, and since Chokhamela held his birth to be the result of a previous life's sin, Ambedkar did not find him a symbol of pride.

**Dani, Shantabai.** 1918–. A political leader and educator from Nashik. The most influential woman in the Ambedkar movement. Recently the subject of a video made by young Dalits.

**Gaikwad, Dadasaheb.** 1902–1968. Bhaurao Krishnarao Gaikwad was Ambedkar's chief lieutenant all his adult life. He was a leading figure in the Nashik satyagraha (1930–1935), and Ambedkar's letters to him are a prime record of the movement's history.

**Gaikwad, Sayajirao Maharaj.** 1875–1939. Ruler of Baroda, a princely state in Gujarat that originated in the Maratha expansion of the eighteenth century. As a non-Brahman reformer, the Gaikwad was instrumental in many educational programs, including sending the young Ambedkar to study at Columbia University in New York.

**Gandhi, Mohandas K.** 1869–1948. In the 1930s, after a conflict with Ambedkar over the nature of political power to be given the Untouchables, Gandhi began using the term "Harijan" (people or children of God) for Untouchables and encouraged help to them. In Moon's narrative, the early effect of the Gandhian concern was helpful in terms of teaching handicrafts in a beneficent way, but he rejected the aid given to students who accepted the term "Harijan." Gandhi's insistence on the patronizing term "Harijan" rather than the realistic "Untouchable" and his opposition to the separate electorates for Untouchables that Ambedkar felt necessary made him an enemy.

**Ghashiram Kotwal.** A powerful official in the court of the *peshwa*, an eighteenth-century ruler of the Maratha federation, remembered for his harsh enforcement of orthodox laws. Also the subject and title of a popular modern musical drama by Vijay Tendulkar.

**Godbole, Wamanrao.** The chief organizer of the conversion ceremony in Nagpur as well as a leading light in the Samata Sainik Dal. Still active today, he is building a large Buddhist center near Nagpur, where he hopes to teach the principles of Buddhism according to Ambedkar's teachings.

**Grace.** Manik Goghate's pen name. A well-known romantic poet from Nagpur, identified as a Mahar but not a participant in the Dalit literary movement.

**Kabir.** A fifteenth-century poet-saint of Varanasi, Kabir left not only a legacy of priceless poetry but a radical egalitarian spirit, some of which was continued in the Kabir sect that spread to the Marathi-speaking area.

**Kalidas.** Poet and playwright of the classical Gupta period, probably fifth century C.E. His epic-length poem *The Cloud Messenger* is evocative of nature and romantic sentiment.

**Khairmode, C. B.** Author of a multivolume biography of Ambedkar in Marathi, begun in 1952.

**Khandekar, V. S.** 1898–1976. One of the greatest Marathi writers, especially famous for romantic novels.

**Kosambi, Dharmanand.** 1871–1947. An internationally famous Pali and Sanskrit scholar who combined learned writing with a popular life of the Buddha and concern for Untouchables.

**Kumbhare, Narayan.** A Mahar from Kamathi mentioned often by Moon as a great leader. His daughter, Sulekhatai Kumbhare, active in the Republican Party founded by Ambedkar, was elected to the Maharashtra State Legislative Assembly in 1999, one of a handful of women.

**Kusumagraj.** Pen name of V. V. Shirwadkar. 1912–1999. Modern poet of great popularity.

**Lata Mangeshkar.** Maharashtra's most popular singer for decades, including the present. Known for "play-back" singing, i.e., dubbed singing in films.

**Lokahitawadi.** 1823–1892. Pen name of Gopal Hari Deshmukh. His *Shatapatre* (One Hundred Letters), which urged change and progress, made him the most effective of the early Brahman reformers.

**Maisaheb.** Ambedkar's second wife, Sharda Kabir, a medical doctor he married twelve years after the death of his first wife, Ramabai.

**Mate, S. M.** A Brahman writer and reformer from Pune, so supportive of Untouchable progress he was known as Mahar Mate.

**Moggallayan.** A disciple of the Buddha.

**Moropant.** An important writer in eighteenth-century Maharashtra. The period when he lived, 1729–1794, is known in literary circles as the Age of Moropant. His scholarly and musical poetry was based on the epics. Most important is the *Aryabharata,* based on the *Mahabharata.* His *Kekavali* has been translated into English.

**Nanasaheb Gavai.** G. A. Gavai, an early Mahar reformer and spokesman from Amraoti. Important as an English-speaking literate and member of the legislative council in Central Provinces and Berar. He did not join the Ambedkar movement.

**Omar Khayyam.** Moon's use of this Arabic poet's name stresses "a jug of wine" rather than "a loaf of bread … and thou" in the familiar line from the *Rubaiyat.*

**Phadke, N. S.** 1894–1978. Together with Khandekar, the most famous writer of the first half of the twentieth century; known for his "Arts for Art's Sake" ideology.

**Phule, Jotirao,** also known as **Mahatma Phule.** 1827–1890. Founder of the Satyashodak Samaj (truth-seeking society), which encouraged the elimination of superstition and Brahman control. Ambedkar dedicated *Who Were the Shudras?* to Phule, and the phrase Phule-Ambedkar is now often used to indicate radical anti-caste thought.

**Rahuji Raja.** The heir of the Bhosle kingdom, rulers of Nagpur until 1853. In Moon's day, he was still accorded respect.

**Rajbhoj, P. N.** A Chambhar (Leatherworker caste) from Pune who was injured in the 1929 temple satyagraha in Pune led by Untouchables and caste Hindu reformers (but not by Congress or Gandhi.) Later he served as secretary in Ambedkar's Scheduled Castes Federation, but then alternated between Congress and the Ambedkar movement. He became a Buddhist after 1956.

**Sai Baba and Gajanand.** Important holy men in Maharashtra. Sai Baba was a sadhu of the late nineteenth and early twentieth centuries, probably of Muslim background, whose center at Shirdi is popular today. His picture is everywhere in Maharashtra since he is considered an auspicious presence associated with economic well-being. Gajanand Maharaj is a twentieth-century religious figure from Vidarbha with a large following.

**Sane Guruji.** 1899–1950. Pen name of Pandurang Sadashiv Sane. A beloved writer of stories, a Gandhian, and an activist who fasted in front of the Pandharpur temple of Vithoba and Rukmini at the time of Independence to secure entrance for Untouchables.

**Sariputra.** A disciple of the Buddha.

**Savarkar, V. D. (Veer).** 1883–1940. Known as "hero" (*vir,* anglicized as Veer), Savarkar, a nationalist revolutionary often imprisoned by the British, was a member and leader of the orthodox Hindu Mahasabha, a pre-Independence political party. But he strongly supported Untouchables' rights, including the Mahad satyagraha for water rights at the Chaudar tank. Moon's story of his eating meat in Nagpur comes as a surprise, since he was in many ways an orthodox Brahman, one of the heroes of the Rashtriya Swayamsevak Sangh (the RSS).

**Shahu Maharaj.** 1874–1922. Shahu Chhatrapati, Maharaja of Kolhapur, was an important non-Brahman reformist prince who aided Ambedkar in his studies in England and later introduced Ambedkar to a "Depressed Classes" conference in 1920 as "your savior."

**Shende, N. R.** A Mahar scholar and writer in Nagpur who did not join the Ambedkar movement but wrote biographies of G. A. Gawai and Kisan Fagoji Bansode, novels, essays, and a book on folklore invaluable for its reference to Mahar life. He served as president of the Vidarbha Sahitya Sangh, the literary society of eastern India.

**Shivaji.** The seventeenth-century founder and ruler of the Maratha kingdom, known as Chhatrapati. An idealized and idolized figure for all Maharashtrians even today. His killing of the Muslim general Afzal Khan in a way that might be seen as trickery is a story known to all schoolchildren as a legend with the theme "the ends justify the means."

**Tajuddin Baba.** A nineteenth-century Vidarbha saint of Muslim background, very popular as an object of devotion in the same way that Sai Baba is everywhere in Maharashtra.

**Thaware, G. M.** A Mahanubhav and a strong Mahar leader in Nagpur who joined with the southern Depressed Classes leader M. C. Rajah in opposition to Ambedkar at the time of the Pune Pact in 1932, which found Ambedkar and Gandhi in conflict over the issue of a separate electorate for Untouchables. An off-and-on supporter of Ambedkar thereafter, he at times supported the Gandhian approach to untouchability; he joined Congress in 1950.

**Tilak, Narayan Waman.** 1861–1919. A poet and one of the rare Brahmans who became a Christian. His hymns are sung today, and his wife's autobiography, Lakshmibai Tilak's *I Follow After,* is a Marathi classic available in English.

**Tukodji Maharaj.** A twentieth-century nationalist and religious figure of great popularity in Vidarbha.

# BIBLIOGRAPHY

## FURTHER READING

Ambedkar, Bhimrao Ramji. *Dr. Babasaheb Ambedkar: Writings and Speeches.* Edited by Vasant Moon. Bombay: Education Department, Government of Maharashtra, 1979–present. Sixteen volumes so far have been published.

Anand, Mulk Raj. *Untouchable.* Preface by E. M. Forster. New Delhi: Arnold-Heineman Publishers, 1983. First published in 1947.

*Dalit International Newsletter.* P.O. Box 932, Waterford, Conn. 06385

Deo, Veena, and Eleanor Zelliot. "Dalit Literature: Twenty-Five Years of Protest? Of Progress?" *Journal of South Asia Literature* 29.2 (1994): 41–68.

Dube, Siddarth. *In the Land of Poverty: Memoirs of an Indian Family 1947–1997.* London: Zed Books, and New York: St. Martin's Press, 1998.

Freeman, James M. *Untouchable: An Untouchable Life History.* Stanford, Cal.: Stanford University Press, 1979.

Hazari (pseud. of Marcus Abraham Malik). *Untouchable: The Autobiography of an Indian Outcaste.* New York: Frederick A. Praeger, 1969. First published in 1951.

Joshi, Barbara R., editor. *Untouchable! Voices of the Dalit Liberation Movement.* London: Zed Books, 1986.

Keer, Dhananjay. *Dr. Ambedkar: Life and Mission.* Bombay: Popular Prakashan, 1962. First published 1954; many editions.

Khare, Ravindra S. *The Untouchable as Himself: Ideology, Identity and Pragmatism among Lucknow Chamars.* Cambridge, Eng.: Cambridge University Press, 1984.

Mahar, J. Michael, editor. *The Untouchables in Contemporary India.* Tucson, Ariz.: University of Arizona Press, 1972.

Mane, Laxman. *Upara: An Outsider.* Translated from the Marathi by A. K. Kamat. New Delhi: Sahitya Akademi, 1997.

Manu, Joseph. "The Pit of No Return" (on Indian wrestling). *Outlook* 40.19 (22 May 2000): 70–73.

Mendelsohn, Oliver, and Marika Vicziany. *The Untouchables: Subordination, Poverty and the State in Modern India.* Cambridge, Eng.: Cambridge University Press, 1998.

Omvedt, Gail. *Dalits and the Democratic Revolution: Dr. Ambedkar and the Dalit Movement in Colonial India.* New Delhi and Thousand Oaks, Cal.: Sage Publications, 1994.

Viramma, Josiane Racine, and Jean-Luc Racine. *Viramma: Life of an Untouchable.* Translated from the French by Will Hobson. London: Verso, 1997.

Zelliot, Eleanor. *From Untouchable to Dalit: Essays on the Ambedkar Movement.* New Delhi: Manohar Publishers and Distributors, 1992, 1996.

# INDEX

NOTE: Page numbers in italics refer to illustrations.

195